The Speeches of President John F. Kennedy

CONTENTS

The Speeches of President John F. Kennedy

ACCEPTANCE OF THE DEMOCRATIC PARTY NOMINATION

(JULY 15, 1960)

Governor Stevenson, Senator Johnson, Mr. Butler, Senator Symington, Senator Humphrey, Speaker Rayburn, Fellow Democrats, I want to express my thanks to Governor Stevenson for his generous and heart-warming introduction.

It was my great honor to place his name in nomination at the 1956 Democratic National Convention, and I am delighted to have his support and his counsel and his advice in the coming months ahead.

With a deep sense of duty and high resolve, I accept your nomination.

I accept it with a full and grateful heart—without reservation—and with only one obligation—the obligation to devote every effort of body, mind and spirit to lead our party back to victory and our Nation back to greatness.

I am grateful too, that you have provided me with such an eloquent statement of our Party's platform. Pledges which are made so eloquently are made to be kept. "The Rights of Man,"—the civil and economic rights essential to the human dignity of all men—are indeed our goal and our first principles. This is a platform on which I can run with enthusiasm and conviction.

And I am grateful, finally, that I can rely in the coming months on so many others—on a distinguished running mate who brings unity to our ticket and strength to our Platform, Lyndon Johnson—on one of the most articulate statesmen of our time, Adlai Stevenson—on a great spokesman for our needs as a Nation and a people, Stuart Symington—and on that fighting campaigner whose support I welcome, President Harry S. Truman—on my traveling companion in Wisconsin and West Virginia, Senator Hubert Humphrey. On Paul Butler, our devoted and courageous

1

Chairman.

I feel a lot safer now that they are on my side again. And I am proud of the contrast with our Republican competitors. For their ranks are apparently so thin that not one challenger has come forth with both the competence and the courage to make theirs an open convention.

I am fully aware of the fact that the Democratic Party, by nominating someone of my faith, has taken on what many regard as a new and hazardous risk—new, at least since 1928. But I look at it this way: the Democratic Party has once again placed its confidence in the American people, and in their ability to render a free, fair judgement—to uphold the Constitution and my oath of office—and to reject any kind of religious pressure or obligation that might directly or indirectly interfere with my conduct of the Presidency in the national interest. My record of fourteen years supporting public education—supporting complete separation of church and state—and resisting pressure from any source on any issue should be clear by now to everyone.

I hope that no American, considering the really critical issues facing this country, will waste his franchise by voting either for me or against me solely on account of my religious affiliation. It is not relevant. I want to stress, what some other political or religious leader may have said on this subject. It is not relevant what abuses may have existed in other countries or in other times. It is not relevant what pressures, if any, might conceivably be brought to bear on me. I am telling you now what you are entitled to know: that my decisions on any public policy will be my own—as an American, a Democrat and a free man.

Under any circumstances, however, the victory that we seek in November will not be easy. We all know that in our hearts. We recognize the power of the forces that will be aligned against us. We know they will invoke the name of Abraham Lincoln on behalf of their candidate—despite the fact that the political career of their candidate has often served to show charity toward none and malice toward for all.

We know that it will not be easy to campaign against a man who has spoken or voted on every known side of every known issue. Mr. Nixon may feel it is his turn now, after the New Deal and the Fair Deal—but before he deals, someone had better cut the cards.

That "someone" may be the millions of Americans who voted for President Eisenhower but balk at his would-be, self-appointed successor.

For just as historians tell us that Richard I was not fit to fill the shoes of bold Henry II—and that Richard Cromwell was not fit to wear the mantle of his uncle—they might add in future years that Richard Nixon did not measure to the footsteps of Dwight D. Eisenhower.

Perhaps he could carry on the party policies—the policies of Nixon, Benson, Dirksen and Goldwater. But this Nation cannot afford such a luxury. Perhaps we could better afford a Coolidge following Harding. And perhaps we could afford a Pierce following Fillmore.

But after Buchanan, this nation needed a Lincoln—after Taft, we needed a Wilson—after Hoover we needed Franklin Roosevelt . . . . And after eight years of drugged and fitful sleep, this nation needs strong, creative Democratic leadership in the White House.

But we are not merely running against Mr. Nixon. Our task is not merely one of itemizing Republican failures. Nor is that wholly necessary. For the families forced from the farm will know how to vote without our telling them. The unemployed miners and textile workers will know how to vote. The old people without medical care—the families without a decent home—the parents of children without adequate food or schools—they all know that it's time for a change.

But I think the American people expect more from us than cries of indignation and attack. The times are too grave, the challenge too urgent, and the stakes too high—to permit the customary passions of political debate. We are not here to curse the darkness, but to light the candle that can guide us through that darkness to a safe and sane future. As Winston Churchill said on taking office some twenty years ago: if we open a quarrel between the present and the past, we shall be in danger of losing the future.

Today our concern must be with the future. For the world is changing. The old era is ending. The old ways will not do.

Abroad, the balance of power is shifting. There are new and more terrible weapons—new and uncertain nations—new pressures of population and deprivation. One-third of the world, it has been said, may be free—but one-third is the victim of cruel repression—and the other one-third is rocked by the pangs of poverty, hunger, and envy. More energy is released by the awakening of these new nations then by the fission of the atom itself.

Meanwhile, Communist influence has penetrated further into Asia, stood astride in the Middle East and now festers some ninety miles off the coast of Florida. Friends have slipped into neutrality—and neutrals into hostility. As our keynoter reminded us, the President who began his career by going to Korea ends it by staying away from Japan.

The world has been close to war before—but now man, who has survived all previous threats to his existence, has taken into his mortal hands the power to exterminate the entire species some seven times over.

Here, at home, the changing face of the future is equally revolutionary. The New Deal and the Fair Deal were bold measures for their generations—but this is a new generation.

A technological revolution on the farm has led us to an output explosion—but we have not yet learned how to harness that explosion usefully, while protecting our farmers' right to full parity income.

An urban population explosion has crowded our schools, cluttered up our suburbs, and increased the squalor of our slums.

A peaceful revolution for human rights—demanding an end to racial discrimination in all parts of our community life has strained at the leashes imposed by timid executive leadership.

A medical revolution has extended the life of our elder citizens without providing the dignity and security those later years deserve. And a revolution of automation finds machines replacing men in the mines and mills of America, without replacing their incomes or their training or their needs to pay the family doctor, grocer and landlord.

There has also been a change—a slippage—in our intellectual and moral strength. Seven lean years of drought and famine have withered a field of ideas. Blight has descended on our regulatory agencies—and a dry rot, beginning in Washington, is seeping into every corner of America—in the payola mentality, the expense account way of life, the confusion between what is legal and what is right. Too many Americans have lost their way, their will, and their sense of historic purpose.

It is a time, in short, for a new generation of leadership—new men to cope with new problems and new opportunities.

All over the world, particularly in the newer nations, young men are coming to power—men who are not bound by the traditions of the past—

men who are not blinded by the old fears and hates and rivalries—young men who can cast off the old slogans and delusions and suspicions.

The Republican nominee-to-be, of course, is also a young man. But his approach is as old as McKinley. His party is the party of the past. His speeches are generalities from Poor Richard's Almanac. Their platform, made up of left-over Democratic planks, has the courage of our old convictions. Their pledge is a pledge to the status quo – and today there can be no status quo.

For I stand tonight facing west on what was once the last frontier. From the lands that stretch three thousand miles behind me, the pioneers of old gave up their safety, their comfort and sometimes their own lives to build a new world here in the West. They were not the captives of their own doubts, the prisoners of their own price tags. Their motto was not "every man for himself" but "all for the common cause." They were determined to make that new world strong and free, to overcome its hazards and its hardships, to conquer the enemies that threatened from without and within.

Today some would say that those struggles are all over—that all the horizons have been explored—that all the battles have been won—that there is no longer an American frontier.

But I trust that no one in this vast assemblage will agree with those sentiments. For the problems are not all solved and the battles are not all won—and we stand today on the edge of a New Frontier—the frontier of the 1960's—a frontier of unknown opportunities and perils—a frontier of unfulfilled hopes and threats.

Woodrow Wilson's New Freedom promised our nation a new political and economic framework. Franklin Roosevelt's New Deal promised security and succor to those in need. But the New Frontier of which I speak is not a set of promises, it is a set of challenges. It sums up not what I intend to offer the American people, but what I intend to ask of them. It appeals to their pride, not to their pocketbook—it holds out the promise of more sacrifice instead of more security.

But I tell you the New Frontier is here, whether we seek it or not. Beyond that frontier are the uncharted areas of science and space, unsolved problems of peace and war, unconquered pockets of ignorance and prejudice, unanswered questions of poverty and surplus. It would be easier to shrink back from that frontier, to look to the safe mediocrity of the past, to be lulled by good intentions and high rhetoric—and those who prefer that course should not cast their votes for me regardless of party.

But I believe the times demand new invention, innovation, imagination, decision. I am asking each of you to be pioneers on that New Frontier. My call is to the young in heart, regardless of age – to all who respond to the Scriptural call: "Be strong and of good courage; be not afraid, neither be thou dismayed."

For courage—not complacency—is our need today—leadership, not salesmanship. And the only valid test of leadership is the ability to lead, and lead vigorously. A tired nation, said David Lloyd George, is a Tory nation, and the United States today cannot afford to be either tired or Tory.

There may be those who wish to hear more—more promises to this group or that—more harsh rhetoric about the men in the Kremlin—more assurances of a golden future, where taxes are always low and subsidies ever high. But my promises are in the platform you have adopted. Our ends will not be won by rhetoric and we can have faith in the future only if we have faith in ourselves.

For the harsh facts of the matter are that we stand on this frontier at a turning-point in history. We must prove all over again whether this nation, or any nation so conceived, can long endure; whether our society, with its freedom of choice, its breadth of opportunity, its range of alternatives, can compete with the single-minded advance of the Communist system.

Can a nation organized and governed such as ours endure? That is the real question. Have we the nerve and the will? Can we carry through in an age where we will witness not only new breakthroughs in weapons of destruction, but also a race for mastery of the sky and the rain, the ocean and the tides, the far side of space and the inside of men's minds?

Are we up to the task—are we equal to the challenge? Are we willing to match the Russian sacrifice of the present for the future, or must we sacrifice our future in order to enjoy the present?

That is the question of the New Frontier. That is the choice our nation must make—a choice that lies not merely between two men or two parties, but between the public interest and private comfort—between national greatness and national decline—between the fresh air of progress and the stale, dank atmosphere of "normalcy"—between determined dedication and creeping mediocrity.

All mankind waits upon our decision. A whole world looks to see what we will do. We cannot fail their trust, we cannot fail to try.

It has been a long road from that first snowy day in New Hampshire to this crowded convention city. Now begins another long journey, taking me into your cities and homes all over America. Give me your help, your hand, your voice, your vote. Recall with me the words of Isaiah: "They that wait upon the Lord shall renew their strength; they shall mount up with wings as eagles; they shall run and not be weary."

As we face the coming challenge, we too shall wait upon the Lord, and ask that he renew our strength, Then shall we be equal to the test. Then shall we not be weary. And then we shall prevail.

Thank you.

ADDRESS TO THE GREATER HOUSTON MINISTERIAL ASSOCIATION

(SEPTEMBER 12, 1960)

Reverend Meza, Reverend Reck, I'm grateful for your generous invitation to speak my views.

While the so-called religious issue is necessarily and properly the chief topic here tonight, I want to emphasize from the outset that we have far more critical issues to face in the 1960 election; the spread of Communist influence, until it now festers 90 miles off the coast of Florida—the humiliating treatment of our President and Vice President by those who no longer respect our power—the hungry children I saw in West Virginia, the old people who cannot pay their doctor bills, the families forced to give up their farms—an America with too many slums, with too few schools, and too late to the moon and outer space.

These are the real issues which should decide this campaign. And they are not religious issues—for war and hunger and ignorance and despair know no religious barriers.

But because I am a Catholic, and no Catholic has ever been elected President, the real issues in this campaign have been obscured—perhaps deliberately, in some quarters less responsible than this. So it is apparently necessary for me to state once again—not what kind of church I believe in, for that should be important only to me—but what kind of America I believe in.

I believe in an America where the separation of church and state is absolute—where no Catholic prelate would tell the President (should he be Catholic) how to act, and no Protestant minister would tell his parishioners for whom to vote—where no church or church school is granted any public funds or political preference—and where no man is denied public office merely because his religion differs from the President who might appoint him or the people who might elect him.

I believe in an America that is officially neither Catholic, Protestant nor Jewish—where no public official either requests or accepts instructions on public policy from the Pope, the National Council of Churches or any other ecclesiastical source—where no religious body seeks to impose its will directly or indirectly upon the general populace or the public acts of its officials—and where religious liberty is so indivisible that an act against one church is treated as an act against all.

For while this year it may be a Catholic against whom the finger of suspicion is pointed, in other years it has been, and may someday be again, a Jew—or a Quaker—or a Unitarian—or a Baptist. It was Virginia's harassment of Baptist preachers, for example, that helped lead to Jefferson's statute of religious freedom. Today I may be the victim—but tomorrow it may be you—until the whole fabric of our harmonious society is ripped at a time of great national peril.

Finally, I believe in an America where religious intolerance will someday end—where all men and all churches are treated as equal—where every man has the same right to attend or not attend the church of his choice—where there is no Catholic vote, no anti-Catholic vote, no bloc voting of any kind—and where Catholics, Protestants and Jews, at both the lay and pastoral level, will refrain from those attitudes of disdain and division which have so often marred their works in the past, and promote instead the American ideal of brotherhood.

That is the kind of America in which I believe. And it represents the kind of Presidency in which I believe—a great office that must neither be humbled by making it the instrument of any one religious group nor tarnished by arbitrarily withholding its occupancy from the members of any one religious group. I believe in a President whose religious views are his own private affair, neither imposed by him upon the Nation or imposed by the Nation upon him as a condition to holding that office.

I would not look with favor upon a President working to subvert the first amendment's guarantees of religious liberty. Nor would, our system of checks and balances permit him to do so—and neither do I look with favor upon those who would work to subvert Article VI of the Constitution by requiring a religious test—even by indirection—for it. If they disagree with that safeguard they should be out openly working to repeal it.

I want a Chief Executive whose public acts are responsible to all groups and obligated to none—who can attend any ceremony, service, or dinner his office may appropriately require of him—and whose fulfillment of his Presidential oath is not limited or conditioned by any religious oath, ritual, or obligation.

This is the kind of America I believe in—and this is the kind I fought for in the South Pacific, and the kind my brother died for in Europe. No one suggested then that we might have a "divided loyalty," that we did "not believe in liberty" or that we belonged to a disloyal group that threatened the "freedoms for which our forefathers died."

And in fact this is the kind of America for which our forefathers died—when they fled here to escape religious test oaths that denied office to members of less favored churches—when they fought for the Constitution, the Bill of Rights, and the Virginia Statute of Religious Freedom—and when they fought at the shrine I visited today, the Alamo. For side by side with Bowie and Crockett died McCafferty and Bailey and Carey—but no one knows whether they were Catholics or not. For there was no religious test at the Alamo.

I ask you tonight to follow in that tradition—to judge me on the basis of my record of 14 years in Congress—on my declared stands against an Ambassador to the Vatican, against unconstitutional aid to parochial schools, and against any boycott of the public schools (which I have attended myself)—instead of judging me on the basis of these pamphlets and publications we all have seen that carefully select quotations out of context from the statements of Catholic church leaders, usually in other countries, frequently in other centuries, and always omitting, of course, the statement of the American Bishops in 1948 which strongly endorsed church-state separation, and which more nearly reflects the views of almost every American Catholic.

I do not consider these other quotations binding upon my public acts—why should you? But let me say, with respect to other countries, that I am wholly opposed to the state being used by any religious group, Catholic or Protestant, to compel, prohibit, or persecute the free exercise of any other religion. And I hope that you and I condemn with equal fervor those nations which deny their Presidency to Protestants and those which deny it to Catholics. And rather than cite the misdeeds of those who differ, I would cite the record of the Catholic Church in such nations as Ireland and France—and the independence of such statesmen as Adenauer and De Gaulle.

But let me stress again that these are my views—for, contrary to common newspaper usage, I am not the Catholic candidate for President. I am the Democratic Party's candidate for President who happens also to be a Catholic. I do not speak for my Church on public matters—and the Church does not speak for me.

Whatever issue may come before me as President—in birth control, divorce, censorship, gambling or any other subject—I will make my decision in accordance with these views, in accordance with what my conscience tells me to be the national interest, and without regard to outside religious pressures or dictates. And no power or threat of punishment could cause me to decide otherwise.

But if the time should ever come—and I do not concede any conflict to be even remotely possible—when my office would require me to either violate my conscience or violate the national interest, then I would resign the office; and I hope any conscientious public servant would do the same.

But I do not intend to apologize for these views to my critics of either Catholic or Protestant faith—nor do I intend to disavow either my views or my Church in order to win this election.

If I should lose on the real issues, I shall return to my seat in the Senate, satisfied that I had tried my best and was fairly judged. But if this election is decided on the basis that 40 million Americans lost their chance of being President on the day they were baptized, then it is the whole Nation that will be the loser, in the eyes of Catholics and non-Catholics around the world, in the eyes of history, and in the eyes of our own people.

But if, on the other hand, I should win the election, then I shall devote every effort of mind and spirit to fulfilling the oath of the Presidency—practically identical, I might add, to the oath I have taken for 14 years in the Congress. For, without reservation, I can "solemnly swear that I will faithfully execute the office of President of the United States, and will to the best of my ability preserve, protect, and defend the Constitution, so help me God."

"CITY UPON A HILL" SPEECH

(JANUARY 9, 1961)

I have welcomed this opportunity to address this historic body, and, through you, the people of Massachusetts to whom I am so deeply indebted for a lifetime of friendship and trust.

For fourteen years I have placed my confidence in the citizens of Massachusetts—and they have generously responded by placing their confidence in me.

Now, on the Friday after next, I am to assume new and broader responsibilities. But I am not here to bid farewell to Massachusetts.

For forty-three years—whether I was in London, Washington, the South Pacific, or elsewhere—this has been my home; and, God willing, wherever I serve this shall remain my home.

It was here my grandparents were born—it is here I hope my grandchildren will be born.

I speak neither from false provincial pride nor artful political flattery. For no man about to enter high office in this country can ever be unmindful of the contribution this state has made to our national greatness.

Its leaders have shaped our destiny long before the great republic was born. Its principles have guided our footsteps in times of crisis as well as in times of calm. Its democratic institutions—including this historic body— have served as beacon lights for other nations as well as our sister states.

For what Pericles said to the Athenians has long been true of this commonwealth: "We do not imitate—for we are a model to others."

And so it is that I carry with me from this state to that high and lonely office to which I now succeed more than fond memories of firm friendships. The enduring qualities of Massachusetts—the common threads woven by the Pilgrim and the Puritan, the fisherman and the farmer, the Yankee and the immigrant—will not be and could not be forgotten in this nation's executive mansion.

They are an indelible part of my life, my convictions, my view of the past, and my hopes for the future.

Allow me to illustrate: During the last sixty days, I have been at the task of constructing an administration. It has been a long and deliberate process. Some have counseled greater speed. Others have counseled more expedient tests.

But I have been guided by the standard John Winthrop set before his shipmates on the flagship Arbella three hundred and thirty-one years ago, as they, too, faced the task of building a new government on a perilous frontier.

"We must always consider," he said, "that we shall be as a city upon a hill—the eyes of all people are upon us."

Today the eyes of all people are truly upon us—and our governments, in every branch, at every level, national, state and local, must be as a city upon a hill—constructed and inhabited by men aware of their great trust and their great responsibilities.

For we are setting out upon a voyage in 1961 no less hazardous than that undertaken by the Arabella in 1630. We are committing ourselves to tasks of statecraft no less awesome than that of governing the Massachusetts Bay Colony, beset as it was then by terror without and disorder within.

History will not judge our endeavors—and a government cannot be selected—merely on the basis of color or creed or even party affiliation. Neither will competence and loyalty and stature, while essential to the utmost, suffice in times such as these.

For of those to whom much is given, much is required. And when at some future date the high court of history sits in judgment on each one of us—recording whether in our brief span of service we fulfilled our responsibilities to the state—our success or failure, in whatever office we may hold, will be measured by the answers to four questions:

First, were we truly men of courage—with the courage to stand up to one's enemies—and the courage to stand up, when necessary, to one's associates—the courage to resist public pressure, as well as private greed?

Secondly, were we truly men of judgment—with perceptive judgment of the future as well as the past—of our own mistakes as well as the mistakes of others—with enough wisdom to know that we did not know, and enough candor to admit it?

Third, were we truly men of integrity—men who never ran out on either the principles in which they believed or the people who believed in them—men who believed in us—men whom neither financial gain nor political ambition could ever divert from the fulfillment of our sacred trust?

Finally, were we truly men of dedication—with an honor mortgaged to no single individual or group, and compromised by no private obligation or aim, but devoted solely to serving the public good and the national interest.

Courage—judgment—integrity—dedicationthese are the historic qualities of the Bay Colony and the Bay State—the qualities which this state has consistently sent to this chamber on Beacon Hill here in Boston and to Capitol Hill back in Washington.

And these are the qualities which, with God's help, this son of Massachusetts hopes will characterize our government's conduct in the four stormy years that lie ahead.

Humbly I ask His help in that undertaking—but aware that on earth His will is worked by men. I ask for your help and your prayers, as I embark on this new and solemn journey.

President John F. Kennedy

INAUGURAL ADDRESS

(JANUARY 20, 1961)

Vice President Johnson, Mr. Speaker, Mr. Chief Justice, President Eisenhower, Vice President Nixon, President Truman, Reverend Clergy, fellow citizens:

We observe today not a victory of party but a celebration of freedom—symbolizing an end as well as a beginning—signifying renewal as well as change. For I have sworn before you and Almighty God the same solemn oath our forebears prescribed nearly a century and three quarters ago.

The world is very different now. For man holds in his mortal hands the power to abolish all forms of human poverty and all forms of human life. And yet the same revolutionary beliefs for which our forebears fought are still at issue around the globe—the belief that the rights of man come not from the generosity of the state but from the hand of God.

We dare not forget today that we are the heirs of that first revolution. Let the word go forth from this time and place, to friend and foe alike, that the torch has been passed to a new generation of Americans—born in this century, tempered by war, disciplined by a hard and bitter peace, proud of our ancient heritage—and unwilling to witness or permit the slow undoing of those human rights to which this nation has always been committed, and to which we are committed today at home and around the world.

Let every nation know, whether it wishes us well or ill, that we shall pay any price, bear any burden, meet any hardship, support any friend, oppose any foe to assure the survival and the success of liberty.

This much we pledge—and more.

To those old allies whose cultural and spiritual origins we share, we pledge the loyalty of faithful friends. United, there is little we cannot do in a host of cooperative ventures. Divided, there is little we can do—for we dare not meet a powerful challenge at odds and split asunder.

To those new states whom we welcome to the ranks of the free, we pledge our word that one form of colonial control shall not have passed away merely to be replaced by a far more iron tyranny. We shall not always expect to find them supporting our view. But we shall always hope to find them strongly supporting their own' freedom—and to remember that, in the past, those who foolishly sought power by riding the back of the tiger ended up inside.

To those peoples in the huts and villages of half the globe struggling to break the bonds of mass misery, we pledge our best efforts to help them help themselves, for whatever period is required—not because the communists may be doing it, not because we seek their votes, but because it is right. If a free society cannot help the many who are poor, it cannot save the few who are rich.

To our sister republics south of our border, we offer a special pledge—to convert our good words into good deeds—in a new alliance for progress—to assist free men and free governments in casting off the chains of poverty. But this peaceful revolution of hope cannot become the prey of hostile powers. Let all our neighbors know that we shall join with them to oppose aggression or subversion anywhere in the Americas. And let every other power know that this Hemisphere intends to remain the master of its own house.

To that world assembly of sovereign states, the United Nations, our last best hope in an age where the instruments of war have far outpaced the instruments of peace, we renew our pledge of support—to prevent it from becoming merely a forum for invective—to strengthen its shield of the new and the weak—and to enlarge the area in which its writ may run.

Finally, to those nations who would make themselves our adversary, we offer not a pledge but a request: that both sides begin anew the quest for peace, before the dark powers of destruction unleashed by science engulf all humanity in planned or accidental self-destruction.

We dare not tempt them with weakness. For only when our arms are sufficient, beyond doubt can we be certain beyond doubt that they will never be employed.

But neither can two great and powerful groups of nations take comfort from our present course—both sides overburdened by the cost of modern weapons, both rightly alarmed by the steady spread of the deadly atom, yet both racing to alter that uncertain balance of terror that stays the hand of mankind's final war.

So let us begin anew—remembering on both sides that civility is not a sign of weakness, and sincerity is always subject to proof. Let us never negotiate out of fear. But let us never fear to negotiate.

Let both sides explore what problems unite us instead of belaboring those problems which divide us.

Let both sides, for the first time, formulate serious and precise proposals for the inspection and control of arms—and bring the absolute power to destroy other nations under the absolute control of all nations.

Let both sides seek to invoke the wonders of science instead of its terrors. Together let us explore the stars, conquer the deserts, eradicate disease, tap the ocean depths and encourage the arts and commerce.

Let both sides unite to heed in all corners of the earth the command of Isaiah—to "undo the heavy burdens . . . (and) let the oppressed go free."

And if a beach-head of cooperation may push back the jungle of suspicion, let both sides join in creating a new endeavor, not a new balance of power, but a new world of law, where the strong are just and the weak secure and the peace preserved.

All this will not be finished in the first one hundred days. Nor will it be finished in the first one thousand days, nor in the life of this Administration, nor even perhaps in our lifetime on this planet. But let us begin.

In your hands, my fellow citizens, more than mine, will rest the final success or failure of our course. Since this country was founded, each generation of Americans has been summoned to give testimony to its national loyalty. The graves of young Americans who answered the call to service surround the globe.

Now the trumpet summons us again—not as a call to bear arms, though arms we need—not as a call to battle, though embattled we are—but a call to bear the burden of a long twilight struggle, year in and year out, "rejoicing in hope, patient in tribulation"—a struggle against the common enemies of man: tyranny, poverty, disease and war itself.

Can we forge against these enemies a grand and global alliance, North and South, East and West, that can assure a more fruitful life for all mankind? Will you join in that historic effort?

In the long history of the world, only a few generations have been granted the role of defending freedom in its hour of maximum danger. I do not shrink from this responsibility—I welcome it. I do not believe that any of us would exchange places with any other people or any other generation. The energy, the faith, the devotion which we bring to this endeavor will light our country and all who serve it—and the glow from that fire can truly light the world.

And so, my fellow Americans: ask not what your country can do for you—ask what you can do for your country.

My fellow citizens of the world: ask not what America will do for you, but what together we can do for the freedom of man.

Finally, whether you are citizens of America or citizens of the world, ask of us here the same high standards of strength and sacrifice which we ask of you. With a good conscience our only sure reward, with history the final judge of our deeds, let us go forth to lead the land we love, asking His blessing and His help, but knowing that here on earth God's work must truly be our own.

STATE OF THE UNION

(JANUARY 30, 1961)

Mr. Speaker, Mr. Vice President, Members of the Congress:

It is a pleasure to return from whence I came. You are among my oldest friends in Washington--and this House is my oldest home. It was here, more than 14 years ago, that I first took the oath of Federal office. It was here, for 14 years, that I gained both knowledge and inspiration from members of both parties in both Houses--from your wise and generous leaders--and from the pronouncements which I can vividly recall, sitting where you now sit--including the programs of two great Presidents, the undimmed eloquence of Churchill, the soaring idealism of Nehru, the steadfast words of General de Gaulle. To speak from this same historic rostrum is a sobering experience. To be back among so many friends is a happy one.

I am confident that that friendship will continue. Our Constitution wisely assigns both joint and separate roles to each branch of the government; and a President and a Congress who hold each other in mutual respect will neither permit nor attempt any trespass. For my part, I shall withhold from neither the Congress nor the people any fact or report, past, present, or future, which is necessary for an informed judgment of our conduct and hazards. I shall neither shift the burden of executive decisions to the Congress, nor avoid responsibility for the outcome of those decisions.

I speak today in an hour of national peril and national opportunity. Before my term has ended, we shall have to test anew whether a nation organized and governed such as ours can endure. The outcome is by no means certain. The answers are by no means clear. All of us together--this Administration, this Congress, this nation-must forge those answers.

But today, were I to offer--after little more than a week in office--

detailed legislation to remedy every national ill, the Congress would rightly wonder whether the desire for speed had replaced the duty of responsibility.

My remarks, therefore, will be limited. But they will also be candid. To state the facts frankly is not to despair the future nor indict the past. The prudent heir takes careful inventory of his legacies, and gives a faithful accounting to those whom he owes an obligation of trust. And, while the occasion does not call for another recital of our blessings and assets, we do have no greater asset than the willingness of a free and determined people, through its elected officials, to face all problems frankly and meet all dangers free from panic or fear.

The present state of our economy is disturbing. We take office in the wake of seven months of recession, three and one-half years of slack, seven years of diminished economic growth, and nine years of falling farm income.

Business bankruptcies have reached their highest level since the Great Depression. Since 1951 farm income has been squeezed down by 25 percent. Save for a brief period in 1958, insured unemployment is at the highest peak in our history. Of some five and one-half million Americans who are without jobs, more than one million have been searching for work for more than four months. And during each month some 150,000 workers are exhausting their already meager jobless benefit rights.

Nearly, one-eighth of those who are without jobs live almost without hope in nearly one hundred especially depressed and troubled areas. The rest include new school graduates unable to use their talents, farmers forced to give up their part-time jobs which helped balance their family budgets, skilled and unskilled workers laid off in such important industries as metals, machinery, automobiles and apparel.

Our recovery from the 1958 recession, moreover, was anemic and incomplete. Our Gross National Product never regained its full potential. Unemployment never returned to normal levels. Maximum use of our national industrial capacity was never restored.

In short, the American economy is in trouble. The most resourceful industrialized country on earth ranks among the last in the rate of economic growth. Since last spring our economic growth rate has actually receded. Business investment is in a decline. Profits have fallen below predicted levels. Construction is off. A million unsold automobiles are in inventory. Fewer people are working--and the average work week has shrunk well below 40 hours. Yet prices have continued to rise--so that now too many Americans have less to spend for items that cost more to buy.

Economic prophecy is at best an uncertain art--as demonstrated by the prediction one year ago from this same podium that 1960 would be, and I quote, "the most prosperous year in our history." Nevertheless, forecasts of continued slack and only slightly reduced unemployment through 1961 and 1962 have been made with alarming unanimity-and this Administration does not intend to stand helplessly by.

We cannot afford to waste idle hours and empty plants while awaiting the end of the recession. We must show the world what a free economy can do--to reduce unemployment, to put unused capacity to work, to spur new productivity, and to foster higher economic growth within a range of sound fiscal policies and relative price stability.

I will propose to the Congress within the next 14 days measures to improve unemployment compensation through temporary increases in duration on a self-supporting basis--to provide more food for the families of the unemployed, and to aid their needy children--to redevelop our areas of chronic labor surplus--to expand the services of the U.S. Employment Offices--to stimulate housing and construction--to secure more purchasing power for our lowest paid workers by raising and expanding the minimum wage--to offer tax incentives for sound plant investment--to increase the development of our natural resources--to encourage price stability--and to take other steps aimed at insuring a prompt recovery and paving the way for increased long-range growth. This is not a partisan program concentrating on our weaknesses--it is, I hope, a national program to realize our national strength.

Efficient expansion at home, stimulating the new plant and technology that can make our goods more competitive, is also the key to the international balance of payments problem. Laying aside all alarmist talk and panicky solutions, let us put that knotty problem in its proper perspective.

It is true that, since 1958, the gap between the dollars we spend or invest abroad and the dollars returned to us has substantially widened. This overall deficit in our balance of payments increased by nearly $11 billion in the 3 years--and holders of dollars abroad converted them to gold in such a quantity as to cause a total outflow of nearly $5 billion of gold from our reserve. The 1959 deficit was caused in large part by the failure of our exports to penetrate foreign markets-the result both of restrictions on our goods and our own uncompetitive prices. The 1960 deficit, on the other hand, was more the result of an increase in private capital outflow seeking new opportunity, higher return or speculative advantage abroad.

Meanwhile this country has continued to bear more than its share of the West's military and foreign aid obligations. Under existing policies, another deficit of $2 billion is predicted for 1961--and individuals in those countries whose dollar position once depended on these deficits for improvement now wonder aloud whether our gold reserves will remain sufficient to meet our own obligations.

All this is cause for concern--but it is not cause for panic. For our monetary and financial position remains exceedingly strong. Including our drawing rights in the International Monetary Fund and the gold reserve held as backing for our currency and Federal Reserve deposits, we have some $22 billion in total gold stocks and other international monetary reserves available-and I now pledge that their full strength stands behind the value of the dollar for use if needed.

Moreover, we hold large assets abroad-the total owed this nation far exceeds the claims upon our reserves--and our exports once again substantially exceed our imports.

In short, we need not--and we shall not-take any action to increase the dollar price of gold from $35 an ounce--to impose exchange controls--to reduce our anti-recession efforts--to fall back on restrictive trade policies-- or to weaken our commitments around the world.

This Administration will not distort the value of the dollar in any fashion. And this is a commitment.

Prudence and good sense do require, however, that new steps be taken to ease the payments deficit and prevent any gold crisis. Our success in world affairs has long depended in part upon foreign confidence in our ability to pay. A series of executive orders, legislative remedies and cooperative efforts with our allies will get underway immediately--aimed at attracting foreign investment and travel to this country-promoting American exports, at stable prices and with more liberal government guarantees and financing--curbing tax and customs loopholes that encourage undue spending of private dollars abroad--and (through OECD, NATO and otherwise) sharing with our allies all efforts to provide for the common defense of the free world and the hopes for growth of the less developed lands. While the current deficit lasts, ways will be found to ease our dollar outlays abroad without placing the full burden on the families of men whom we have asked to serve our Flag overseas.

In short, whatever is required will be done to back up all our efforts abroad, and to make certain that, in the future as in the past, the dollar is as "sound as a dollar."

But more than our exchange of international payments is out of balance. The current Federal budget for fiscal 1961 is almost certain to show a net deficit. The budget already submitted for fiscal 1962 will remain in balance only if the Congress enacts all the revenue measures requested--and only if an earlier and sharper up-turn in the economy than my economic advisers now think likely produces the tax revenues estimated. Nevertheless, a new Administration must of necessity build on the spending and revenue estimates already submitted. Within that framework, barring the development of urgent national defense needs or a worsening of the economy, it is my current intention to advocate a program of expenditures which, including revenues from a stimulation of the economy, will not of and by themselves unbalance the earlier Budget.

However, we will do what must be done. For our national household is cluttered with unfinished and neglected tasks. Our cities are being engulfed in squalor. Twelve long years after Congress declared our goal to be "a decent home and a suitable environment for every American family," we still have 25 million Americans living in substandard homes. A new housing program under a new Housing and Urban Affairs Department will be needed this year.

Our classrooms contain 2 million more children than they can properly have room for, taught by 90,000 teachers not properly qualified to teach. One third of our most promising high school graduates are financially unable to continue the development of their talents. The war babies of the 1940's, who overcrowded our schools in the 1950's, are now descending in 1960 upon our colleges-with two college students for every one, ten years from now--and our colleges are ill prepared. We lack the scientists, the engineers and the teachers our world obligations require. We have neglected oceanography, saline water conversion, and the basic research that lies at the root of all progress. Federal grants for both higher and public school education can no longer be delayed.

Medical research has achieved new wonders--but these wonders are too often beyond the reach of too many people, owing to a lack of income (particularly among the aged), a lack of hospital beds, a lack of nursing homes and a lack of doctors and dentists. Measures to provide health care for the aged under Social Security, and to increase the supply of both facilities and personnel, must be undertaken this year.

Our supply of clean water is dwindling. Organized and juvenile crimes cost the taxpayers millions of dollars each year, making it essential that we have improved enforcement and new legislative safeguards. The denial of constitutional rights to some of our fellow Americans on account of race-- at the ballot box and elsewhere--disturbs the national conscience, and subjects us to the charge of world opinion that our democracy is not equal to the high promise of our heritage. Morality in private business has not been sufficiently spurred by morality in public business. A host of problems and projects in all 50 States, though not possible to include in this Message, deserves-and will receive--the attention of both the Congress and the Executive Branch. On most of these matters, Messages will be sent to the Congress within the next two weeks.

But all these problems pale when placed beside those which confront us around the world. No man entering upon this office, regardless of his party, regardless of his previous service in Washington, could fail to be staggered upon learning--even in this brief 10 day period--the harsh enormity of the trials through which we must pass in the next four years. Each day the crises multiply. Each day their solution grows more difficult. Each day we draw nearer the hour of maximum danger, as weapons spread and hostile forces grow stronger. I feel I must inform the Congress that our analyses over the last ten days make it clear that--in each of the principal areas of crisis--the tide of events has been running out and time has not been our friend.

In Asia, the relentless pressures of the Chinese Communists menace the security of the entire area--from the borders of India and South Viet Nam to the jungles of Laos, struggling to protect its newly-won independence. We seek in Laos what we seek in all Asia, and, indeed, in all of the world- freedom for the people and independence for the government. And this Nation shall persevere in our pursuit of these objectives. In Africa, the Congo has been brutally torn by civil strife, political unrest and public disorder. We shall continue to support the heroic efforts of the United Nations to restore peace and order--efforts which are now endangered by mounting tensions, unsolved problems, and decreasing support from many member states.

In Latin America, Communist agents seeking to exploit that region's peaceful revolution of hope have established a base on Cuba, only 90 miles from our shores. Our objection with Cuba is not over the people's drive for a better life. Our objection is to their domination by foreign and domestic tyrannies. Cuban social and economic reform should be encouraged. Questions of economic and trade policy can always be negotiated. But Communist domination in this Hemisphere can never be negotiated.

We are pledged to work with our sister republics to free the Americas of all such foreign domination and all tyranny, working toward the goal of a free hemisphere of free governments, extending from Cape Horn to the Arctic Circle.

In Europe our alliances are unfulfilled and in some disarray. The unity of NATO has been weakened by economic rivalry and partially eroded by national interest. It has not yet fully mobilized its resources nor fully achieved a common outlook. Yet no Atlantic power can meet on its own the mutual problems now facing us in defense, foreign aid, monetary reserves, and a host of other areas; and our close ties with those whose hopes and interests we share are among this Nation's most powerful assets.

Our greatest challenge is still the world that lies beyond the Cold War--but the first great obstacle is still our relations with the Soviet Union and Communist China. We must never be lulled into believing that either power has yielded its ambitions for world domination--ambitions which they forcefully restated only a short time ago. On the contrary, our task is to convince them that aggression and subversion will not be profitable routes to pursue these ends. Open and peaceful competition--for prestige, for markets, for scientific achievement, even for men's minds--is something else again. For if Freedom and Communism were to compete for man's allegiance in a world at peace, I would look to the future with ever increasing confidence.

To meet this array of challenges--to fulfill the role we cannot avoid on the world scene--we must reexamine and revise our whole arsenal of tools: military, economic and political.

One must not overshadow the other: On the Presidential Coat of Arms, the American eagle holds in his right talon the olive branch, while in his left he holds a bundle of arrows. We intend to give equal attention to both.

First, we must strengthen our military tools. We are moving into a period of uncertain risk and great commitment in which both the military and diplomatic possibilities require a Free World force so powerful as to make any aggression clearly futile. Yet in the past, lack of a consistent, coherent military strategy, the absence of basic assumptions about our national requirements and the faulty estimates and duplication arising from inter-service rivalries have all made it difficult to assess accurately how adequate--or inadequate--our defenses really are.

I have, therefore, instructed the Secretary of Defense to reappraise our entire defense strategy--our ability to fulfill our commitments-the effectiveness, vulnerability, and dispersal of our strategic bases, forces and warning systems--the efficiency and economy of our operation and organization-the elimination of obsolete bases and installations-and the adequacy, modernization and mobility of our present conventional and nuclear forces and weapons systems in the light of present and future dangers. I have asked for preliminary conclusions by the end of February-- and I then shah recommend whatever legislative, budgetary or executive action is needed in the light of these conclusions.

In the meantime, I have asked the Defense Secretary to initiate immediately three new steps most clearly needed now:

First, I have directed prompt attention to increase our air-lift capacity. Obtaining additional air transport mobility--and obtaining it now--will better assure the ability of our conventional forces to respond, with discrimination and speed, to any problem at any spot on the globe at any moment's notice. In particular it will enable us to meet any deliberate effort to avoid or divert our forces by starting limited wars in widely scattered parts of the globe.

I have directed prompt action to step up our Polaris submarine program. Using unobligated ship-building funds now (to let contracts originally scheduled for the next fiscal year) will build and place on station-- at least nine months earlier than planned-substantially more units of a crucial deterrent--a fleet that will never attack first, but possess sufficient powers of retaliation, concealed beneath the seas, to discourage any aggressor from launching an attack upon our security.

I have directed prompt action to accelerate our entire missile program. Until the Secretary of Defense's reappraisal is completed, the emphasis here will be largely on improved organization and decision making--on cutting down the wasteful duplications and the time-lag that have handicapped our whole family of missiles. If we are to keep the peace, we need an invulnerable missile force powerful enough to deter any aggressor from even threatening an attack that he would know could not destroy enough of our force to prevent his own destruction. For as I said upon taking the oath of office: "Only when our arms are sufficient beyond doubt can we be certain beyond doubt that they will never be employed."

Secondly, we must improve our economic tools. Our role is essential and unavoidable in the construction of a sound and expanding economy for the entire non-communist world, helping other nations build the strength to meet their own problems, to satisfy their own aspirations--to surmount their own dangers. The problems in achieving this goal are towering and unprecedented-the response must be towering and unprecedented as well, much as Lend-Lease and the Marshall Plan were in earlier years, which brought such fruitful results.

I intend to ask the Congress for authority to establish a new and more effective program for assisting the economic, educational and social development of other countries and continents. That program must stimulate and take more effectively into account the contributions of our allies, and provide central policy direction for all our own programs that now so often overlap, conflict or diffuse our energies and resources. Such a program, compared to past programs, will require

--more flexibility for short run emergencies

--more commitment to long term development --new attention to education at all levels --greater emphasis on the recipient nation's role, their effort, their purpose, with greater social justice for their people, broader distribution and participation by their people and more efficient public administration and more efficient tax systems of their own

--and orderly planning for national and regional development instead of a piecemeal approach.

I hope the Senate will take early action approving the Convention establishing the Organization for Economic Cooperation and Development. This will be an important instrument in sharing with our allies this development effort--working toward the time when each nation will contribute in proportion to its ability to pay. For, while we are prepared to assume our full share of these huge burdens, we cannot and must not be expected to bear them alone.

To our sister republics to the south, we have pledged a new alliance for progress-alianza para progreso. Our goal is a free and prosperous Latin America, realizing for all its states and all its citizens a degree of economic and social progress that matches their historic contributions of culture, intellect and liberty. To start this nation's role at this time in that alliance of neighbors, I am recommending the following:

--That the Congress appropriate in full the $500 million fund pledged by the Act of Bogota, to be used not as an instrument of the Cold War, but as a first step in the sound development of the Americas.

--That a new Inter-Departmental Task Force be established under the leadership of the Department of State, to coordinate at the highest level all policies and programs of concern to the Americas.

--That our delegates to the OAS, working with those of other members, strengthen that body as an instrument to preserve the peace and to prevent foreign domination anywhere in the Hemisphere.

--That, in cooperation with other nations, we launch a new hemispheric attack on illiteracy and inadequate educational opportunities to all levels; and, finally,

--That a Food-for-Peace mission be sent immediately to Latin America to explore ways in which our vast food abundance can be used to help end hunger and malnutrition in certain areas of suffering in our own hemisphere.

This Administration is expanding its Food-for-Peace Program in every possible way. The product of our abundance must be used more effectively to relieve hunger and help economic growth in all corners of the globe. And I have asked the Director of this Program to recommend additional ways in which these surpluses can advance the interests of world peace--including the establishment of world food reserves.

An even more valuable national asset is our reservoir of dedicated men and women-not only on our college campuses but in every age group--who have indicated their desire to contribute their skills, their efforts, and a part of their lives to the fight for world order. We can mobilize this talent through the formation of a National Peace Corps, enlisting the services of all those with the desire and capacity to help foreign lands meet their urgent needs for trained personnel.

Finally, while our attention is centered on the development of the noncommunist world, we must never forget our hopes for the ultimate freedom and welfare of the Eastern European peoples. In order to be prepared to help re-establish historic ties of friendship, I am asking the Congress for increased discretion to use economic tools in this area whenever this is found to be clearly in the national interest. This will require amendment of the Mutual Defense Assistance Control Act along the lines I proposed as a member of the Senate, and upon which the Senate voted last summer. Meanwhile, I hope to explore with the Polish government the possibility of using our frozen Polish funds on projects of peace that will demonstrate our abiding friendship for and interest in the people of Poland.

Third, we must sharpen our political and diplomatic tools the means of cooperation and agreement on which an enforceable world order must ultimately rest.

I have already taken steps to coordinate and expand our disarmament effort--to increase our programs of research and study-and to make arms control a central goal of our national policy under my direction. The deadly arms race, and the huge resources it absorbs, have too long overshadowed all else we must do. We must prevent that arms race from spreading to new nations, to new nuclear powers and to the reaches of outer space. We must make certain that our negotiators are better informed and better prepared-- to formulate workable proposals of our own and to make sound judgments about the proposals of others.

I have asked the other governments concerned to agree to a reasonable delay in the talks on a nuclear test ban--and it is our intention to resume negotiations prepared to reach a final agreement with any nation that is equally willing to agree to an effective and enforceable treaty.

We must increase our support of the United Nations as an instrument to end the Cold War instead of an arena in which to fight it. In recognition of its increasing importance and the doubling of its membership

--we are enlarging and strengthening our own mission to the U.N.

--we shall help insure that it is properly financed.

--we shall work to see that the integrity of the office of the Secretary-General is maintained.

--And I would address a special plea to the smaller nations of the world--to join with us in strengthening this organization, which is far more essential to their security than it is to ours--the only body in the world where no nation need be powerful to be secure, where every nation has an equal voice, and where any nation can exert influence not according to the strength of its armies but according to the strength of its ideas. It deserves the support of all.

Finally, this Administration intends to explore promptly all possible areas of cooperation with the Soviet Union and other nations "to invoke the wonders of science instead of its terrors." Specifically, I now invite all nations--including the Soviet Union--to join with us in developing a weather prediction program, in a new communications satellite program and in preparation for probing the distant planets of Mars and Venus, probes which may someday unlock the deepest secrets of the universe.

Today this country is ahead in the science and technology of space, while the Soviet Union is ahead in the capacity to lift large vehicles into orbit. Both nations would help themselves as well as other nations by ten moving these endeavors from the bitter and wasteful competition of the Cold War. The United States would be willing to join with the Soviet Union and the scientists of all nations in a greater effort to make the fruits of this new knowledge available to all-and, beyond that, in an effort to extend farm technology to hungry nations--to wipe out disease--to increase the exchanges of scientists and. their knowledge--and to make our own laboratories available to technicians of other lands who lack the facilities to pursue their own work. Where nature makes natural allies of us all, we can demonstrate that beneficial relations are possible even with those with whom we most deeply disagree-and this must someday be the basis of world peace and world law.

I have commented on the state of the domestic economy, our balance of payments, our Federal and social budget and the state of the world. I would like to conclude with a few remarks about the state of the Executive branch. We have found it full of honest and useful public servants--but their capacity to act decisively at the exact time action is needed has too often been muffled in the morass of committees, timidities and fictitious theories which have created a growing gap between decision and execution, between planning and reality. In a time of rapidly deteriorating situations at home and abroad, this is bad for the public service and particularly bad for the country; and we mean to make a change.

I have pledged myself and my colleagues in the cabinet to a continuous encouragement of initiative, responsibility and energy in serving the public interest. Let every public servant know, whether his post is high or low, that a man's rank and reputation in this Administration will be determined by the size of the job he does, and not by the size of his staff, his office or his budget. Let it be clear that this Administration recognizes the value of dissent and daring--that we greet healthy controversy as the hallmark of healthy change. Let the public service be a proud and lively career. And let every man and woman who works in any area of our national government, in any branch, at any level, be able to say with pride and with honor in future years: "I served the United States government in that hour of our nation's need."

For only with complete dedication by us all to the national interest can we bring our country through the troubled years that lie ahead. Our problems are critical. The tide is unfavorable. The news will be worse before it is better. And while hoping and working for the best, we should prepare ourselves now for the worst.

We cannot escape our dangers--neither must we let them drive us into panic or narrow isolation. In many areas of the world where the balance of power already rests with our adversaries, the forces of freedom are sharply divided. It is one of the ironies of our time that the techniques of a harsh and repressive system should be able to instill discipline and ardor in its servants--. while the blessings of liberty have too often stood for privilege, materialism and a life of case.

But I have a different view of liberty.

Life in 1961 will not be easy. Wishing it, predicting it, even asking for it, will not make it so. There will be further setbacks before the tide is turned. But turn it we must. The hopes of all mankind rest upon us--not simply upon those of us in this chamber, but upon the peasant in Laos, the fisherman in Nigeria, the exile from Cuba, the spirit that moves every man and Nation who shares our hopes for freedom and the future. And in the final analysis, they rest most of all upon the pride and perseverance of our fellow citizens of the great Republic.

In the words of a great President, whose birthday we honor today, closing his final State of the Union Message sixteen years ago, "We pray that we may be worthy of the unlimited opportunities that God has given us.".

REMARKS ON THE YOUTH FITNESS PROGRAM

(FEBRUARY 21, 1961)

Ladies and Gentlemen, Mr. Secretary:

I want to express my great appreciation at the opportunity to be here with you, and to express my thanks to all of you for having attended this conference.

I asked those members of the Cabinet who felt they were physically fit to come here today, and I am delighted that Mr. Udall and Mr. Robert Kennedy and Governor Ribicoff responded to the challenge.

Some years ago, another President of the United States who was also interested in physical fitness, Mr. Theodore Roosevelt, expressed some ambition that--I think members of the armed services would improve their physical fitness. As there was some question about his, you will recall that he then rode a horse for a hundred miles.

We don't have to prove it in 1961. We take it for granted that the members of the administration are all physically fit and our presence here today is an effort to encourage all of you in your work.

Since the time of the ancient Greeks, we have always felt that there was a close relationship between a strong, vital mind and physical fitness. It is our hope that using the influence of the National Government that we can expand this strong spirit among American men and women, that they will concern themselves with this phase of their personal development.

We do not want in the United States a nation of spectators. We want a nation of participants in the vigorous life. This is not a matter which can be settled, of course, from Washington. It is really a matter which starts with each individual family. It is my hope that mothers and fathers, stretching across the United States, will be concerned about this phase of their children's development, that the communities will be concerned to make it possible for young boys and girls to participate actively in the physical life, and that men and women who have reached the age of maturity will concern themselves with maintaining their own participation in this phase of national vigor--national life.

I am hopeful that we can develop here today, with your help and suggestions, a program which will inspire our country to be concerned. I don't think we have to read these tests which we have seen so much of during the last 10 years to realize that because of the generosity of nature, because of the way our society is organized, that there has been less emphasis on national vigor, national vitality, physical well-being, than there has been in many other countries of the world.

I want to do better. And I think you want to do better. We want to make sure that as our life becomes more sophisticated, as we become more urbanized, that we don't lose this very valuable facet of our national character: physical vitality, which is tied into qualities of character, which is tied into qualities of intellectual vigor and vitality.

So I think that you are performing a real service in being here. We want your suggestions and ideas. This has to flow two ways, and we want the flow today to. come from you to tell us how you think we can use the influence of the National Government-its prestige--in order to increase the emphasis which we can place in every community across the country, in every home, in this most important program.

I am particularly glad that we have here today teachers from over 67 countries who have been teaching in the United States and traveling through it, and who have now come to the National Capital before they return home. I hope they realize how much we learn from them--this is a two-way street, and all of these program which have brought hundreds of teachers in the last 15 to 20 years, which have brought them to all parts of the country; that each of you leaves behind you an understanding of the problems and opportunities of your country, your culture, your civilization, what you believe; and by your looking at us, we see something of ourselves.

This is a program which we benefit from. In many ways, I think, we are the greater beneficiary, and I hope that when you go back to your countries, that you will tell them something of what we are trying to do here. You will tell them, though we may not always realize our high ambitions and our high goals, that nevertheless we are attempting to advance ourselves, and that there is tremendous interest in what is going on in the world around us.

During the fall, I spoke, as many Members of Congress have spoken, about a Peace Corps. I am hopeful that it will be possible to bring that into realization, but what has been most interesting has been the great response of young men and women who desire not merely to serve the United States, but who desire to serve the cause of freedom which is common I think to all countries and to all people.

I hope that when the Peace Corps ultimately is organized, and young men and women go out around the world, that they will place their greatest emphasis on teaching; and secondly, that they will learn themselves far more than they will teach, and that we will therefore have another link which binds us to the world around us.

I want to express my thanks to all of you, whether you come from across the sea or here in the United States. We are all involved in this great effort together. And therefore I wish you well. I express my thanks to all of you. I want you to know that we here in Washington are intimately concerned with the matters in which you are engaged.

Thank you.

ESTABLISHMENT OF THE PEACE CORPS

(MARCH 1, 1961)

I have today signed an Executive Order providing for the establishment of a Peace Corps on a temporary pilot basis. I am also sending to Congress a message proposing authorization of a permanent Peace Corps. This Corps will be a pool of trained American men and women sent overseas by the U.S. Government or through private institutions and organizations to help foreign countries meet their urgent needs for skilled manpower.

It is our hope to have 500 or more people in the field by the end of the year. The initial reactions to the Peace Corps proposal are convincing proof that we have, in this country, an immense reservoir of such men and women—anxious to sacrifice their energies and time and toil to the cause of world peace and human progress.

In establishing our Peace Corps we intend to make full use of the resources and talents of private institutions and groups. Universities, voluntary agencies, labor unions and industry will be asked to share in this effort—contributing diverse sources of energy and imagination—making it clear that the responsibility for peace is the responsibility of our entire society.

We will only send abroad Americans who are wanted by the host country—who have a real job to do—and who are qualified to do that job. Programs will be developed with care, and after full negotiation, in order to make sure that the Peace Corps is wanted and will contribute to the welfare of other people. Our Peace Corps is not designed as an instrument of diplomacy or propaganda or ideological conflict. It is designed to permit our people to exercise more fully their responsibilities in the great common cause of world development.

Life in the Peace Corps will not be easy. There will be no salary and allowances will be at a level sufficient only to maintain health and meet basic needs. Men and women will be expected to work and live alongside the nationals of the country in which they are stationed—doing the same work, eating the same food, talking the same language.

But if the life will not be easy, it will be rich and satisfying. For every young American who participates in the Peace Corps—who works in a foreign land—will know that he or she is sharing in the great common task of bringing to man that decent way of life which is the foundation of freedom and a condition of peace.

ADDRESS TO THE DIPLOMATIC CORPS
OF LATIN AMERICA

(MARCH 13, 1961)

It is a great pleasure for Mrs. Kennedy and for me, for the Vice President and Mrs. Johnson, and for the Members of Congress, to welcome the Ambassadorial Corps of our Hemisphere, our long time friends, to the White House today. One hundred and thirty-nine years ago this week the United States, stirred by the heroic struggle of its fellow Americans, urged the independence and recognition of the new Latin American Republics. It was then, at the dawn of freedom throughout this hemisphere, that Bolivar spoke of his desire to see the Americas fashioned into the greatest region in the world, "greatest," he said, "not so much by virtue of her area and her wealth, as by her freedom and her glory."

Never in the long history of our hemisphere has this dream been nearer to fulfillment, and never has it been in greater danger.

The genius of our scientists has given us the tools to bring abundance to our land, strength to our industry, and knowledge to our people. For the first time we have the capacity to strike off the remaining bonds of poverty and ignorance--to free our people for the spiritual and intellectual fulfillment which has always been the goal of our civilization.

Yet at this very moment of maximum opportunity, we confront the same forces which have imperiled America throughout its history--the alien forces which once again seek to impose the despotisms of the Old World on the people of the New.

I have asked you to come here today so that I might discuss these challenges and these dangers.

We meet together as firm and ancient friends, united by history and experience and by our determination to advance the values of American civilization. For this New World of ours is not a mere accident of geography. Our continents are bound together by a common history, the endless exploration of new frontiers. Our nations are the product of a common struggle, the revolt from colonial rule. And our people share a common heritage, the quest for the dignity and the freedom of man.

The revolutions which gave us birth ignited, in the words of Thomas Paine, "a spark never to be extinguished." And across vast, turbulent continents these American ideals still stir man's struggle for national independence and individual freedom. But as we welcome the spread of the American revolution to other lands, we must also remember that our own struggle--the revolution which began in Philadelphia in 1776, and in Caracas in 1811--is not yet finished. Our hemisphere's mission is not yet completed. For our unfulfilled task is to demonstrate to the entire world that man's unsatisfied aspiration for economic progress and social justice can best be achieved by free men working within a framework of democratic institutions. If we can do this in our own hemisphere, and for our own people, we may yet realize the prophecy of the great Mexican patriot, Benito Juarez, that "democracy is the destiny of future humanity."

As a citizen of the United States let me be the first to admit that we North Americans have not always grasped the significance of this common mission, just as it is also true that many in your own countries have not fully understood the urgency of the need to lift people from poverty and ignorance and despair. But we must turn from these mistakes from the failures and the misunderstandings of the past to a future full of peril, but bright with hope.

Throughout Latin America, a continent rich in resources and in the spiritual and cultural achievements of its people, millions of men and women suffer the daily degradations of poverty and hunger. They lack decent shelter or protection from disease. Their children are deprived of the education or the jobs which are the gateway to a better life. And each day the problems grow more urgent. Population growth is outpacing economic growth--low living standards are further endangered--and discontent--the discontent of a people who know that abundance and the tools of progress are at last within their reach--that discontent is growing. In the words of Jose Figueres, "once dormant peoples are struggling upward toward the sun, toward a better life."

If we are to meet a problem so staggering in its dimensions, our approach must itself be equally bold--an approach consistent with the majestic concept of Operation Pan America. Therefore I have called on all people of the hemisphere to join in a new Alliance for Progress--Alianza para Progreso--a vast cooperative effort, unparalleled in magnitude and nobility of purpose, to satisfy the basic needs of the American people for homes, work and land, health and schools--techo, trabajo y tierra, salud y escuela,

First, I propose that the American Republics begin on a vast new Ten Year Plan for the Americas, a plan to transform the 1960's into a historic decade of democratic progress.

These 10 years will be the years of maximum progress-maximum effort, the years when the greatest obstacles must be overcome, the years when the need for assistance will be the greatest.

And if we are successful, if our effort is bold enough and determined enough, then the close of this decade will mark the beginning of a new era in the American experience. The living standards of every American family will be on the rise, basic education will be available to all, hunger will be a forgotten experience, the need for massive outside help will have passed, most nations will have entered a period of self-sustaining growth, and though there will be still much to do, every American Republic will be the master of its own revolution and its own hope and progress.

Let me stress that only the most determined efforts of the American nations themselves can bring success to this effort. They, and they alone, can mobilize their resources, enlist the energies of their people, and modify their social patterns so that all, and not just a privileged few, share in the fruits of growth. If this effort is made, then outside assistance will give vital impetus to progress; without it, no amount of help will advance the welfare of the people.

Thus if the countries of Latin America are ready to do their part, and I am sure they are, then I believe the United States, for its part, should help provide resources of a scope and magnitude sufficient to make this bold development plan a success--just as we helped to provide, against equal odds nearly, the resources adequate to help rebuild the economies of Western Europe. For only an effort of towering dimensions can ensure fulfillment of our plan for a decade of progress.

Secondly, I will shortly request a ministerial meeting of the Inter-American Economic and Social Council, a meeting at which we can begin the massive planning effort which will be at the heart of the Alliance for Progress.

For if our Alliance is to succeed, each Latin nation must formulate long-range plans for its own development, plans which establish targets and priorities, ensure monetary stability, establish the machinery for vital social change, stimulate private activity and initiative, and provide for a maximum national effort. These plans will be the foundation of our development effort, and the basis for the allocation of outside resources.

A greatly strengthened IA-ECOSOC, working with the Economic Commission for Latin America and the Inter-American Development Bank, can assemble the leading economists and experts of the hemisphere to help each country develop its own development plan--and provide a continuing review of economic progress in this hemisphere.

Third, I have this evening signed a request to the Congress for $500 million as a first step in fulfilling the Act of Bogota. This is the first large-scale Inter-American effort, instituted by my predecessor President Eisenhower, to attack the social barriers which block economic progress. The money will be used to combat illiteracy, improve the productivity and use of their land, wipe out disease, attack archaic tax and land tenure structures, provide educational opportunities, and offer a broad range of projects designed to make the benefits of increasing abundance available to all. We will begin to commit these funds as soon as they are appropriated.

Fourth, we must support all economic integration which is a genuine step toward larger markets and greater competitive opportunity. The fragmentation of Latin American economies is a serious barrier to industrial growth. Projects such as the Central American common market and free trade areas in South America can help to remove these obstacles.

Fifth, the United States is ready to cooperate in serious, case-by-case examinations of commodity market problems. Frequent violent change in commodity prices seriously injure the economies of many Latin American countries, draining their resources and stultifying their growth. Together we must find practical methods of bringing an end to this pattern.

Sixth, we will immediately step up our Food for Peace emergency program, help establish food reserves in areas of recurrent drought, help provide school lunches for children, and offer feed grains for use in rural development. For hungry men and women cannot wait for economic discussions or diplomatic meetings--their need is urgent--and their hunger rests heavily on the conscience of their fellow men.

Seventh, all the people of the hemisphere must be allowed to share in the expanding wonders of science--wonders which have captured man's imagination, challenged the powers of his mind, and given him the tools for rapid progress. I invite Latin American scientists to work with us in new projects in fields such as medicine and agriculture, physics and astronomy, and desalinization, to help plan for regional research laboratories in these and other fields, and to strengthen cooperation between American universities and laboratories.

We also intend to expand our science teacher training programs to include Latin American instructors, to assist in establishing such programs in other American countries, and translate and make available revolutionary new teaching materials in physics, chemistry, biology, and mathematics, so that the young of all nations may contribute their skills to the advance of science.

Eighth, we must rapidly expand the training of those needed to man the economies of rapidly developing countries. This means expanded technical training programs, for which the Peace Corps, for example, will be available when needed. It also means assistance to Latin American universities, graduate schools, and research institutes.

We welcome proposals in Central America for intimate cooperation in higher education--cooperation which can achieve a regional effort of increased effectiveness and excellence. We are ready to help fill the gap in trained manpower, realizing that our ultimate goal must be a basic education for all who wish to learn.

Ninth, we reaffirm our pledge to come to the defense of any American nation whose independence is endangered. As its confidence in the collective security system of the OAS spreads, it will be possible to devote to constructive use a major share of those resources now spent on the instruments of war. Even now, as the government of Chile has said, the time has come to take the first steps toward sensible limitations of arms. And the new generation of military leaders has shown an increasing awareness that armies cannot only defend their countries--they can, as we have learned through our own Corps of Engineers, they can help to build them.

Tenth, we invite our friends in Latin America to contribute to the enrichment of life and culture in the United States. We need teachers of your literature and history and tradition, opportunities for our young people to study in your universities, access to your music, your art, and the thought of your great philosophers. For we know we have much to learn.

In this way you can help bring a fuller spiritual and intellectual life to the people of the United States--and contribute to understanding and mutual respect among the nations of the hemisphere.

With steps such as these, we propose to complete the revolution of the Americas, to build a hemisphere where all men can hope for a suitable standard of living, and all can live out their lives in dignity and in freedom.

To achieve this goal political freedom must accompany material progress. Our Alliance for Progress is an alliance of free governments, and it must work to eliminate tyranny from a hemisphere in which it has no rightful place. Therefore let us express our special friendship to the people of Cuba and the Dominican Republic--and the hope they will soon rejoin the society of free men, uniting with us in common effort.

This political freedom must be accompanied by social change. For unless necessary social reforms, including land and tax reform, are freely made--unless we broaden the opportunity for all of our people--unless the great mass of Americans share in increasing prosperity--then our alliance, our revolution, our dream, and our freedom will fail. But we call for social change by free men-change in the spirit of Washington and Jefferson, of Bolivar and San Martin and Martin--not change which seeks to impose on men tyrannies which we cast out a century and a half ago. Our motto is what it has always been--progress yes, tyranny no-progreso si, tirania no!

But our greatest challenge comes from within--the task of creating an American civilization where spiritual and cultural values are strengthened by an ever-broadening base of material advance--where, within the rich diversity of its own traditions, each nation is free to follow its own path towards progress.

The completion of our task will, of course, require the efforts of all governments of our hemisphere. But the efforts of governments alone will never be enough. In the end, the people must choose and the people must help themselves.

And so I say to the men and women of the Americas--to the campesino in the fields, to the obrero in the cities, to the estudiante in the schools-- prepare your mind and heart for the task ahead--call forth your strength and let each devote his energies to the betterment of all, so that your children and our children in this hemisphere can find an ever richer and a freer life.

Let us once again transform the American continent into a vast crucible of revolutionary ideas and efforts--a tribute to the power of the creative energies of free men and women--an example to all the world that liberty and progress walk hand in hand. Let us once again awaken our American revolution until it guides the struggle of people everywhere--not with an imperialism of force or fear--but the rule of courage and freedom and hope for the future of man.

President John F. Kennedy

ADDRESS TO THE AMERICAN ASSOCIATION OF NEWSPAPER EDITORS

(APRIL 20, 1961)

Mr. Catledge, members of the American Society of Newspaper Editors, ladies and gentlemen:

The President of a great democracy such as ours, and the editors of great newspapers such as yours, owe a common obligation to the people: an obligation to present the facts, to present them with candor, and to present them in perspective. It is with that obligation in mind that I have decided in the last 24 hours to discuss briefly at this time the recent events in Cuba.

On that unhappy island, as in so many other arenas of the contest for freedom, the news has grown worse instead of better. I have emphasized before that this was a struggle of Cuban patriots against a Cuban dictator. While we could not be expected to hide our sympathies, we made it repeatedly clear that the armed forces of this country would not intervene in any way.

Any unilateral American intervention, in the absence of an external attack upon ourselves or an ally, would have been contrary to our traditions and to our international obligations. But let the record show that our restraint is not inexhaustible. Should it ever appear that the inter-American doctrine of non-interference merely conceals or excuses a policy of nonaction--if the nations of this Hemisphere should fail to meet their commitments against outside Communist penetration-then I want it clearly understood that this Government will not hesitate in meeting its primary obligations which are to the security of our Nation!

Should that time ever come, we do not intend to be lectured on "intervention" by those whose character was stamped for all time on the bloody streets of Budapest! Nor would we expect or accept the same outcome which this small band of gallant Cuban refugees must have known that they were chancing, determined as they were against heavy odds to pursue their courageous attempts to regain their Island's freedom.

But Cuba is not an island unto itself; and our concern is not ended by mere expressions of nonintervention or regret. This is not the first time in either ancient or recent history that a small band of freedom fighters has engaged the armor of totalitarianism.

It is not the first time that Communist tanks have rolled over gallant men and women fighting to redeem the independence of their homeland. Nor is it by any means the final episode in the eternal struggle of liberty against tyranny, anywhere on the face of the globe, including Cuba itself.

Mr. Castro has said that these were mercenaries. According to press reports, the final message to be relayed from the refugee forces on the beach came from the rebel commander when asked if he wished to be evacuated. His answer was: "I will never leave this country." That is not the reply of a mercenary. He has gone now to join in the mountains countless other guerrilla fighters, who are equally determined that the dedication of those who gave their lives shall not be forgotten, and that Cuba must not be abandoned to the Communists. And we do not intend to abandon it either!

The Cuban people have not yet spoken their final piece. And I have no doubt that they and their Revolutionary Council, led by Dr. Cardona--and members of the families of the Revolutionary Council, I am informed by the Doctor yesterday, are involved themselves in the Islands--will continue to speak up for a free and independent Cuba.

Meanwhile we will not accept Mr. Castro's attempts to blame this nation for the hatred which his onetime supporters now regard his repression. But there are from this sobering episode useful lessons for us all to learn. Some may be still obscure, and await further information. Some are clear today.

First, it is clear that the forces of communism are not to be underestimated, in Cuba or anywhere else in the world. The advantages of a police state--its use of mass terror and arrests to prevent the spread of free dissent--cannot be overlooked by those who expect the fall of every fanatic tyrant. If the self-discipline of the free cannot match the iron discipline of the mailed fist--in economic, political, scientific and all the other kinds of struggles as well as the military--then the peril to freedom will continue to rise.

Secondly, it is clear that this Nation, in concert with all the free nations of this hemisphere, must take an ever closer and more realistic look at the menace of external Communist intervention and domination in Cuba. The American people are not complacent about Iron Curtain tanks and planes less than 90 miles from their shore. But a nation of Cuba's size is less a threat to our survival than it is a base for subverting the survival of other free nations throughout the hemisphere. It is not primarily our interest or our security but theirs which is now, today, in the greater peril. It is for their sake as well as our own that we must show our will.

The evidence is clear--and the hour is late. We and our Latin friends will have to face the fact that we cannot postpone any longer the real issue of survival of freedom in this hemisphere itself. On that issue, unlike perhaps some others, there can be no middle ground. Together we must build a hemisphere where freedom can flourish; and where any free nation under outside attack of any kind can be assured that all of our resources stand ready to respond to any request for assistance.

Third, and finally, it is clearer than ever that we face a relentless struggle in every corner of the globe that goes far beyond the clash of armies or even nuclear armaments. The armies are there, and in large number. The nuclear armaments are there. But they serve primarily as the shield behind which subversion, infiltration, and a host of other tactics steadily advance, picking off vulnerable areas one by one in situations which do not permit our own armed intervention.

Power is the hallmark of this offensive-power and discipline and deceit. The legitimate discontent of yearning people is exploited. The legitimate trappings of self-determination are employed. But once in power, all talk of discontent is repressed, all self-determination disappears, and the promise of a revolution of hope is betrayed, as in Cuba, into a reign of terror. Those who on instruction staged automatic "riots" in the streets of free nations over the efforts of a small group of young Cubans to regain their freedom should recall the long roll call of refugees who cannot now go back--to Hungary, to North Korea, to North Viet-Nam, to East Germany, or to Poland, or to any of the other lands from which a steady stream of refugees pours forth, in eloquent testimony to the cruel oppression now holding sway in their homeland.

We dare not fail to see the insidious nature of this new and deeper struggle. We dare not fail to grasp the new concepts, the new tools, the new sense of urgency we will need to combat it--whether in Cuba or South Viet-Nam. And we dare not fail to realize that this struggle is taking place every day, without fanfare, in thousands of villages and markets--day and night-- and in classrooms all over the globe.

The message of Cuba, of Laos, of the rising din of Communist voices in Asia and Latin America--these messages are all the same. The complacent, the self-indulgent the soft societies are about to be swept away with the debris of history. Only the strong, only the industrious, only the determined, only the courageous, only the visionary who determine the real nature of our struggle can possibly survive.

No greater task faces this country or this administration. No other challenge is more deserving of our every effort and energy. Too long we have fixed our eyes on traditional military needs, on armies prepared to cross borders, on missiles poised for flight. Now it should be clear that this is no longer enough--that our security may be lost piece by piece, country by country, without the firing of a single missile or the crossing of a single border.

We intend to profit from this lesson. We intend to reexamine and reorient our forces of all kinds--our tactics and our institutions here in this community. We intend to intensify our efforts for a struggle in many ways more difficult than war, where disappointment will often accompany us.

For I am convinced that we in this country and in the free world possess the necessary resource, and the skill, and the added strength that comes from a belief in the freedom of man. And I am equally convinced that history will record the fact that this bitter struggle reached its climax in the late 1950's and the early 1960's. Let me then make clear as the President of the United States that I am determined upon our system's survival and success, regardless of the cost and regardless of the peril!

SPECIAL MESSAGE TO THE CONGRESS ON TAXATION

(APRIL 20, 1961)

To the Congress of the United States:

A strong and sound Federal tax system is essential to America's future. Without such a system, we cannot maintain our defenses and give leadership to the free world. Without such a system, we cannot render the public services necessary for enriching the lives of our people and furthering the growth of our economy.

The tax system must be adequate to meet our public needs. It must meet them fairly, calling on each of us to contribute his proper share to the cost of government. It must encourage efficient use of our resources. It must promote economic stability and stimulate economic growth. Economic expansion in turn creates a growing tax base, thus increasing revenue and thereby enabling us to meet more readily our public needs, as well as our needs as private individuals.

A strong and sound Federal tax system is essential to America's future. Without such a system, we cannot maintain our defenses and give leadership to the free world. Without such a system, we cannot render the public services necessary for enriching the lives of our people and furthering the growth of our economy.

The tax system must be adequate to meet our public needs. It must meet them fairly, calling on each of us to contribute his proper share to the cost of government. It must encourage efficient use of our resources. It must promote economic stability and stimulate economic growth. Economic expansion in turn creates a growing tax base, thus increasing revenue and thereby enabling us to meet more readily our public needs, as well as our needs as private individuals.

This message recognizes the basic soundness of our tax structure. But it also recognizes the changing needs and standards of our economic and international position, and the constructive reform needs to keep our tax system up to date and to maintain its equity. Previous messages have emphasized the need for prompt Congressional and Executive action to alleviate the deficit in our international balance of payments--to increase the modernization, productivity and competitive status of American industry-- to stimulate the expansion and growth of our economy--to eliminate to the extent possible economic injustice within our own society--and to maintain the level of revenues requested in my predecessor's Budget. In each of these endeavors, tax policy has an important role to play and necessary tax changes are herein proposed.

The elimination of certain defects and inequities as proposed below will provide revenue gains to offset the tax reductions offered to stimulate the economy. Thus no net loss of revenue is involved in this set of proposals. I wish to emphasize here that they are a "set"--and that considerations of both revenue and equity, as well as the interrelationship of many of the proposals, urge their consideration as a unit.

I am instructing the Secretary of the Treasury to furnish the Committee on Ways and Means of the House a detailed explanation of these proposals in connection with their legislative consideration.

I. LONG-RANGE TAX REFORM

While it is essential that the Congress receive at this time this Administration's proposals for urgent and obvious tax adjustments needed to fulfill the aims listed above, time has not permitted the comprehensive review necessary for a tax structure which is so complicated and so critically important to so many people. This message is but a first though urgent step along the road to constructive reform.

I am directing the Secretary of the Treasury, building on recent tax studies of the Congress, to undertake the research and preparation of a comprehensive tax reform program to be placed before the next session of the Congress.

Progressing from these studies, particularly those of the Committee on Ways and Means and the Joint Economic Committee, the program should be aimed at providing a broader and more uniform tax base, together with an appropriate rate structure. We can thereby work toward the goal of a higher rate of economic growth, a more equitable tax structure, and a simpler tax law. I know these objectives are shared by--and, at this particular time of year, acutely desired by--the vast majority of the American people.

In meeting the demands of war finance, the individual income tax moved from a selective tax imposed on the wealthy to the means by which the great majority of our citizens participates in paying for well over one-half of our total budget receipts. It is supplemented by the corporation income tax, which provides for another quarter of the total.

This emphasis on income taxation has been a sound development. But so many taxpayers have become so preoccupied with so many tax-saving devices that business decisions are interfered with, and the efficient functioning of the price system is distorted.

Moreover, special provisions have developed into an increasing source of preferential treatment to various groups. Whenever one taxpayer is permitted to pay less, someone else must be asked to pay more. The uniform distribution of the tax burden is thereby disturbed and higher rates are made necessary by the narrowing of the tax base. Of course, some departures from uniformity are needed to promote desirable social or economic objectives of overriding importance which can be achieved most effectively through the tax mechanism. But many of the preferences which have developed do not meet such a test and need to be reevaluated in our tax reform program.

It will be a major aim of our tax reform program to reverse this process, by broadening the tax base and reconsidering the rate structure. The result should be a tax system that is more equitable, more efficient and more conducive to economic growth.

II. TAX INCENTIVE FOR MODERNIZATION AND EXPANSION

The history of our economy has been one of rising productivity, based on improvement in skills, advances in technology, and a growing supply of more efficient tools and equipment. This rise has been reflected in rising wages and standards of living for our workers, as well as a healthy rate of growth for the economy as a whole. It has also been the foundation of our leadership in world markets, even as we enjoyed the highest wage rates in the world.

Today, as we face serious pressure on our balance of payments position, we must give special attention to the modernization of our plant and equipment. Forced to reconstruct after wartime devastation, our friends abroad now possess a modern industrial system helping to make them formidable competitors in world markets. If our own goods are to compete with foreign goods in price and quality, both at home and abroad, we shall need the most efficient plant and equipment.

At the same time, to meet the needs of a growing population and labor force, and to achieve a rising per capita income and employment level, we need a high and rising level of both private and public capital formation. In my preceding messages, I have proposed programs to meet some of our needs for such capital formation in the public area, including investment in intangible capital such as education and research, as well as investment in physical capital such as buildings and highways. I am now proposing additional incentives for the modernization and expansion of private plant and equipment.

Inevitably, capital expansion and modernization-now frequently under the name of automation--alter established modes of production. Great benefits result and are distributed widely--but some hardships result as well. This places heavy responsibilities on public policy, not to retard modernization and capital expansion but to promote growth and ameliorate hardships when they do occur--to maintain a high level of demand and employment, so that those who are displaced will be reabsorbed quickly into new positions--and to assist in retraining and finding new jobs for such displaced workers. We are developing, through such measures as the Area Redevelopment Bill and a strengthened Employment Service, as well as assistance to the unemployed, the programs designed to achieve these objectives.

High capital formation can be sustained only by a high and rising level of demand for goods and service. Indeed, the investment incentive itself can contribute materially to achieving the prosperous economy under which this incentive will make its maximum contribution to economic growth. Rather than delaying its adoption until all excess capacity has disappeared and unemployment is low, we should take this step now to strengthen our anti-recession program, stimulate employment and increase our export markets.

Additional expenditures on plant and equipment will immediately create more jobs in the construction, lumber, steel, cement, machinery and other related capital goods industries. The staffing of these new plants--and filling the orders for new export markets--will require additional employees. The additional wages of these workers will help create still more jobs in consumer goods and service industries. The increase in jobs resulting from a full year's operation of such an incentive is estimated at about half a million.

Specifically, therefore, I recommend enactment of an investment tax incentive in the form of a tax credit of

--15% of all new plant and equipment investment expenditures in excess of current depreciation allowances

--6% of such expenditures below this level but in excess of 50% of depreciation allowances; with

--10% on the first $5,000 of new investment as a minimum credit.

This credit would be taken as an offset against the firm's tax liability, up to an overall limitation of 30% in the reduction of that liability in any one year. It would be separate from and in addition to depreciation of the eligible new investment at cost. It would be available to individually owned businesses as well as corporate enterprises, and apply to eligible investment expenditures made after January 1 of this year. To remain a real incentive and make a maximum contribution to those areas of capital expansion and modernization where it is most needed, and to permit efficient administration, eligible investment expenditures would be limited to expenditures on new plant and equipment, on assets located in .the United States, and on assets with a life of six years or more. Investments by public utilities other than transportation would be excluded, as would be investment in residential construction including apartments and hotels.

Of the eligible firms, it is expected that many small firms would be able to take advantage of the minimum credit of 10% on the first $5000 of new investment which is designed to provide a helpful stimulus to the many small businesses in need of modernization. Other small firms, subject to a 30% tax rate, would strive to be eligible for the full 15% credit--the equivalent for such firms of a deduction from their gross income for tax purposes of 50% of the cost of new investment. Among the remaining firms, it is expected that a majority would be induced to make new investments in modern plant and equipment in excess of their depreciation in order to earn the 15% credit. New and growing firms would be particularly benefited. The 6% credit for those whose new investment expenditures fall between 50% and 100% of their depreciation allowances is designed to afford some substantial incentive to the depressed or hesitant firm which knows it cannot yet achieve the 15% credit.

In arriving at this form of tax encouragement to investment, careful consideration was given to other alternatives. If the credit were given across-the-board to all new investment, a much larger revenue loss would result from those expenditures which would have been undertaken anyway or represent no new level of effort. Our objective is to provide the largest possible inducement to new investment which would not otherwise be undertaken. Thus the plan recommended above would involve the same revenue loss--approximately $1.7 billion--as only a 7 percent credit across-the-board to all new investment.

The use of current depreciation allowances as the threshold above which the higher rate of credit would apply recommends itself for a number of reasons. Depreciation reflects the average level of investment over the past, but is a less restrictive and more stable test than the use of an average of investment expenditures for a period such as the preceding five years. In addition, the depreciation allowances themselves in effect supply tax-free funds for investment up to this level. We now propose a tax credit-which would help to secure funds needed for the additional investment beyond that level.

The proposed credit, in terms of the revenue loss involved, will also be much more effective as an inducement to investment than an outright reduction in the rate of corporation income tax. Its benefits would be distributed more broadly, since the proposed credit will apply to individuals and partnerships as well as corporations. It will also be more effective as a direct incentive to corporate investment, and increase available funds more specifically in those corporations most likely to use them for additional investment. In short, whereas the credit will have the advantage of focusing on the profitability of new investment, much of the revenue loss under a general corporate rate reduction would be diverted into raising the profitability of old investment.

It is true that this advantage of focusing entirely on new investment is shared by the alternative strongly urged by some--a tax change permitting more rapid depreciation of new assets (be it accelerated depreciation or an additional depreciation allowance for the first year). But the proposed investment credit would be superior, in my view, for a number of reasons. In the first place, the determination of the length of an asset's life and proper methods of depreciation have a normal and important function in determining taxable income, wholly apart from any considerations of incentive; and they should not be altered or manipulated for other purposes that would interfere with this function. It may be that on examination some of the existing depreciation rules will be found to be outmoded and inequitable; but that is a question that should be separated from investment incentives. A review of these rules and methods is underway in the Treasury Department as a part of its overall tax reform study to determine whether changes are appropriate and, if so, what form they should take. Adoption of the proposed incentive credit would in no way foreclose later action on these aspects of depreciation.

In the second place, an increase in tax depreciation tends to be recorded in the firm's accounts, thereby raising current costs and acting as a deterrent to price reduction. The proposed investment credit would not share this defect.

Finally, it is clear that the tax credit would be more effective in inducing new investment for the same revenue loss. The entire credit would be reflected immediately in the increased funds available for investment without increasing the company's future tax liability. A speed-up in depreciation only postpones the timing of the tax liability on profits from the investment to a later date--an increase in profitability not comparable to that of an outright tax credit. Yet accelerated depreciation is much more costly in immediate revenues.

For example, on an average investment, a tax credit of 15% would bring the same return to the firm as an additional first year depreciation of over 50% of the cost of the investment. Yet the immediate revenue loss to the Treasury from such additional depreciation would be twice as much, and would remain considerably higher for many years. The incentive to new investment our economy needs, and which this recommendation would provide at a revenue loss of $ 1.7 billion, could be supplied by an initial write-off only at an immediate cost of $3.4 billion.

I believe this investment tax credit will become a useful and continuous part of our tax structure. But it will be a new venture and remain in need of review. Moreover, it may prove desirable for the Congress to modify the credit from time to time, so as to adapt it to the needs of a changing economy. I strongly urge its adoption in this session.

III. TAX TREATMENT OF FOREIGN INCOME

Changing economic conditions at home and abroad, the desire to achieve greater equity in taxation, and the strains which have developed in our balance of payments position in the last few years, compel us to examine critically certain features of our tax system which, in conjunction with the tax system of other countries, consistently favor United States private investment abroad compared with investment in our own economy.

1. Elimination of tax deferral privileges in developed countries and "tax haven" deferral privileges in all countries. Profits earned abroad by American firms operating through foreign subsidiaries are, under present tax laws, subject to United States tax only when they are returned to the parent company in the form of dividends. In some cases, this tax deferral has made possible indefinite postponement of the United States tax; and, in those countries where income taxes are lower than in the United States, the ability to defer the payment of U.S. tax by retaining income in the subsidiary companies provides a tax advantage for companies operating through overseas subsidiaries that is not available to companies operating solely in the United States. Many American investors properly made use of this deferral in the conduct of their foreign investment. Though changing conditions now make continuance of the privilege undesirable, such change of policy implies no criticism of the investors who so utilize this privilege.

The undesirability of continuing deferral is underscored where deferral has served as a shelter for tax escape through the unjustifiable use of tax havens such as Switzerland. Recently more and more enterprises organized abroad by American firms have arranged their corporate structures--aided by artificial arrangements between parent and subsidiary regarding intercompany pricing, the transfer of patent licensing rights, the shifting of management fees, and similar practices which maximize the accumulation of profits in the tax haven--so as to exploit the multiplicity of foreign tax systems and international agreements in order to reduce sharply or eliminate completely their tax liabilities both at home and abroad.

To the extent that these tax havens and other tax deferral privileges result in U.S. firms investing or locating abroad largely for tax reasons, the efficient allocation of international resources is upset, the initial drain on our already adverse balance of payments is never fully compensated, and profits are retained and reinvested abroad which would otherwise be invested in the United States. Certainly since the postwar reconstruction of Europe and Japan has been completed, there are no longer foreign policy reasons for providing tax incentives for foreign investment in the economically advanced countries.

If we are seeking to curb tax havens, if we recognize that the stimulus of tax deferral is no longer needed for investment in the developed countries, and if we are to emphasize investment in this country in order to stimulate our economy and our plant modernization, as well as ease our balance of payments deficit, we can no longer afford existing tax treatment of foreign income.

I therefore recommend that legislation be adopted which would, after a two-step transitional period, tax each year American corporations on their current share of the undistributed profits realized in that year by subsidiary corporations organized in economically advanced countries. This current taxation would also apply to individual shareholders of closely-held corporations in those countries. Since income taxes paid abroad are properly a credit against the United States income tax, this would subject the income from such business activities to essentially the same tax rates as business activities conducted in the United States. To permit firms to adjust their operations to this change, I also recommend that this result be achieved in equal steps over a two-year period, under which only one-half of the profits would be affected during 1962. Where the foreign taxes paid have been close to the U.S. rates, the impact of this change would be small.

This proposal will maintain United States investment in the developed countries at the level justified by market forces. American enterprise abroad will continue to compete with foreign firms. With their access to capital markets at home and abroad, their advanced technical know-how, their energy, resourcefulness and many other advantages, American firms will continue to occupy their rightful place in the markets of the world. While the rate of expansion of some American business operations abroad may be reduced through the withdrawal of tax deferral such reduction would be consistent with the efficient distribution of capital resources in the world, our balance of payments needs, and fairness to competing firms located in our own country.

At the same time, I recommend that tax deferral be continued for income from investment in the developing economies. The free world has a strong obligation to assist in the development of these economies, and private investment has an important contribution to make. Continued income tax deferral for these areas will be helpful in this respect. In addition, the proposed elimination of income tax deferral on United States earnings in industrialized countries should enhance the relative attraction of investment in the less developed countries.

On the other hand, I recommend elimination of the "tax haven" device anywhere in the world, even in the underdeveloped countries, through the elimination of tax deferral privileges for those forms of activities, such as trading, licensing, insurance and others, that typically seek out tax haven methods of operation. There is no valid reason to permit their remaining

61

untaxed regardless of the country in which they are located.

2. Taxation of Foreign Investment Companies. For some years now we have witnessed substantial outflows of capital from the United States into investment companies created abroad whose principal justification lies in the tax benefits which their method of operation produces. I recommend that these tax benefits be removed and that income derived through such foreign investment companies be treated in substantially the same way as income from domestic investment companies.

3. Taxation of American Citizens Abroad. It is no more justifiable to provide tax exemptions for individuals living in the developed countries than it is to provide tax inducements for capital investment there. Nor should we permit totally unjustified tax benefits to be obtained by those Americans whose choice of residence is dictated primarily by their desire to minimize taxes.

I, therefore, recommend:

--that the total tax exemption now accorded the earned income of American citizens residing abroad be completely terminated for those residing in economically advanced countries;

--that this exemption for earned income be limited to $20,000 for those residing in the less developed countries; and

--that the exemption of $20,000 of earned income now accorded those citizens who stay (but do not reside) abroad for 17 out of 18 months also be completely terminated for those living or traveling in the economically advanced countries.

4. Estate Tax on Property Located Abroad. I recommend that the exclusion from the estate tax accorded real property situated abroad be terminated. With the adoption several years ago of the credit for foreign taxes under the estate tax, there is no justification for the continued exemption of such property.

5. Allowance for Foreign Tax on Dividends. Finally, the method by which the credit for foreign income taxes is computed in the case of dividends involves a double allowance for foreign income taxes and should be corrected.

These proposals, along with more detailed and technical changes needed to improve the taxation of foreign income, are expected to reduce substantially our balance of payments deficit and to increase revenues by at least $250 million per year.

IV. CORRECTION OF OTHER STRUCTURAL DEFECTS

I next recommend a number of measures to remove other serious defects in the income tax structure. These changes, while making a beginning toward the comprehensive tax reform program mentioned above, will provide sufficient revenue gains to offset the cost of the investment tax credit and keep the revenue-producing potential of our tax structure intact.

1. Withholding on Interest and Dividends. Our system of combined withholding and voluntary reporting on wages and salaries under the individual income tax has served us well. Introduced during the war when the income tax was extended to millions of new taxpayers, the wage-withholding system has been one of the most important and successful advances in our tax system in recent times. Initial difficulties were quickly overcome, and the new system helped the taxpayer no less than the tax collector.

It is the more unfortunate, therefore, that the application of the withholding principle has remained incomplete. Withholding does not apply to dividends and interest, with the result that substantial amounts of such income, particularly interest, improperly escape taxation. It is estimated that about $3 billion of taxable interest and dividends are unreported each year. This is patently unfair to those who must as a result bear a larger share of the tax burden. Re-cipients of dividends and interest should pay their tax no less than those who receive wage and salary income, and the tax should be paid just as promptly. Large continued avoidance of tax on the part of some has a steadily demoralizing effect on the compliance of others.

This gap in reporting has not been appreciably lessened by educational programs. Nor can it be effectively closed by intensified enforcement measures, except by the expenditure of inordinate amounts of time and money. Withholding on corporate dividends and on investment type interest, such as interest paid on taxable government and corporate securities and savings accounts, is both necessary and practicable.

I, therefore, recommend the enactment of legislation to provide for a 20% withholding rate on corporate dividends and taxable investment type interest, effective January 1, 1962, under a system which would not require the preparation of withholding statements to be sent to recipients. It would thus place a relatively light burden of compliance on the payers of interest and dividends--certainly less than that placed on payers of wages and salaries--while at the same time largely solving the compliance problem for most of the taxpayers receiving dividends and interest. Steps will also be taken to avoid hardships for recipients who are not subject to tax.

The remaining need for compliance, largely in the high income group subject to a higher tax rate, would be met through the concentration of enforcement devices on taxpayers in these brackets. Introduction of equipment for the automatic processing of information returns would be especially helpful for this purpose and would thus supplement the extension of withholding.

Enactment of this proposal is estimated to increase revenue by $600 million per year.

2. Repeal of the Dividend Credit and Exclusion. The present law provides for an exclusion from income of the first $50 of dividends received from domestic corporations and for a 4% credit against tax of such dividend income in excess of $50. These provisions were enacted in 1954. Proponents argued that they would encourage capital formation through equity investment, and that they would provide a partial offset to the so-called double taxation of dividend income. It is now clear that they serve neither purpose well; and I, therefore, recommend the repeal of both the dividend credit and exclusion.

The dividend credit and exclusion are not an efficient stimulus to capital expansion in the form of plant and equipment. The revenue losses resulting from these provisions are spread over a large volume of outstanding shares rather than being concentrated on new shares; and the stimulating effects of the provisions are thus greatly diluted, resulting in relatively little increases in the supply of equity funds and a relatively slight reduction in the cost of equity financing. In fact, such reduction as does occur is more likely to benefit large corporations with easy access to the capital market, while being of little use to small firms which are not so favorably situated. Insofar as raising the profitability of new investment in plant and equipment is concerned, the tax investment credit proposed above would be far more effective since it is offered to the corporation, where the actual investment decision is made.

The dividend credit and exclusion are equally inadequate as a solution to the so-called problem of double taxation. Whatever may be the merits of the arguments respecting the existence of double taxation, the provisions of the 1954 Act clearly do not offer an appropriate remedy. They greatly overcompensate the dividend recipient in the high income bracket, while giving either insufficient or no relief to shareholders with smaller income.

This point deserves emphasis. For viewed simply as a means of tax reduction, the dividend credit is. wholly inequitable. The distribution of its benefits is highly favorable to the taxpayers in the upper income groups who receive the major part of dividend income. Only about 10 percent of dividend income accrues to those with incomes below $5,000; about 80 percent of it accrues to that 6.5% of taxpayers whose incomes exceed $10,000 a year. Similarly, dividend income is a sharply rising fraction of total income as we move up the income scale. Thus, dividend income is about 1 percent of all income from all sources for those taxpayers with incomes of $3,000 to $5,000; but it constitutes more than 25 percent of the income for those with $100,000 to $150,000 of income, and about 50 percent for those with incomes over $1,000,000,

The role of the dividend credit should not be confused with the broader question of tax rates applicable to high incomes. These high rates deserve re-examination; and this is one of the problems which will be examined in the context of next year's tax reform. But if top bracket rates were to be reduced, the dividend credit is not the way to do it. Rate reductions, if appropriate, should apply no less to those with high incomes from other sources, such as professional and salaried people whose tax position is particularly difficult today.

If the credit is eliminated, the $50 exclusion should also be discarded for similar reasons. The tax saving from the exclusion is substantially greater for a dividend recipient with a high income than for a recipient with low income. Moreover, on equity grounds, there is no reason for giving tax reduction to that small fraction of low income tax payers who receive dividends in contrast to those who must live on wages, interest, rents or other forms of income.

The 1954 formula therefore is a dead-end and should be rescinded, effective December 31 of this year. The estimated revenue gain is $450 million per year.

3. Expense Accounts. In recent years widespread abuses have developed through the use of the expense account. Too many firms and individuals have devised means of deducting too many personal living expenses as business expenses, thereby charging a large part of their cost to the Federal Government. Indeed, expense account living has become a byword in the

American scene.

This is a matter of national concern, affecting not only our public revenues, our sense of fairness, and our respect for the tax system, but our moral and business practices as well. This widespread distortion of our business and social structure is largely a creature of the tax system, and the time has come when our tax laws should cease their encouragement of luxury spending as a charge on the Federal treasury. The slogan--"It's deductible"--should pass from our scene.

Tighter enforcement of present legislation will not suffice. Even though in some instances entertainment and related expenses have an association with the needs of business, they nevertheless confer substantial tax-free personal benefits to the recipients. In other cases, deductions are obtained by disguising personal expenses as business outlays. But under present law, it is extremely difficult to separate out and disallow such pseudo-business expenditures. New legislation is needed to deal with the problem.

I, therefore, recommend that the cost of such business entertainment and the maintenance of entertainment facilities (such as yachts and hunting lodges) be disallowed in full as a tax deduction and that restrictions be imposed on the deductibility of business gifts, expenses of business trips combined with vacations, and excessive personal living expenses incurred on business travel away from home.

I feel confident that these measures will be welcomed by the American people. I am also confident that business firms, now forced to emulate the expense account favors of their competitors, however unsound or uneconomical such practices may be, will welcome the removal of this pressure. These measures will strengthen both our tax structure and the moral fibre of our society. These provisions should be effective as of January 1, 1962 and are estimated to increase Treasury receipts by at least $250 million per year.

4. Capital Gains on Sale of Depreciable Business Property. Another flaw which should be corrected at this time relates to the taxation of gains on the sale of depreciable business property. Such gains are now taxed at the preferential rate applicable to capital gains, even though they represent ordinary income.

This situation arises because the statutory rate of depreciation may not coincide with the actual decline in the value of the asset. While the taxpayer holds the property, depreciation is taken as a deduction from ordinary income. Upon its resale, where the amount of depreciation allowable exceeds the decline in the actual value of the asset so that a gain occurs, this gain under present law is taxed at the preferential capital gains rate. The advantages resulting from this practice have been increased by the liberalization of depreciation rates.

Our capital gains concept should not encompass this kind of income. This inequity should be eliminated, and especially so in view of the proposed investment credit. We should not encourage through tax incentives the further acquisition of such property as long as this loophole remains.

I therefore recommend that capital gains treatment be withdrawn from gains on the disposition of depreciable property, both personal and real property, to the extent that depreciation has been deducted for such property by the seller in previous years, permitting only the excess of the sales price over the original cost to be treated as a capital gain. The remainder should be treated as ordinary income. This reform should immediately become effective as to all sales taking place after the date of enactment. It is estimated to raise revenue by $200 million annually.

5. Cooperatives and Financial Institutions. Another area of the tax laws which calls for attention is the treatment of cooperatives, private lending institutions, and fire and casualty insurance companies.

Contrary to the intention of Congress, substantial income from certain cooperative enterprises, reflecting business operations, is not being taxed either to the cooperative organization itself or its members. This situation must be corrected in a manner that is fair and just to both the cooperatives and competing businesses.

The present inequity has resulted from court decisions which held patronage refunds in certain forms to be non-taxable. I recommend that the law be clarified so that all earnings are taxable to either the cooperatives or to their patrons, assessing the patron on the earnings that are allocated to him as patronage dividends or refunds in scrip or cash. The withholding principle recommended above should also be applied to patronage dividends or refunds so that the average patron receiving scrip will, in effect, be given the cash to pay his tax on his patronage dividend or refund. The cooperatives should not be penalized by the assessment of a patronage tax upon dividends or refunds taxable to the patron but left in the business as a substitute for the sale of securities to obtain additional equity capital. The exemption for rural electric cooperatives and credit unions should be continued.

The tax provisions applicable to fire and casualty insurance companies, originally adopted in 1942, need to be reviewed in the light of current conditions. Many of these companies, organized on the mutual or reciprocal basis are now taxed under a special formula which does not take account of their underwritings gains and thus results in an inequitable distribution of the tax burden among various types of companies. Consideration should be given to taxing mutual or reciprocal companies on a basis similar to stock companies, following the pattern of similar treatment of stock and mutual enterprise in the life insurance field.

Some of the most important types of private savings and lending institutions in the country are accorded tax deductible reserve provisions which substantially reduce or eliminate their Federal income tax liability. These provisions should be reviewed with the aim of assuring non-discriminatory treatment.

Remedial legislation in these fields would enlarge the revenues and contribute to a fair and sound tax structure.

V. TAX ADMINISTRATION

One of the major characteristics of our tax system, and one in which we can take a great deal of pride, is that it operates primarily through individual self-assessment. The integrity of such a system depends upon the continued willingness of the people honestly and accurately to discharge this annual price of citizenship. To the extent that some people are dishonest or careless in their dealings with the government, the majority is forced to carry a heavier tax burden.

For voluntary serf-assessment to be both meaningful and productive of revenues, the citizens must not only have confidence in the fairness of the tax laws, but also in their uniform and vigorous enforcement of these laws. If non-compliance by the few continues unchecked, the confidence of the many in our self-assessment system will be shaken and one of the cornerstones of our government weakened.

I have in this message already recommended the application of withholding to dividends and interest and revisions to halt the abuses of expense accounts. These measures will improve taxpayer compliance and raise the regard of taxpayers for the fairness of our system. In addition, I propose three further measures to improve the tax enforcement machinery.

1. Taxpayer Account Numbers. The Internal Revenue Service has begun the installation of automatic data processing equipment to improve administration of the growing job of tax collection and enforcement. A system of identifying taxpayer account numbers, which would make possible the bringing together of all tax data for any one particular taxpayer, is an essential part of such an improved collection and enforcement program.

For this purpose, social security numbers would be used by taxpayers already having them. The small minority currently without such numbers' would be assigned numbers which these persons could later use as well for social security purposes if needed. The numbers would be entered on tax returns, information returns, and related documents.

I recommend that legislation be enacted to authorize the use of taxpayer account numbers beginning January 1, 1962 to identify taxpayer accounts throughout the processing and record keeping operations of the Internal Revenue Service.

2. Increased Audit Coverage. The examination of tax returns is the essence of the enforcement process. The number of examining personnel of the Internal Revenue Service, however, has been consistently inadequate to cope with the audit workload. Consequently, it has been unable to audit carefully many of the returns which should be so examined. Anticipated growth in our population will, of course, increase this enforcement problem.

Related to broadened tax audit is the criminal enforcement program of the Revenue Service. Here, the guiding principle is the creation of a deterrent to tax evasion and to maintain or, if possible, increase voluntary compliance with all taxing statutes. This means placing an appropriate degree of investigative emphasis on all types of tax violations, in all geographical areas, and identifying violations of substance in all income brackets regardless of occupation, business or profession.

Within this framework of a balanced enforcement effort, the Service is placing special investigative emphasis on returns filed by persons receiving income from illegal sources. I have directed all Federal law enforcement agencies to cooperate fully with the Attorney General in a drive against organized crime, and to utilize their resources to the maximum extent in conducting investigations of individuals engaged in criminal activity on a major scale. With the foregoing in mind, I have directed the Secretary of the

Treasury to provide through the Internal Revenue Service a maximum effort in this field.

To fulfill these requirements for improved audits, enforcement and anti-crime investigation, it is essential that the Service be provided additional resources which will pay their own cost many times over. In furthering the Service's long-range plans, the prior Administration asked additional appropriations of $27.4 million to hire about 3,500 additional personnel during fiscal 1962, including provisions for the necessary increases in space and modern equipment vital to the efficient operation of the Service. To meet the commitments described above, this Administration reviewed these proposals and recommended that they be increased by another $7 million and 765 additional personnel to expedite the expansion and criminal enforcement programs. The pending alternative of only 1,995 additional personnel, or less than one-half of the number requested, this Administration would constitute little more than the additional employees needed each year during the 1960's just to keep up with the estimated growth in number and complexity of returns filed. Thus I must again strongly urge the Congress to give its full support to my original request. These increases will safeguard the long-term adequacy of the nation's traditional voluntary compliance system and, at the same time, return the added appropriations several times over in added revenue.

3. Inventory Reporting. It is increasingly apparent that the manipulation of inventories has become a frequent method of avoiding taxes. Current laws and regulations generally permit the use of inventory methods which are acceptable in recognized accounting practice. Deviations from these methods, which are not always easy to detect during examination of tax returns, can often lead to complete non-payment of taxes until the inventories are liquidated; and, for some taxpayers, this represents permanent tax reduction. The understating of the valuation of inventories is the device most frequently used.

I have directed the Internal Revenue Service to give increasing attention to this area of tax avoidance, through a stepped-up emphasis on both the verification of the amounts reported as inventories and an examination of methods used in arriving at their reported valuation.

VI. TAX RATE EXTENSION

As recommended by my predecessor, it is again necessary that Congress enact an extension of present corporation income and excise tax rates otherwise scheduled for reduction or termination on July 1, 1961 Such extension has been adopted by the Congress on a number of previous occasions, and our present revenue requirements make such extension absolutely necessary again this year.

In the absence of such legislation, the corporate tax rate would be decreased 5 percentage points, from 52 percent to 47 percent, excise tax rates on distilled spirits, beer, wines, cigarettes, passenger automobiles, automobile parts and accessories, and the transportation of persons would also decline; and the excise tax on general telephone service would expire. We cannot afford the loss of these revenues at this time.

VII. AVIATION FUEL

The last item on the agenda relates to aviation fuel. The two previous Administrations have urged that civil aviation, a mature and growing industry, be required to pay a fair share of the costs of operating and improving the Federal airways system. The rapidly mounting costs of these essential services to air transportation makes the imposition of user charges more imperative now than ever before. The most efficient method for recovering a portion of these costs equitably from the airway users is through a tax on aviation fuel. Present law provides for a net tax of 2 cents a gallon on aviation gasoline but no tax on jet fuel. The freedom from tax of jet fuel is inequitable and is resulting in substantial revenue losses due to the transition to jet power and the resulting decline in gasoline consumption.

My predecessor recommended a flat 41/2 cent tax for both aviation gasoline and jet fuels. Such a request, however, appears to be unrealistic in view of the current financial condition of the airline industry. Therefore, I recommend:

--extending the present net 2-cent rate on aviation gasoline to jet fuels;

--holding this uniform rate covering both types of fuel at the 2-cent level for fiscal 1962; and

--providing for annual increments in this rate of 1/2 cent after fiscal year 1962 until the portion of the cost of the airways properly allocable to civil aviation is substantially recovered by this tax.

The immediate increase in revenue from this proposal is modest in comparison with anticipated airways costs; and the annual gradation of further increases is intended to moderate the impact of the tax on the air carrier industry. Should future economic or other developments warrant, a more rapid increase in the fuel tax will be recommended. The decline from the revenues estimated by my predecessor is not large, and will be met by the reforms previously proposed. I repeat my earlier recommendation that, consistent with the user charge principle, revenues from the aviation fuels tax be retained in the general fund rather than diverted to the highway trust fund.

CONCLUSION

The legislation recommended in this message offers a first step toward the broader objective of tax reform. The immediate need is for encouraging economic growth through modernization and capital expansion, and to remove tax preferences for foreign investment which are no longer needed and which impair our balance of payments position. A beginning is made also toward removing some of the more glaring defects in the tax structure. The revenue gain in these proposals will offset the revenue cost of the investment credit. Finally, certain rate extensions are needed to maintain the revenue potential of our fiscal system.

These items need to be done now; but they are a first step only. They will be followed next year by a second set of proposals, aimed at thorough income tax reform. Their purpose will be to broaden and unify the income tax base, and to review the entire rate structure in the light of these revisions. Let us join in solving these immediate problems in the coming months, and then join in further action to strengthen the foundations of our revenue system.

"PRESIDENT AND THE PRESS" SPEECH

(APRIL 27, 1961)

Mr. Chairman, ladies and gentlemen:

I appreciate very much your generous invitation to be here tonight.

You bear heavy responsibilities these days and an article I read some time ago reminded me of how particularly heavily the burdens of present day events bear upon your profession.

You may remember that in 1851 the New York Herald Tribune, under the sponsorship and publishing of Horace Greeley, employed as its London correspondent an obscure journalist by the name of Karl Marx.

We are told that foreign correspondent Marx, stone broke, and with a family ill and undernourished, constantly appealed to Greeley and Managing Editor Charles Dana for an increase in his munificent salary of $5 per installment, a salary which he and Engels ungratefully labeled as the "lousiest petty bourgeois cheating."

But when all his financial appeals were refused, Marx looked around for other means of livelihood and fame, eventually terminating his relationship with the Tribune and devoting his talents full time to the cause that would bequeath to the world the seeds of Leninism, Stalinism, revolution and the Cold War.

If only this capitalistic New York newspaper had treated him more kindly; if only Marx had remained a foreign correspondent, history might have been different. And I hope all publishers will bear this lesson in mind the next time they receive a poverty-stricken appeal for a small increase in the expense account from an obscure newspaper.

I have selected as the title of my remarks tonight "The President and the Press." Some may suggest that this would be more naturally worded "The

President Versus the Press." But those are not my sentiments tonight.

It is true, however, that when a well-known diplomat from another country demanded recently that our State Department repudiate certain newspaper attacks on his colleague it was unnecessary for us to reply that this Administration was not responsible for the press, for the press had already made it clear that it was not responsible for this Administration.

Nevertheless, my purpose here tonight is not to deliver the usual assault on the so-called one-party press. On the contrary, in recent months I have rarely heard any complaints about political bias in the press except from a few Republicans. Nor is it my purpose tonight to discuss or defend the televising of Presidential press conferences. I think it is highly beneficial to have some 20,000,000 Americans regularly sit in on these conferences to observe, if I may say so, the incisive, the intelligent and the courteous qualities displayed by your Washington correspondents.

Nor, finally, are these remarks intended to examine the proper degree of privacy which the press should allow to any President and his family.

If in the last few months your White House reporters and photographers have been attending church services with regularity, that has surely done them no harm.

On the other hand, I realize that your staff and wire service photographers may be complaining that they do not enjoy the same green privileges at the local golf courses which they once did.

It is true that my predecessor did not object as I do to pictures of one's golfing skill in action. But neither on the other hand did he ever bean a Secret Service man. My topic tonight is a more sober one of concern to publishers as well as editors.

I want to talk about our common responsibilities in the face of a common danger. The events of recent weeks may have helped to illuminate that challenge for some; but the dimensions of its threat have loomed large on the horizon for many years. Whatever our hopes may be for the future—for reducing this threat or living with it—there is no escaping either the gravity or the totality of its challenge to our survival and to our security—a challenge that confronts us in unaccustomed ways in every sphere of human activity.

This deadly challenge imposes upon our society two requirements of direct concern both to the press and to the President—two requirements that may seem almost contradictory in tone, but which must be reconciled and fulfilled if we are to meet this national peril. I refer, first, to the need for far greater public information; and, second, to the need for far greater official secrecy.

The very word "secrecy" is repugnant in a free and open society; and we are as a people inherently and historically opposed to secret societies, to secret oaths and to secret proceedings. We decided long ago that the dangers of excessive and unwarranted concealment of pertinent facts far outweighed the dangers which are cited to justify it. Even today, there is little value in opposing the threat of a closed society by imitating its arbitrary restrictions. Even today, there is little value in insuring the survival of our nation if our traditions do not survive with it. And there is very grave danger that an announced need for increased security will be seized upon by those anxious to expand its meaning to the very limits of official censorship and concealment. That I do not intend to permit to the extent that it is in my control. And no official of my Administration, whether his rank is high or low, civilian or military, should interpret my words here tonight as an excuse to censor the news, to stifle dissent, to cover up our mistakes or to withhold from the press and the public the facts they deserve to know.

But I do ask every publisher, every editor, and every newsman in the nation to reexamine his own standards, and to recognize the nature of our country's peril. In time of war, the government and the press have customarily joined in an effort, based largely on self-discipline, to prevent unauthorized disclosures to the enemy. In time of "clear and present danger," the courts have held that even the privileged rights of the First Amendment must yield to the public's need for national security.

Today no war has been declared—and however fierce the struggle may be—it may never be declared in the traditional fashion. Our way of life is under attack. Those who make themselves our enemy are advancing around the globe. The survival of our friends is in danger. And yet no war has been declared, no borders have been crossed by marching troops, no missiles have been fired.

If the press is awaiting a declaration of war before it imposes the self-discipline of combat conditions, then I can only say that no war ever posed a greater threat to our security. If you are awaiting a finding of "clear and present danger," then I can only say that the danger has never been more clear and its presence has never been more imminent.

It requires a change in outlook, a change in tactics, a change in missions—by the government, by the people, by every businessman or labor leader, and by every newspaper. For we are opposed around the world by a monolithic and ruthless conspiracy that relies primarily on covert means for expanding its sphere of influence—on infiltration instead of invasion, on subversion instead of elections, on intimidation instead of free choice, on guerrillas by night instead of armies by day. It is a system which has conscripted vast human and material resources into the building of a tightly knit, highly efficient machine that combines military, diplomatic, intelligence, economic, scientific and political operations.

Its preparations are concealed, not published. Its mistakes are buried, not headlined. Its dissenters are silenced, not praised. No expenditure is questioned, no rumor is printed, no secret is revealed. It conducts the Cold War, in short, with a war-time discipline no democracy would ever hope or wish to match.

Nevertheless, every democracy recognizes the necessary restraints of national security—and the question remains whether those restraints need to be more strictly observed if we are to oppose this kind of attack as well as outright invasion.

For the facts of the matter are that this nation's foes have openly boasted of acquiring through our newspapers information they would otherwise hire agents to acquire through theft, bribery or espionage; that details of this nation's covert preparations to counter the enemy's covert operations have been available to every newspaper reader, friend and foe alike; that the size, the strength, the location and the nature of our forces and weapons, and our plans and strategy for their use, have all been pinpointed in the press and other news media to a degree sufficient to satisfy any foreign power; and that, in at least one case, the publication of details concerning a secret mechanism whereby satellites were followed required its alteration at the expense of considerable time and money.

The newspapers which printed these stories were loyal, patriotic, responsible and well-meaning. Had we been engaged in open warfare, they undoubtedly would not have published such items. But in the absence of open warfare, they recognized only the tests of journalism and not the tests of national security. And my question tonight is whether additional tests should not now be adopted.

That question is for you alone to answer. No public official should answer it for you. No governmental plan should impose its restraints against your will. But I would be failing in my duty to the Nation, in considering all of the responsibilities that we now bear and all of the means at hand to meet those responsibilities, if I did not commend this problem to your attention, and urge its thoughtful consideration.

On many earlier occasions, I have said—and your newspapers have constantly said—that these are times that appeal to every citizen's sense of sacrifice and self-discipline. They call out to every citizen to weigh his rights and comforts against his obligations to the common good. I cannot now believe that those citizens who serve in the newspaper business consider themselves exempt from that appeal.

I have no intention of establishing a new Office of War Information to govern the flow of news. I am not suggesting any new forms of censorship or new types of security classifications. I have no easy answer to the dilemma that I have posed, and would not seek to impose it if I had one. But I am asking the members of the newspaper profession and the industry in this country to reexamine their own responsibilities, to consider the degree and the nature of the present danger, and to heed the duty of self-restraint which that danger imposes upon us all.

Every newspaper now asks itself, with respect to every story: "Is it news?" All I suggest is that you add the question: "Is it in the interest of the national security?" And I hope that every group in America—unions and businessmen and public officials at every level—will ask the same question of their endeavors, and subject their actions to this same exacting test.

And should the press of America consider and recommend the voluntary assumption of specific new steps or machinery, I can assure you that we will cooperate whole-heartedly with those recommendations.

Perhaps there will be no recommendations. Perhaps there is no answer to the dilemma faced by a free and open society in a cold and secret war. In times of peace, any discussion of this subject, and any action that results, are both painful and without precedent. But this is a time of peace and peril which knows no precedent in history.

It is the unprecedented nature of this challenge that also gives rise to your second obligation—an obligation which I share. And that is our obligation to inform and alert the American people—to make certain that they possess all the facts that they need, and understand them as well—the perils, the prospects, the purposes of our program and the choices that we face.

No President should fear public scrutiny of his program. For from that scrutiny comes understanding; and from that understanding comes support or opposition. And both are necessary. I am not asking your newspapers to support the Administration, but I am asking your help in the tremendous task of informing and alerting the American people. For I have complete confidence in the response and dedication of our citizens whenever they are fully informed.

I not only could not stifle controversy among your readers—I welcome it. This Administration intends to be candid about its errors; for, as a wise man once said: "An error doesn't become a mistake until you refuse to correct it." We intend to accept full responsibility for our errors; and we expect you to point them out when we miss them.

Without debate, without criticism, no Administration and no country can succeed—and no republic can survive. That is why the Athenian law-maker Solon decreed it a crime for any citizen to shrink from controversy. And that is why our press was protected by the First Amendment—the only business in America specifically protected by the Constitution—not primarily to amuse and entertain, not to emphasize the trivial and the sentimental, not to simply "give the public what it wants"—but to inform, to arouse, to reflect, to state our dangers and our opportunities, to indicate our crises and our choices, to lead, mold, educate and sometimes even anger public opinion.

This means greater coverage and analysis of international news—for it is no longer far away and foreign but close at hand and local. It means greater attention to improved understanding of the news as well as improved transmission. And it means, finally, that government at all levels, must meet its obligation to provide you with the fullest possible information outside the narrowest limits of national security—and we intend to do it.

It was early in the Seventeenth Century that Francis Bacon remarked on three recent inventions already transforming the world: the compass, gunpowder and the printing press. Now the links between the nations first forged by the compass have made us all citizens of the world, the hopes and threats of one becoming the hopes and threats of us all. In that one world's efforts to live together, the evolution of gunpowder to its ultimate limit has warned mankind of the terrible consequences of failure.

And so it is to the printing press—to the recorder of man's deeds, the keeper of his conscience, the courier of his news—that we look for strength and assistance, confident that with your help man will be what he was born to be: free and independent.

President John F. Kennedy

REMARKS AT GEORGE WASHINGTON

(MAY 3, 1961)

Mr. President:

I want to express my appreciation to the President and to the Fellows of this University for the honor that they have bestowed upon me. My wife beat me to this honor by about 8 or 9 years. It took her 2 years to get this degree and it took me 2 minutes, but in any case we are both grateful.

I am also glad to be here because this University bears the distinguished name of the father of our country, George Washington. It is a matter of great interest that there has been an intimate relationship between the great political leaders of our country and our colleges and universities.

This University bears the name of George Washington, which showed his understanding in his day of the necessity of a free society to produce educated men and women. John Adams and John Quincy Adams from my own State of Massachusetts had an intimate relationship with Harvard University. Both of them, I believe, were members of the board of overseers. In both of their lives, Harvard and its development played a major part.

Washington and Lee shows an intimate relationship, for General Lee, the fact that he was willing to devote his life at the end of the war to educating the men and women of the South, indicated his understanding of this basic precept. Woodrow Wilson, Theodore Roosevelt--and all the rest.

I don't think that there has ever been a time when we have had greater need for those qualities which a university produces. I know that many people feel that a democracy is a divided system, that where the Communists are certain in purpose and certain in execution, we debate and talk and are unable to meet their consistency and their perseverance.

I do not hold that view. There are many disadvantages which a free society bears with it in a cold war struggle, but I believe over the long run that people do want to be free, that they desire to develop their own personalities and their own potentials, that democracy permits them to do so. And that it is the job of schools and colleges such as this to provide the men and women who will with their sense of discipline and purpose and understanding contribute to the maintenance of free societies here and around the world.

A hundred years ago, George William Curtis of my own State asked a body of educators during the Kansas-Nebraska controversy, "Would you have counted him a friend of ancient Greece who quietly discussed the theory of patriotism on that hot summer day through whose hopeless and immortal hours Leonidas and the three hundred stood at Thermopylae for liberty? Was John Milton to conjugate Greek verbs in his library when the liberty of Englishmen was imperiled?" No, quite obviously, the duty of the educated man or woman, the duty of the scholar, is to give his objective sense, his sense of liberty to the maintenance of our society at a critical time.

This is our opportunity, as well as our responsibility; and I am particularly glad to be here today when we are witnessing the swearing-in of a new President. Many years ago, as most of you know, at Harvard University somebody came around and asked for President Lowell. They said, "He's in Washington seeing Mr. Taft." I know that some other day, when they are asking for the President of your University, they will say that he is over at the White House seeing Mr. Kennedy.

They understood at Harvard, and you understood here, the relative importance of a University President and a President of the United States.

Thank you.

ADDRESS BEFORE THE CANADIAN PARLIAMENT

(MAY 17, 1961)

Mr. Speaker of the Senate, Mr. Speaker of the House, Mr. Prime Minister, Members of the Canadian Houses of Parliament, distinguished guests and friends:

I am grateful for the generous remarks and kind sentiments toward my country and myself, Mr. Prime Minister. We in the United States have an impression that this country is made up of descendants of the English and the French. But I was glad to hear some applause coming from the very back benches when you mentioned Ireland. I am sure they are making progress forward. Je me sens vraiment entre amis.

It is a deeply felt honor to address this distinguished legislative body. And yet may I say that I feel very much at home with you here today. For one-third of my life was spent in the Parliament of my own country-the United States Congress.

There are some differences between this body and my own, the most noticeable to me is the lofty appearance of statesmanship which is on the faces of the Members of the--Senators who realize that they will never have to place their cause before the people again!

I feel at home also here because I number in my own State of Massachusetts many friends and former constituents who are of Canadian descent. Among the voters of Massachusetts who were born outside the United States, the largest group by far was born in Canada. Their vote is enough to determine the outcome of an election, even a Presidential election. You can understand that having been elected President of the United States by less than 140 thousand votes out of 60 million, that I am very conscious of these statistics!

The warmth of your hospitality symbolizes more than merely the courtesy which may be accorded to an individual visitor. They symbolize the enduring qualities of amity and honor which have characterized our countries' relations for so many decades.

Nearly forty years ago, a distinguished Prime Minister of this country took the part of the United States at a disarmament conference. He said, "They may not be angels but they are at least our friends."

I must say that I do not think that we probably demonstrated in that forty years that we are angels yet, but I hope we have demonstrated that we are at least friends. And I must say that I think in these days where hazard is our constant companion, that friends are a very good thing to have.

The Prime Minister was the first of the leaders from other lands who was invited to call upon me shortly after I entered the White House; and this is my first trip--the first trip of my wife and myself outside of our country's borders. It is just and fitting, and appropriate and traditional, that I should come here to Canada--across a border that knows neither guns nor guerrillas.

But we share more than a common border. We share a common heritage, traced back to those early settlers who traveled from the beachheads of the Maritime Provinces and New England to the far reaches of the Pacific Coast. Henry Thoreau spoke a common sentiment for them all: "Eastward I go only by force, Westward I go free. I must walk towards Oregon and not towards Europe." We share common values from the past, a common defense line at present, and common aspirations for the future-our future, and indeed the future of all mankind.

Geography has made us neighbors. History has made us friends. Economics has made us partners. And necessity has made us allies. Those whom nature hath so joined together, let no man put asunder.

What unites us is far greater than what divides us. The issues and irritants that inevitably affect all neighbors are small deed in comparison with the issues that we face together--above all the somber threat now posed to the whole neighborhood of this continent--in fact, to the whole community of nations. But our alliance is born, not of fear, but of hope. It is an alliance that advances what we are for, as well as opposes what we are against.

And so it is that when we speak of our common attitudes and relationships, Canada and the United States speak in 1961 in terms of unity. We do not seek the unanimity that comes to those who water down all issues to the lowest common denominator--or to those who conceal their differences behind fixed smiles--or to those who measure unity by standards of popularity and affection, instead of trust and respect.

We are allies. This is a partnership, not an empire. We are bound to have differences and disappointments--and we are equally bound to bring them out into the open, to settle them where they can be settled, and to respect each other's views when they cannot be settled.

Thus ours is the unity of equal and independent nations, co-tenants of the same continent, heirs of the same legacy, and fully sovereign associates in the same historic endeavor: to preserve freedom for ourselves and all who wish it. To that endeavor we must bring great material and human resources, the result of separate cultures and independent economies. And above all, that endeavor requires a free and full exchange of new and different ideas on all issues and all undertakings.

For it is clear that no free nation can stand alone to meet the threat of those who make themselves our adversaries--that no free nation can retain any illusions about the nature of the threat--and that no free nation can remain indifferent to the steady erosion of freedom around the globe.

It is equally clear that no Western nation on its own can help those less-developed lands to fulfill their hopes for steady progress.

And finally, it is clear that in an age where new forces are asserting their strength around the globe--when the political shape of the hemispheres are changing rapidly-nothing is more vital than the unity of the United States and of Canada.

And so my friends of Canada, whatever problems may exist or arise between us, I can assure you that my associates and I will be ever ready to discuss them with you, and to take whatever steps we can to remove them. And whatever those problems may be, I can also assure you that they shrink in comparison with the great and awesome tasks that await us as free and peace-loving nations.

So let us fix our attention, not on those matters that vex us as neighbors, but on the issues that face us as leaders. Let us look southward as part of the Hemisphere with whose fate we are both inextricably bound. Let us look eastward as part of the North Atlantic Community upon whose strength and will so many depend. Let us look westward to Japan, to the newly emerging lands of Asia and Africa and the Middle East, where lie the people upon whose fate and choice the struggle for freedom may ultimately depend. And let us look at the world in which we live and hope to go on living--and at the way of life for which Canadians--and I was reminded again of this this morning, on my visit to your War Memorial--and Americans alike have always been willing to give up their lives in nearly every generation, if necessary to defend and preserve freedom.

First, if you will, consider our mutual hopes for this Hemisphere. Stretching virtually from Pole to Pole, the nations of the Western Hemisphere are bound together by the laws of economics as well as geography, by a common dedication to freedom as well as a common history of fighting for it. To make this entire area more secure against aggression of all kinds--to defend it against the encroachment of international communism in this Hemisphere--and to see our sister states fulfill their hopes and needs for economic and social reform and development-are surely all challenges confronting your nation, and deserving of your talents and resources, as well as ours.

To be sure, it would mean an added responsibility; but yours is not a nation that shrinks from responsibility. The Hemisphere is a family into which we were born--and we cannot turn our backs on it in time of trouble. Nor can we stand aside from its great adventure of development. I believe that all of the free members of the Organization of American States would be heartened and strengthened by any increase in your Hemispheric role. Your skills, your resources, your judicious perception at the council table-- even when it differs from our own view--are all needed throughout the inter-American Community. Your country and mine are partners in North American affairs--can we not now become partners in inter-American affairs?

Secondly, let us consider our mutual hopes for the North Atlantic Community.

Our NATO alliance is still, as it was when it was founded, the world's greatest bulwark of freedom. But the military balance of power has been changing. Enemy tactics and weaponry have been changing. We can stand still only at our peril.

NATO force structures were originally devised to meet the threat of a massive conventional attack, in a period of Western nuclear monopoly.

Now, if we are to meet the defense requirements of the 1960's, the NATO countries must push forward simultaneously along two lines:

First, we must strengthen the conventional capability of our Alliance as a matter of the highest priority.

To this end, we in the United States are taking steps to increase the strength and mobility of our forces and to modernize their equipment. To the same end, we will maintain our forces now on the European Continent and will increase their conventional capabilities. We look to our NATO Allies to assign an equally high priority to this same essential task.

Second, we must make certain that nuclear weapons will continue to be available for the defense of the entire Treaty area, and that these weapons are at all times under close and flexible political control that meets the needs of all the NATO countries. We are prepared to join our Allies in working out suitable arrangements for this purpose. To make clear our own intentions and commitments to the defense of-Western Europe, the United States will commit to the NATO command five--and subsequently still more--Polaris atomic-missile submarines, which are defensive weapons, subject to any agreed NATO guidelines on their control and use, and responsive to the needs of all members but still credible in an emergency. Beyond this, we look to the possibility of eventually establishing a NATO sea-borne force, which would be truly multi-lateral in ownership and control, if this should be desired and found feasible by our Allies, once NATO's non-nuclear goals have been achieved.

Both of these measures--improved conventional forces and increased nuclear forces--are put forward in recognition of the fact that the defense of Europe and the assurances that can be given to the people of Europe and the defense of North America are indivisible--in the hope that no aggressor will mistake our desire for peace with our determination to respond instantly to any attack with whatever force is appropriate-and in the conviction that the time has come for all members of the NATO community to further increase and integrate their respective forces in the NATO command area, coordinating and sharing in research, development, production, storage, defense, command and training at all levels of armaments. So let us begin. Our opponents are watching to see if we in the West are divided. They take courage when we are. We must not let them be deceived or in doubt about our willingness to maintain our own freedom.

Third, let us turn to the less-developed nations in the southern half of the globe-those who struggle to escape the bonds of mass misery which appeals to our hearts as well as to our hopes. Both your nation and mine have recognized our responsibilities to these new nations. Our people have given generously, if not always effectively. We could not do less. And now we must do more.

For our historic task in this embattled age is not merely to defend freedom. It is to extend its writ and strengthen its covenant-to peoples of different cultures and creeds and colors, whose policy or economic system may differ from ours, but whose desire to be free is no less fervent than our own. Through the Organization for Economic Cooperation and Development and the Development Assistance Group, we can pool our vast resources and skills, and make available the kind of long-term capital, planning and know-how without which these nations will never achieve independent and viable economies, and without which our efforts will be tragically wasted. I propose further that the OECD establish a Development Center, where citizens and officials, and students and professional men of the Atlantic area and the less-developed world can meet to study in common the problems of economic development.

If we in the Atlantic Community can more closely coordinate our own economic policies--and certainly the OECD provides the framework if we but use it, and I hope that you will join as we are seeking to join to use it-- then surely our potential economic resources are adequate to meet our responsibility. Consider, for example, the unsurpassed productivity of our farms. Less than 8 percent of the American working force is on our farms; less than 11 percent of the Canadian working force is on yours. Fewer men on fewer acres than any nation on earth--but free men on free acres can produce here in North America all the food that a hungry world could use-- while all the collective farms and forced labor of the communist system produce one shortage after another. This is a day-to-day miracle of our free societies, easy to forget at a time when our minds are caught up in the glamour of beginning the exploration of space.

As the new nations emerge into independence, they face a choice: Shall they develop by the method of consent, or by turning their freedom over to the system of totalitarian control. In making that decision they should look long and hard at the tragedy now being played out in the villages of Communist China.

If we can work closely together to make our food surpluses a blessing instead of a curse, no man, woman or child need go hungry. And if each of the more fortunate nations can bear its fair share of the effort to help the less-fortunate--not merely those with whom we have traditional ties, but all who are willing and able to achieve meaningful growth and dignity--then this decade will surely be a turning-point in the history of the human family.

Finally, let me say just a few words about the world in which we live. We should not misjudge the force of the challenge that we face--a force that is powerful as well as insidious, that inspires dedication as well as fear, that uses means we cannot adopt to achieve ends we cannot permit.

Nor can we mistake the nature of the struggle. It is not for concessions or territory. It is not simply between different systems. It is an age old battle for the survival of liberty itself. And our great advantage-and we must never forget it--is that the irresistible tide that began five hundred years before the birth of Christ in ancient Greece is for freedom, and against tyranny. And that is the wave of the future--and the iron hand of totalitarianism can ultimately neither seize it nor turn it back. In the words of Macaulay: "A single breaker may recede, but the tide is coming in."

So we in the Free World are not without hope. We are not without friends. And we are not without resources to defend ourselves and those who are associated with us. Believing in the peaceful settlement of disputes in the defense of human rights, we are working throughout the United Nations, and through regional and other associations, to lessen the risks, the tensions and the means and opportunity for aggression that have been mounting so rapidly throughout the world. In these councils of peace--in the UN Emergency Force in the Middle East, in the Congo, in the International Control Commission in South East Asia, in the Ten Nations Commission on Disarmament-Canada has played a leading, important, and constructive role.

If we can contain the powerful struggle of ideologies, and reduce it to manageable proportions, we can proceed with the transcendent task of disciplining the nuclear weapons which shadow our lives, and of finding a widened range of common enterprises between ourselves and those who live under communist rule. For, in the end, we live on one planet and we are part of one human family; and whatever the struggles that confront us, we must lose no chance to move forward towards a world of law and a world of disarmament.

At the conference table and in the minds of men, the Free World's cause is strengthened because it is just. But it is strengthened even more by the dedicated efforts of free men and free nations. As the great parliamentarian Edmund Burke said, "The only thing necessary for the triumph of evil is for good men to do nothing." And that in essence is why I am here today. This trip is more than a consultation--more than a good-will visit. It is an act of faith--faith in your country, in your leaders--faith in the capacity of two great neighbors to meet their common problems--and faith in the cause of freedom, in which we are so intimately associated.

THE GOAL OF SENDING A MAN TO THE MOON

(MAY 25, 1961)

Mr. Speaker, Mr. Vice President, my copartners in Government, gentlemen and ladies:

The Constitution imposes upon me the obligation to "from time to time give to the Congress information of the State of the Union." While this has traditionally been interpreted as an annual affair, this tradition has been broken in extraordinary times.

These are extraordinary times. And we face an extraordinary challenge. Our strength as well as our convictions have imposed upon this nation the role of leader in freedom's cause.

No role in history could be more difficult or more important. We stand for freedom. That is our conviction for ourselves—that is our only commitment to others. No friend, no neutral and no adversary should think otherwise. We are not against any man—or any nation—or any system— except as it is hostile to freedom. Nor am I here to present a new military doctrine, bearing any one name or aimed at any one area. I am here to promote the freedom doctrine.

The great battleground for the defense and expansion of freedom today is the whole southern half of the globe—Asia, Latin America, Africa and the Middle East—the lands of the rising peoples. Their revolution is the greatest in human history. They seek an end to injustice, tyranny, and exploitation. More than an end, they seek a beginning.

And theirs is a revolution which we would support regardless of the Cold War, and regardless of which political or economic route they should choose to freedom.

For the adversaries of freedom did not create the revolution; nor did they create the conditions which compel it. But they are seeking to ride the crest of its wave—to capture it for themselves.

Yet their aggression is more often concealed than open. They have fired no missiles; and their troops are seldom seen. They send arms, agitators, aid, technicians and propaganda to every troubled area. But where fighting is required, it is usually done by others—by guerrillas striking at night, by assassins striking alone—assassins who have taken the lives of four thousand civil officers in the last twelve months in Vietnam alone—by subversives and saboteurs and insurrectionists, who in some cases control whole areas inside of independent nations.1

1 At this point the following paragraph, which appears in fine text as signed and transmitted to the Senate and House of Representatives, was omitted in the reading of the message:

They possess a powerful intercontinental striking force, large forces for conventional war, a well-trained underground in nearly every country, the power to conscript talent and manpower for any purpose, the capacity for quick decisions, a closed society without dissent or free information, and long experience in the techniques of violence and subversion. They make the most of their scientific successes, their economic progress and their pose as a foe of colonialism and friend of popular revolution. They prey on unstable or unpopular governments, unsealed, or unknown boundaries, unfilled hopes, convulsive change, massive poverty, illiteracy, unrest and frustration.

With these formidable weapons, the adversaries of freedom plan to consolidate their territory—to exploit, to control, and finally to destroy the hopes of the world's newest nations; and they have ambition to do it before the end of this decade. It is a contest of will and purpose as well as force and violence—a battle for minds and souls as well as lives and territory. And in that contest, we cannot stand aside.

We stand, as we have always stood from our earliest beginnings, for the independence and equality of all nations. This nation was born of revolution and raised in freedom. And we do not intend to leave an open road for despotism.

There is no single simple policy which meets this challenge. Experience has taught us that no one nation has the power or the wisdom to solve all the problems of the world or manage its revolutionary tides—that extending our commitments does not always increase our security—that any initiative carries with it the risk of a temporary defeat—that nuclear weapons cannot prevent subversion—that no free people can be kept free without will and energy of their own—and that no two nations or situations are exactly alike.

Yet there is much we can do—and must do. The proposals I bring before you are numerous and varied. They arise from the host of special opportunities and dangers which have become increasingly clear in recent months. Taken together, I believe that they can mark another step forward in our effort as a people. I am here to ask the help of this Congress and the nation in approving these necessary measures.

II. ECONOMIC AND SOCIAL PROGRESS AT HOME

The first and basic task confronting this nation this year was to turn recession into recovery. An affirmative anti-recession program, initiated with your cooperation, supported the natural forces in the private sector; and our economy is now enjoying renewed confidence and energy. The recession has been halted. Recovery is under way.

But the task of abating unemployment and achieving a full use of our resources does remain a serious challenge for us all. Large-scale unemployment during a recession is bad enough, but large-scale unemployment during a period of prosperity would be intolerable.

I am therefore transmitting to the Congress a new Manpower Development and Training program, to train or retrain several hundred thousand workers, particularly in those areas where we have seen chronic unemployment as a result of technological factors in new occupational skills over a four-year period, in order to replace those skills made obsolete by automation and industrial change with the new skills which the new processes demand.

It should be a satisfaction to us all that we have made great strides in restoring world confidence in the dollar, halting the outflow of gold and improving our balance of payments. During the last two months, our gold stocks actually increased by seventeen million dollars, compared to a loss of 635 million dollars during the last two months of 1960. We must maintain this progress—and this will require the cooperation and restraint of everyone. As recovery progresses, there will be temptations to seek unjustified price and wage increases. These we cannot afford. They will only handicap our efforts to compete abroad and to achieve full recovery here at home. Labor and management must—and I am confident that they will— pursue responsible wage and price policies in these critical times. I look to the President's Advisory Committee on Labor-Management Policy to give a strong lead in this direction.

Moreover, if the budget deficit now increased by the needs of our security is to be held within manageable proportions, it will be necessary to hold tightly to prudent fiscal standards; and I request the cooperation of the Congress in this regard—to refrain from adding funds or programs, desirable as they may be, to the Budget—to end the postal deficit, as my predecessor also recommended, through increased rates—a deficit incidentally, this year, which exceeds the fiscal 1962 cost of all the space and defense measures that I am submitting today—to provide full pay-as-you-go highway financing—and to close those tax loopholes earlier specified. Our security and progress cannot be cheaply purchased; and their price must be found in what we all forego as well as what we all must pay.

III. ECONOMIC AND SOCIAL PROGRESS ABROAD

I stress the strength of our economy because it is essential to the strength of our nation. And what is true in our case is true in the case of other countries. Their strength in the struggle for freedom depends on the strength of their economic and their social progress.

We would be badly mistaken to consider their problems in military terms alone. For no amount of arms and armies can help stabilize those governments which are unable or unwilling to achieve social and economic reform and development. Military pacts cannot help nations whose social injustice and economic chaos invite insurgency and penetration and subversion. The most skillful counter-guerrilla efforts cannot succeed where the local population is too caught up in its own misery to be concerned about the advance of communism.

But for those who share this view, we stand ready now, as we have in the past, to provide generously of our skills, and our capital, and our food to assist the peoples of the less-developed nations to reach their goals in freedom—to help them before they are engulfed in crisis.

This is also our great opportunity in 1961. If we grasp it, then subversion to prevent its success is exposed as an unjustifiable attempt to keep these nations from either being free or equal. But if we do not pursue it, and if they do not pursue it, the bankruptcy of unstable governments, one by one, and of unfilled hopes will surely lead to a series of totalitarian receiverships.

Earlier in the year, I outlined to the Congress a new program for aiding emerging nations; and it is my intention to transmit shortly draft legislation to implement this program, to establish a new Act for International Development, and to add to the figures previously requested, in view of the swift pace of critical events, an additional 250 million dollars for a Presidential Contingency Fund, to be used only upon a Presidential determination in each case, with regular and complete reports to the Congress in each case, when there is a sudden and extraordinary drain upon our regular funds which we cannot foresee—as illustrated by recent events in Southeast Asia—and it makes necessary the use of this emergency reserve. The total amount requested—now raised to 2.65 billion dollars—is both minimal and crucial. I do not see how anyone who is concerned—as we all are—about the growing threats to freedom around the globe—and who is asking what more we can do as a people—can weaken or oppose the single most important program available for building the frontiers of freedom.

IV.

All that I have said makes it clear that we are engaged in a world-wide struggle in which we bear a heavy burden to preserve and promote the ideals that we share with all mankind, or have alien ideals forced upon them. That struggle has highlighted the role of our Information Agency. It is essential that the funds previously requested for this effort be not only approved in full, but increased by 2 million, 400 thousand dollars, to a total of 121 million dollars.

This new request is for additional radio and television to Latin America and Southeast Asia. These tools are particularly effective and essential in the cities and villages of those great continents as a means of reaching millions of uncertain peoples to tell them of our interest in their fight for freedom. In Latin America, we are proposing to increase our Spanish and Portuguese broadcasts to a total of 154 hours a week, compared to 42 hours today, none of which is in Portuguese, the language of about one-third of the people of South America. The Soviets, Red Chinese and satellites already broadcast into Latin America more than 134 hours a week in Spanish and Portuguese. Communist China alone does more public information broadcasting in our own hemisphere than we do. Moreover, powerful propaganda broadcasts from Havana now are heard throughout Latin America, encouraging new revolutions in several countries.

Similarly, in Laos, Vietnam, Cambodia, and Thailand, we must communicate our determination and support to those upon whom our hopes for resisting the communist tide in that continent ultimately depend. Our interest is in the truth.

V. OUR PARTNERSHIP FOR SELF-DEFENSE

But while we talk of sharing and building and the competition of ideas, others talk of arms and threaten war. So we have learned to keep our defenses strong—and to cooperate with others in a partnership of self-defense. The events of recent weeks have caused us to look anew at these efforts.

The center of freedom's defense is our network of world alliances, extending from NATO, recommended by a Democratic President and approved by a Republican Congress, to SEATO, recommended by a Republican President and approved by a Democratic Congress. These alliances were constructed in the 1940's and 1950's—it is our task and responsibility in the 1960's to strengthen them.

To meet the changing conditions of power—and power relationships have changed—we have endorsed an increased emphasis on NATO's conventional strength. At the same time we are affirming our conviction that the NATO nuclear deterrent must also be kept strong. I have made clear our intention to commit to the NATO command, for this purpose, the 5 Polaris submarines originally suggested by President Eisenhower, with the possibility, if needed, of more to come.

Second, a major part of our partnership for self-defense is the Military Assistance Program. The main burden of local defense against local attack, subversion, insurrection or guerrilla warfare must of necessity rest with local forces. Where these forces have the necessary will and capacity to cope with such threats, our intervention is rarely necessary or helpful. Where the will is present and only capacity is lacking, our Military Assistance Program can be of help.

But this program, like economic assistance, needs a new emphasis. It cannot be extended without regard to the social, political and military reforms essential to internal respect and stability. The equipment and training provided must be tailored to legitimate local needs and to our own foreign and military policies, not to our supply of military stocks or a local leader's desire for military display. And military assistance can, in addition to its military purposes, make a contribution to economic progress, as do our own Army Engineers.

In an earlier message, I requested 1.6 billion dollars for Military Assistance, stating that this would maintain existing force levels, but that I could not foresee how much more might be required. It is now clear that this is not enough. The present crisis in Southeast Asia, on which the Vice President has made a valuable report—the rising threat of communism in Latin America-the increased arms traffic in Africa—and all the new pressures on every nation found on the map by tracing your fingers along the borders of the Communist bloc in Asia and the Middle East—all make clear the dimension of our needs.

I therefore request the Congress to provide a total of 1.885 billion dollars for Military Assistance in the coming fiscal year—an amount less than that requested a year ago—but a minimum which must be assured if we are to help those nations make secure their independence. This must be prudently and wisely spent—and that will be our common endeavor. Military and economic assistance has been a heavy burden on our citizens for a long time, and I recognize the strong pressures against it; but this battle is far from over, it is reaching a crucial stage, and I believe we should participate in it. We cannot merely state our opposition to totalitarian advance without paying the price of helping those now under the greatest pressure.

VI. OUR OWN MILITARY AND INTELLIGENCE

In line with these developments, I have directed a further reinforcement of our own capacity to deter or resist non-nuclear aggression. In the conventional field, with one exception, I find no present need for large new levies of men. What is needed is rather a change of position to give us still further increases in flexibility.

Therefore, I am directing the Secretary of Defense to undertake a reorganization and modernization of the Army's divisional structure, to increase its non-nuclear firepower, to improve its tactical mobility in any environment, to insure its flexibility to meet any direct or indirect threat, to facilitate its coordination with our major allies, and to provide more modern mechanized divisions in Europe and bring their equipment up to date, and new airborne brigades in both the Pacific and Europe.

And secondly, I am asking the Congress for an additional 100 million dollars to begin the procurement task necessary to re-equip this new Army structure with the most modern material. New helicopters, new armored personnel carriers, and new howitzers, for example, must be obtained now.

Third, I am directing the Secretary of Defense to expand rapidly and substantially, in cooperation with our Allies, the orientation of existing forces for the conduct of nonnuclear war, para-military operations and sub-limited or unconventional wars.

In addition, our special forces and unconventional warfare units will be increased and reoriented. Throughout the services new emphasis must be placed on the special skills and languages which are required to work with local populations.

Fourth, the Army is developing plans to make possible a much more rapid deployment of a major portion of its highly trained reserve forces. When these plans are completed and the reserve is strengthened, two combat-equipped divisions, plus their supporting forces, a total of 89,000 men, could be ready in an emergency for operations with but 3 weeks notice—2 more divisions with but 5 weeks notice—and six additional divisions and their supporting forces, making a total of 10 divisions, could be deployable with less than 8 weeks' notice. In short, these new plans will allow us to almost double the combat power of the Army in less than two months, compared to the nearly nine months heretofore required.

Fifth, to enhance the already formidable ability of the Marine Corps to respond to limited war emergencies, I am asking the Congress for 60 million dollars to increase the Marine Corps strength to 190,000 men. This will increase the initial impact and staying power of our three Marine divisions and three air wings, and provide a trained nucleus for further expansion, if necessary for self-defense.

Finally, to cite one other area of activities that are both legitimate and necessary as a means of self-defense in an age of hidden perils, our whole intelligence effort must be reviewed, and its coordination with other elements of policy assured. The Congress and the American people are entitled to know that we will institute whatever new organization, policies, and control are necessary.

VII. CIVIL DEFENSE

One major element of the national security program which this nation has never squarely faced up to is civil defense. This problem arises not from present trends but from national inaction in which most of us have participated. In the past decade we have intermittently considered a variety of programs, but we have never adopted a consistent policy. Public considerations have been largely characterized by apathy, indifference and skepticism; while, at the same time, many of the civil defense plans have been so far-reaching and unrealistic that they have not gained essential support.

This Administration has been looking hard at exactly what civil defense can and cannot do. It cannot be obtained cheaply. It cannot give an assurance of blast protection that will be proof against surprise attack or guaranteed against obsolescence or destruction. And it cannot deter a nuclear attack.

We will deter an enemy from making a nuclear attack only if our retaliatory power is so strong and so invulnerable that he knows he would be destroyed by our response. If we have that strength, civil defense is not needed to deter an attack. If we should ever lack it, civil defense would not be an adequate substitute.

But this deterrent concept assumes rational calculations by rational men. And the history of this planet, and particularly the history of the 20th century, is sufficient to remind us of the possibilities of an irrational attack, a miscalculation, an accidental war, for a war of escalation in which the stakes by each side gradually increase to the point of maximum danger which cannot be either foreseen or deterred. It is on this basis that civil defense can be readily justifiable—as insurance for the civilian population in case of an enemy miscalculation. It is insurance we trust will never be needed—but insurance which we could never forgive ourselves for foregoing in the event of catastrophe.

Once the validity of this concept is recognized, there is no point in delaying the initiation of a nation-wide long-range program of identifying present fallout shelter capacity and providing shelter in new and existing structures. Such a program would protect millions of people against the hazards of radioactive fallout in the event of large-scale nuclear attack. Effective performance of the entire program not only requires new legislative authority and more funds, but also sound organizational arrangements.

Therefore, under the authority vested in me by Reorganization Plan No. 1 of 1958, I am assigning responsibility for this program to the top civilian authority already responsible for continental defense, the Secretary of Defense. It is important that this function remain civilian, in nature and leadership; and this feature will not be changed.

The Office of Civil and Defense Mobilization will be reconstituted as a small staff agency to assist in the coordination of these functions. To more accurately describe its role, its title should be changed to the Office of Emergency Planning.

As soon as those newly charged with these responsibilities have prepared new authorization and appropriation requests, such requests will be transmitted to the Congress for a much strengthened Federal-State civil defense program. Such a program will provide Federal funds for identifying fallout shelter capacity in existing structures, and it will include, where appropriate, incorporation of shelter in Federal buildings, new requirements for shelter in buildings constructed with Federal assistance, and matching grants and other incentives for constructing shelter in State and local and private buildings.

Federal appropriations for civil defense in fiscal 1962 under this program will in all likelihood be more than triple the pending budget requests; and they will increase sharply in subsequent years. Financial participation will also be required from State and local governments and from private citizens. But no insurance is cost-free; and every American citizen and his community must decide for themselves whether this form of survival insurance justifies the expenditure of effort, time and money. For myself, I am convinced that it does.

VIII. DISARMAMENT

I cannot end this discussion of defense and armaments without emphasizing our strongest hope: the creation of an orderly world where disarmament will be possible. Our aims do not prepare for war—they are efforts to discourage and resist the adventures of others that could end in war.

That is why it is consistent with these efforts that we continue to press for properly safeguarded disarmament measures. At Geneva, in cooperation with the United Kingdom, we have put forward concrete proposals to make clear our wish to meet the Soviets half way in an effective nuclear test ban treaty—the first significant but essential step on the road towards disarmament. Up to now, their response has not been what we hoped, but Mr. Dean returned last night to Geneva, and we intend to go the last mile in patience to secure this gain if we can.

Meanwhile, we are determined to keep disarmament high on our agenda—to make an intensified effort to develop acceptable political and technical alternatives to the present arms race. To this end I shall send to the Congress a measure to establish a strengthened and enlarged Disarmament Agency.

IX. SPACE

Finally, if we are to win the battle that is now going on around the world between freedom and tyranny, the dramatic achievements in space which occurred in recent weeks should have made clear to us all, as did the Sputnik in 1957, the impact of this adventure on the minds of men everywhere, who are attempting to make a determination of which road they should take. Since early in my term, our efforts in space have been under review. With the advice of the Vice President, who is Chairman of the National Space Council, we have examined where we are strong and where we are not, where we may succeed and where we may not. Now it is time to take longer strides—time for a great new American enterprise—time for this nation to take a clearly leading role in space achievement, which in many ways may hold the key to our future on earth.

I believe we possess all the resources and talents necessary. But the facts of the matter are that we have never made the national decisions or marshaled the national resources required for such leadership. We have never specified long-range goals on an urgent time schedule, or managed our resources and our time so as to insure their fulfillment.

Recognizing the head start obtained by the Soviets with their large rocket engines, which gives them many months of lead-time, and recognizing the likelihood that they will exploit this lead for some time to come in still more impressive successes, we nevertheless are required to make new efforts on our own. For while we cannot guarantee that we shall one day be first, we can guarantee that any failure to make this effort will make us last. We take an additional risk by making it in full view of the world, but as shown by the feat of astronaut Shepard, this very risk enhances our stature when we are successful. But this is not merely a race. Space is open to us now; and our eagerness to share its meaning is not governed by the efforts of others. We go into space because whatever mankind must undertake, free men must fully share.

I therefore ask the Congress, above and beyond the increases I have earlier requested for space activities, to provide the funds which are needed to meet the following national goals:

First, I believe that this nation should commit itself to achieving the goal, before this decade is out, of landing a man on the moon and returning him safely to the earth. No single space project in this period will be more impressive to mankind, or more important for the long-range exploration of space; and none will be so difficult or expensive to accomplish. We propose to accelerate the development of the appropriate lunar space craft. We propose to develop alternate liquid and solid fuel boosters, much larger than any now being developed, until certain which is superior. We propose additional funds for other engine development and for unmanned explorations—explorations which are particularly important for one purpose which this nation will never overlook: the survival of the man who first makes this daring flight. But in a very real sense, it will not be one man going to the moon—if we make this judgment affirmatively, it will be an entire nation. For all of us must work to put him there.

Secondly, an additional 23 million dollars, together with 7 million dollars already available, will accelerate development of the Rover nuclear rocket. This gives promise of some day providing a means for even more exciting and ambitious exploration of space, perhaps beyond the moon, perhaps to the very end of the solar system itself.

Third, an additional 50 million dollars will make the most of our present leadership, by accelerating the use of space satellites for world-wide communications.

Fourth, an additional 75 million dollars—of which 53 million dollars is for the Weather Bureau—will help give us at the earliest possible time a satellite system for world-wide weather observation.

Let it be clear—and this is a judgment which the Members of the Congress must finally make—let it be clear that I am asking the Congress and the country to accept a firm commitment to a new course of action—a course which will last for many years and carry very heavy costs: 531 million dollars in fiscal '62—an estimated seven to nine billion dollars additional over the next five years. If we are to go only half way, or reduce our sights in the face of difficulty, in my judgment it would be better not to go at all.

Now this is a choice which this country must make, and I am confident that under the leadership of the Space Committees of the Congress, and the Appropriating Committees, that you will consider the matter carefully.

It is a most important decision that we make as a nation. But all of you have lived through the last four years and have seen the significance of space and the adventures in space, and no one can predict with certainty what the ultimate meaning will be of mastery of space.

I believe we should go to the moon. But I think every citizen of this country as well as the Members of the Congress should consider the matter carefully in making their judgment, to which we have given attention over many weeks and months, because it is a heavy burden, and there is no sense in agreeing or desiring that the United States take an affirmative position in outer space, unless we are prepared to do the work and bear the burdens to make it successful. If we are not, we should decide today and this year.

This decision demands a major national commitment of scientific and technical manpower, materiel and facilities, and the possibility of their diversion from other important activities where they are already thinly spread. It means a degree of dedication, organization and discipline which have not always characterized our research and development efforts. It means we cannot afford undue work stoppages, inflated costs of material or talent, wasteful interagency rivalries, or a high turnover of key personnel.

New objectives and new money cannot solve these problems. They could in fact, aggravate them further—unless every scientist, every engineer, every serviceman, every technician, contractor, and civil servant gives his personal pledge that this nation will move forward, with the full speed of freedom, in the exciting adventure of space.

X. CONCLUSION

In conclusion, let me emphasize one point. It is not a pleasure for any President of the United States, as I am sure it was not a pleasure for my predecessors, to come before the Congress and ask for new appropriations which place burdens on our people. I came to this conclusion with some reluctance. But in my judgment, this is a most serious time in the life of our country and in the life of freedom around the globe, and it is the obligation, I believe, of the President of the United States to at least make his recommendations to the Members of the Congress, so that they can reach their own conclusions with that judgment before them. You must decide yourselves, as I have decided, and I am confident that whether you finally decide in the way that I have decided or not, that your judgment—as my judgment—is reached on what is in the best interests of our country.

In conclusion, let me emphasize one point: that we are determined, as a nation in 1961 that freedom shall survive and succeed—and whatever the peril and set-backs, we have some very large advantages.

The first is the simple fact that we are on the side of liberty—and since the beginning of history, and particularly since the end of the Second World War, liberty has been winning out all over the globe.

A second great asset is that we are not alone. We have friends and allies all over the world who share our devotion to freedom. May I cite as a symbol of traditional and effective friendship the great ally I am about to visit—France. I look forward to my visit to France, and to my discussion with a great Captain of the Western World, President de Gaulle, as a meeting of particular significance, permitting the kind of close and ranging consultation that will strengthen both our countries and serve the common purposes of world-wide peace and liberty. Such serious conversations do not require a pale unanimity—they are rather the instruments of trust and understanding over a long road.

A third asset is our desire for peace. It is sincere, and I believe the world knows it. We are proving it in our patience at the test-ban table, and we are proving it in the UN where our efforts have been directed to maintaining that organization's usefulness as a protector of the independence of small nations. In these and other instances, the response of our opponents has not been encouraging.

Yet it is important to know that our patience at the bargaining table is nearly inexhaustible, though our credulity is limited—that our hopes for peace are unfailing, while our determination to protect our security is resolute. For these reasons I have long thought it wise to meet with the Soviet Premier for a personal exchange of views. A meeting in Vienna turned out to be convenient for us both; and the Austrian government has kindly made us welcome. No formal agenda is planned and no negotiations will be undertaken; but we will make dear America's enduring concern is for both peace and freedom—that we are anxious to live in harmony with the Russian people—that we seek no conquests, no satellites, no riches—that we seek only the day when "nation shall not lift up sword against nation, neither shall they learn war any more."

Finally, our greatest asset in this struggle is the American people—their willingness to pay the price for these programs—to understand and accept a long struggle—to share their resources with other less fortunate people—to meet the tax levels and close the tax loopholes I have requested—to exercise self-restraint instead of pushing up wages or prices, or over-producing certain crops, or spreading military secrets, or urging unessential expenditures or improper monopolies or harmful work stoppages—to serve in the Peace Corps or the Armed Services or the Federal Civil Service or the Congress—to strive for excellence in their schools, in their cities and in their physical fitness and that of their children—to take part in Civil Defense—to pay higher postal rates, and higher payroll taxes and higher teachers' salaries, in order to strengthen our society—to show friendship to students and visitors from other lands who visit us and go back in many cases to be the future leaders, with an image of America—and I want that image, and I know you do, to be affirmative and positive—and, finally, to practice democracy at home, in all States, with all races, to respect each other and to protect the Constitutional rights of all citizens.

I have not asked for a single program which did not cause one or all Americans some inconvenience, or some hardship, or some sacrifice. But they have responded—and you in the Congress have responded to your duty—and I feel confident in asking today for a similar response to these new and larger demands. It is heartening to know, as I journey abroad, that our country is united in its commitment to freedom—and is ready to do its duty.

REPORT TO THE AMERICAN PEOPLE
ON RETURNING FROM EUROPE

(JUNE 6, 1961)

Good evening, my fellow citizens:

I returned this morning from a week-long trip to Europe and I want to report to you on that trip in full. It was in every sense an unforgettable experience. The people of Paris, of Vienna, of London, were generous in their greeting. They were heartwarming in their hospitality, and their graciousness to my wife is particularly appreciated.

We knew of course that the crowds and the shouts were meant in large measure for the country that we represented, which is regarded as the chief defender of freedom. Equally memorable was the pageantry of European history and their culture that is very much a part of any ceremonial reception, to lay a wreath at the Arc de Triomphe, to dine at Versailles, and Schonbrunn Palace, and with the Queen of England. These are the colorful memories that will remain with us for many years to come. Each of the three cities that we visited--Paris, Vienna, and London--have existed for many centuries, and each serves as a reminder that the Western civilization that we seek to preserve has flowered over many years, and has defended itself over many centuries. But this was not a ceremonial trip. Two aims of American foreign policy, above all others, were the reason for the trip: the unity of the free world, whose strength is the security of us all, and the eventual achievement of a lasting peace. My trip was devoted to the advancement of these two aims.

To strengthen the unity of the West, our journey opened in Paris and closed in London. My talks with General de Gaulle were profoundly encouraging to me. Certain differences in our attitudes on one or another problem became insignificant in view of our common commitment to defend freedom. Our alliance, I believe, became more secure; the friendship of our nation, I hope--with theirs--became firmer; and the relations between the two of us who bear responsibility became closer, and I hope were marked by confidence. I found General de Gaulle far more interested in our frankly stating our position, whether or not it was his own, than in appearing to agree with him when we do not. But he knows full well the true meaning of an alliance. He is after all the only major leader of World War II who still occupies a position of great responsibility. His life has been one of unusual dedication; he is a man of extraordinary personal character, symbolizing the new strength and the historic grandeur of France. Throughout our discussions he took the long view of France and the world at large. I found him a wise counselor for the future, and an informative guide to the history that he has helped to make. Thus we had a valuable meeting.

I believe that certain doubts and suspicions that might have come up in a long time--I believe were removed on both sides. Problems which proved to be not of substance but of wording or procedure were cleared away. No question, however sensitive, was avoided. No area of interest was ignored, and the conclusions that we reached will be important for the future--in our agreement on defending Berlin, on working to improve the defenses of Europe, on aiding the economic and political independence of the underdeveloped world, including Latin America, on spurring European economic unity, on concluding successfully the conference on Laos, and on closer consultations and solidarity in the Western alliance.

General de Gaulle could not have been more cordial, and I could not have more confidence in any man. In addition to his individual strength of character, the French people as a whole showed vitality and energy which were both impressive and gratifying. Their recovery from the postwar period is dramatic, their productivity is increasing, and they are steadily building their stature in both Europe and Africa, and thus, I left Paris for Vienna with increased confidence in Western unity and strength.

The people of Vienna know what it is to live under occupation, and they know what it is to live in freedom. Their welcome to me as President of this country should be heartwarming to us all. I went to Vienna to meet the leader of the Soviet Union, Mr. Khrushchev. For 2 days we met in sober, intensive conversation, and I believe it is my obligation to the people, to the Congress, and to our allies to report on those conversations candidly and publicly.

Mr. Khrushchev and I had a very full and frank exchange of views on the major issues that now divide our two countries. I will tell you now that it was a very sober 2 days. There was no discourtesy, no loss of tempers, no threats or ultimatums by either side; no advantage or concession was either gained or given; no major decision was either planned or taken; no

108

spectacular progress was either achieved or pretended.

This kind of informal exchange may not be as exciting as a full-fledged summit meeting with a fixed agenda and a large corps of advisers, where negotiations are attempted and new agreements sought, but this was not intended to be and was not such a meeting, nor did we plan any future summit meetings at Vienna.

But I found this meeting with Chairman Khrushchev, as somber as it was, to be immensely useful. I had read his speeches and of his policies. I had been advised on his views. I had been told by other leaders of the West, General de Gaulle, Chancellor Adenauer, Prime Minister Macmillan, what manner of man he was.

But I bear the responsibility of the Presidency of the United States, and it is my duty to make decisions that no adviser and no ally can make for me. It is my obligation and responsibility to see that these decisions are as informed as possible, that they are based on as much direct, firsthand knowledge as possible.

I therefore thought it was of immense importance that I know Mr. Khrushchev, that I gain as much insight and understanding as I could on his present and future policies. At the same time, I wanted to make certain Mr. Khrushchev knew this country and its policies, that he understood our strength and our determination, and that he knew that we desired peace with all nations of every kind.

I wanted to present our views to him directly, precisely, realistically, and with an opportunity for discussion and clarification. This was done. No new aims were stated in private that have not been stated in public on either side. The gap between us was not, in such a short period, materially reduced, but at least the channels of communications were opened more fully, at least the chances of a dangerous misjudgment on either side should now be less, and at least the men on whose decisions the peace in part depends have agreed to remain in contact.

This is important, for neither of us tried to merely please the other, to agree merely to be agreeable, to say what the other wanted to hear. And just as our judicial system relies on witnesses appearing in court and on cross-examination, instead of hearsay testimony or affidavits on paper, so, too, was this direct give-and-take of immeasurable value in making clear and precise what we considered to be vital, for the facts of the matter are that the Soviets and ourselves give wholly different meanings to the same words--war, peace, democracy, and popular will.

We have wholly different views of right and wrong, of what is an internal affair and what is aggression, and, above all, we have wholly different concepts of where the world is and where it is going.

Only by such a discussion was it possible for me to be sure that Mr. Khrushchev knew how differently we view the present and the future. Our views contrasted sharply but at least we knew better at the end where we both stood. Neither of us was there to dictate a settlement or to convert the other to a cause or to concede our basic interests. But both of us were there, I think, because we realized that each nation has the power to inflict enormous damage upon the other, that such a war could and should be avoided if at all possible, since it would settle no dispute and prove no doctrine, and that care should thus be taken to prevent our conflicting interests from so directly confronting each other that war necessarily ensued. We believe in a system of national freedom and independence. He believes in an expanding and dynamic concept of world communism, and the question was whether these two systems can ever hope to live in peace without permitting any loss of security or any denial of the freedom of our friends. However difficult it may seem to answer this question in the affirmative as we approach so many harsh tests, I think we owe it to all mankind to make every possible effort. That is why I considered the Vienna talks to be useful. The somber mood that they conveyed was not cause for elation or relaxation, nor was it cause for undue pessimism or fear. It simply demonstrated how much work we in the free world have to do and how long and hard a struggle must be our fate as Americans in this generation as the chief defenders of the cause of liberty. The one area which afforded some immediate prospect of accord was Laos. Both sides recognized the need to reduce the dangers in that situation. Both sides endorsed the concept of a neutral and independent Laos, much in the manner of Burma or Cambodia.

Of critical importance to the current conference on Laos in Geneva, both sides recognized the importance of an effective cease-fire. It is urgent that this be translated into new attitudes at Geneva, enabling the International Control Commission to do its duty, to make certain that a cease-fire is enforced and maintained. I am hopeful that progress can be made on this matter in the coming days at Geneva for that would greatly improve international atmosphere.

No such hope emerged, however with respect to the other deadlocked Geneva conference, seeking a treaty to ban nuclear tests. Mr. Khrushchev made it clear that there could not be a neutral administrator--in his opinion because no one was truly neutral; that a Soviet veto would have to apply to acts of enforcement; that inspection was only a subterfuge for espionage, in the absence of total disarmament; and that the present test ban negotiations appeared futile. In short, our hopes for an end to nuclear tests, for an end to the spread of nuclear weapons, and for some slowing down of the arms race have been struck a serious blow. Nevertheless, the stakes are too important for us to abandon the draft treaty we have offered at Geneva.

But our most somber talks were on the subject of Germany and Berlin. I made it clear to Mr. Khrushchev that the security of Western Europe and therefore our own security are deeply involved in our presence and our access rights to West Berlin, that those rights are based on law and not on sufferance, and that we are determined to maintain those rights at any risk, and thus meet our obligation to the people of West Berlin, and their right to choose their own future.

Mr. Khrushchev, in turn, presented his views in detail, and his presentation will be the subject of further communications. But we are not seeking to change the present situation. A binding German peace treaty is a matter for all who were at war with Germany, and we and our allies cannot abandon our obligations to the people of West Berlin.

Generally, Mr. Khrushchev did not talk in terms of war. He believes the world will move his way without resort to force. He spoke of his nation's achievements in space. He stressed his intention to outdo us in industrial production, to out-trade us, to prove to the world the superiority of his system over ours. Most of all, he predicted the triumph of communism in the new and less developed countries.

He was certain that the tide there was moving his way, that the revolution of rising peoples would eventually be a Communist revolution, and that the so-called wars of liberation, supported by the Kremlin, would replace the old methods of direct aggression and invasion.

In the 1940's and early fifties, the great danger was from Communist armies marching across free borders, which we saw in Korea. Our nuclear monopoly helped to prevent this in other areas. Now we face a new and different threat. We no longer have a nuclear monopoly. Their missiles, they believe, will hold off our missiles, and their troops can match our troops should we intervene in these so-called wars of liberation. Thus, the local conflict they support can turn in their favor through guerrillas or insurgents or subversion. A small group of disciplined Communists could exploit discontent and misery in a country where the average income may be $60 or $70 a year, and seize control, therefore, of an entire country without Communist troops ever crossing any international frontier. This is the Communist theory.

But I believe just as strongly that time will prove it wrong, that liberty and independence and self-determination--not communism-is the future of man, and that free men have the will and the resources to win the struggle for freedom. But it is clear that this struggle in this area of the new and poorer nations will be a continuing crisis of this decade.

Mr. Khrushchev made one point which I wish to pass on. He said there are many disorders throughout the world, and he should not be blamed for them all. He is quite right. It is easy to dismiss as Communist-inspired every anti-government or anti-American riot, every overthrow of a corrupt regime, or every mass protest against misery and despair. These are not all Communist-inspired. The Communists move in to exploit them, to infiltrate their leadership, to ride their crest to victory. But the Communists did not create the conditions which caused them.

In short, the hopes for freedom in these areas which see so much poverty and illiteracy, so many children who are sick, so many children-who die in the first year, so many families without homes, so many families without hope--the future for freedom in these areas rests with the local peoples and their governments.

If they have the will to determine their own future, if their governments have the support of their own people, if their honest and progressive measures--helping their people--have inspired confidence and zeal, then no guerrilla or insurgent action can succeed. But where those conditions do not exist, a military guarantee against external attack from across a border offers little protection against internal decay.

Yet all this does not mean that our Nation and the West and the free world can only sit by. On the contrary, we have an historic opportunity to help these countries build their societies until they are so strong and broadly based that only an outside invasion could topple them, and that threat, we know, can be stopped.

We can train and equip their forces to resist Communist-supplied insurrections. We can help develop the industrial and agricultural base on which new living standards can be built. We can encourage better administration and better education and better tax and land distribution and a better life for the people.

All this and more we can do because we have the talent and the resources to do it, if we will only use and share them. I know that there is a great deal of feeling in the United States that we have carried the burden of economic assistance long enough, but these countries that we are now supporting-stretching all the way along from the top of Europe through the Middle East, down through Saigon--are now subject to great efforts internally, in many of them, to seize control.

If we're not prepared to assist them in making a better life for their people, then I believe that the prospects for freedom in those areas are uncertain. We must, I believe, assist them if we are determined to meet with commitments of assistance our words against the Communist advance. The burden is heavy; we have carried it for many years. But I believe that this fight is not over. This battle goes on, and we have to play our part in it. And therefore I hope again that we will assist these people so that they can remain free.

It was fitting that Congress opened its hearings on our new foreign military and economic aid programs in Washington at the very time that Mr. Khrushchev's words in Vienna were demonstrating as nothing else could the need for that very program. It should be well run, effectively administered, but I believe we must do it, and I hope that you, the American people, will support it again, because I think it's vitally important to the security of these areas. There is no use talking against the Communist advance unless we're willing to meet our responsibilities, however burdensome they may be.

I do not justify this aid merely on the grounds of anti-Communism. It is a recognition of our opportunity and obligation to help these people be free, and we are not alone.

I found that the people of France, for example, were doing far more in Africa in the way of aiding independent nations than our own country was. But I know that foreign aid is a burden that is keenly felt and I can only say that we have no more crucial obligation now.

My stay in England was short but the visit gave me a chance to confer privately again with Prime Minister Macmillan, just as others of our party in Vienna were conferring yesterday with General de Gaulle and Chancellor Adenauer. We all agreed that there is work to be done in the West and from our conversations have come agreed steps to get on with that work. Our day in London, capped by a meeting with Queen Elizabeth and Prince Philip was a strong reminder at the end of a long journey that the West remains united in its determination to hold to its standards.

May I conclude by saying simply that I am glad to be home. We have on this trip admired splendid places and seen stirring sights, but we are glad to be home. No demonstration of support abroad could mean so much as the support which you, the American people, have so generously given to our country. With that support I am not fearful of the future. We must be patient. We must be determined. We must be courageous. We must accept both risks and burdens, but with the will and the work freedom will prevail.

Good night, and thank you very much.

Good evening, my fellow citizens:

I returned this morning from a week-long trip to Europe and I want to report to you on that trip in full. It was in every sense an unforgettable experience. The people of Paris, of Vienna, of London, were generous in their greeting. They were heartwarming in their hospitality, and their graciousness to my wife is particularly appreciated.

We knew of course that the crowds and the shouts were meant in large measure for the country that we represented, which is regarded as the chief defender of freedom. Equally memorable was the pageantry of European history and their culture that is very much a part of any ceremonial reception, to lay a wreath at the Arc de Triomphe, to dine at Versailles, and Schonbrunn Palace, and with the Queen of England. These are the colorful memories that will remain with us for many years to come. Each of the three cities that we visited--Paris, Vienna, and London--have existed for many centuries, and each serves as a reminder that the Western civilization that we seek to preserve has flowered over many years, and has defended itself over many centuries. But this was not a ceremonial trip. Two aims of American foreign policy, above all others, were the reason for the trip: the unity of the free world, whose strength is the security of us all, and the eventual achievement of a lasting peace. My trip was devoted to the advancement of these two aims.

To strengthen the unity of the West, our journey opened in Paris and closed in London. My talks with General de Gaulle were profoundly encouraging to me. Certain differences in our attitudes on one or another problem became insignificant in view of our common commitment to defend freedom. Our alliance, I believe, became more secure; the friendship of our nation, I hope--with theirs--became firmer; and the relations between the two of us who bear responsibility became closer, and I hope were marked by confidence. I found General de Gaulle far more interested in our frankly stating our position, whether or not it was his own, than in appearing to agree with him when we do not. But he knows full well the true meaning of an alliance. He is after all the only major leader of World War II who still occupies a position of great responsibility. His life has been one of unusual dedication; he is a man of extraordinary personal character, symbolizing the new strength and the historic grandeur of France. Throughout our discussions he took the long view of France and the world at large. I found him a wise counselor for the future, and an informative guide to the history that he has helped to make. Thus we had a valuable meeting.

I believe that certain doubts and suspicions that might have come up in a long time--I believe were removed on both sides. Problems which proved to be not of substance but of wording or procedure were cleared away. No question, however sensitive, was avoided. No area of interest was ignored, and the conclusions that we reached will be important for the future--in our agreement on defending Berlin, on working to improve the defenses of Europe, on aiding the economic and political independence of the underdeveloped world, including Latin America, on spurring European economic unity, on concluding successfully the conference on Laos, and on closer consultations and solidarity in the Western alliance.

General de Gaulle could not have been more cordial, and I could not have more confidence in any man. In addition to his individual strength of character, the French people as a whole showed vitality and energy which were both impressive and gratifying. Their recovery from the postwar period is dramatic, their productivity is increasing, and they are steadily building their stature in both Europe and Africa, and thus, I left Paris for Vienna with increased confidence in Western unity and strength.

The people of Vienna know what it is to live under occupation, and they know what it is to live in freedom. Their welcome to me as President of this country should be heartwarming to us all. I went to Vienna to meet the leader of the Soviet Union, Mr. Khrushchev. For 2 days we met in sober, intensive conversation, and I believe it is my obligation to the people, to the Congress, and to our allies to report on those conversations candidly and publicly.

Mr. Khrushchev and I had a very full and frank exchange of views on the major issues that now divide our two countries. I will tell you now that it was a very sober 2 days. There was no discourtesy, no loss of tempers, no threats or ultimatums by either side; no advantage or concession was either gained or given; no major decision was either planned or taken; no spectacular progress was either achieved or pretended.

This kind of informal exchange may not be as exciting as a full-fledged summit meeting with a fixed agenda and a large corps of advisers, where negotiations are attempted and new agreements sought, but this was not intended to be and was not such a meeting, nor did we plan any future summit meetings at Vienna.

But I found this meeting with Chairman Khrushchev, as somber as it was, to be immensely useful. I had read his speeches and of his policies. I had been advised on his views. I had been told by other leaders of the West, General de Gaulle, Chancellor Adenauer, Prime Minister Macmillan, what manner of man he was.

But I bear the responsibility of the Presidency of the United States, and it is my duty to make decisions that no adviser and no ally can make for me. It is my obligation and responsibility to see that these decisions are as informed as possible, that they are based on as much direct, firsthand knowledge as possible.

I therefore thought it was of immense importance that I know Mr. Khrushchev, that I gain as much insight and understanding as I could on his present and future policies. At the same time, I wanted to make certain Mr. Khrushchev knew this country and its policies, that he understood our strength and our determination, and that he knew that we desired peace with all nations of every kind.

I wanted to present our views to him directly, precisely, realistically, and with an opportunity for discussion and clarification. This was done. No new aims were stated in private that have not been stated in public on either side. The gap between us was not, in such a short period, materially reduced, but at least the channels of communications were opened more fully, at least the chances of a dangerous misjudgment on either side should now be less, and at least the men on whose decisions the peace in part depends have agreed to remain in contact.

This is important, for neither of us tried to merely please the other, to agree merely to be agreeable, to say what the other wanted to hear. And just as our judicial system relies on witnesses appearing in court and on cross-examination, instead of hearsay testimony or affidavits on paper, so, too, was this direct give-and-take of immeasurable value in making clear and precise what we considered to be vital, for the facts of the matter are that the Soviets and ourselves give wholly different meanings to the same words--war, peace, democracy, and popular will.

We have wholly different views of right and wrong, of what is an internal affair and what is aggression, and, above all, we have wholly different concepts of where the world is and where it is going.

Only by such a discussion was it possible for me to be sure that Mr. Khrushchev knew how differently we view the present and the future. Our views contrasted sharply but at least we knew better at the end where we both stood. Neither of us was there to dictate a settlement or to convert the other to a cause or to concede our basic interests. But both of us were there, I think, because we realized that each nation has the power to inflict enormous damage upon the other, that such a war could and should be avoided if at all possible, since it would settle no dispute and prove no doctrine, and that care should thus be taken to prevent our conflicting interests from so directly confronting each other that war necessarily ensued. We believe in a system of national freedom and independence. He believes in an expanding and dynamic concept of world communism, and the question was whether these two systems can ever hope to live in peace without permitting any loss of security or any denial of the freedom of our friends. However difficult it may seem to answer this question in the affirmative as we approach so many harsh tests, I think we owe it to all mankind to make every possible effort. That is why I considered the Vienna talks to be useful. The somber mood that they conveyed was not cause for elation or relaxation, nor was it cause for undue pessimism or fear. It simply demonstrated how much work we in the free world have to do and how long and hard a struggle must be our fate as Americans in this generation as the chief defenders of the cause of liberty. The one area which afforded some immediate prospect of accord was Laos. Both sides recognized the need to reduce the dangers in that situation. Both sides endorsed the concept of a neutral and independent Laos, much in the manner of Burma or Cambodia.

Of critical importance to the current conference on Laos in Geneva, both sides recognized the importance of an effective cease-fire. It is urgent that this be translated into new attitudes at Geneva, enabling the International Control Commission to do its duty, to make certain that a cease-fire is enforced and maintained. I am hopeful that progress can be made on this matter in the coming days at Geneva for that would greatly improve international atmosphere.

No such hope emerged, however with respect to the other deadlocked

Geneva conference, seeking a treaty to ban nuclear tests. Mr. Khrushchev made it clear that there could not be a neutral administrator--in his opinion because no one was truly neutral; that a Soviet veto would have to apply to acts of enforcement; that inspection was only a subterfuge for espionage, in the absence of total disarmament; and that the present test ban negotiations appeared futile. In short, our hopes for an end to nuclear tests, for an end to the spread of nuclear weapons, and for some slowing down of the arms race have been struck a serious blow. Nevertheless, the stakes are too important for us to abandon the draft treaty we have offered at Geneva.

But our most somber talks were on the subject of Germany and Berlin. I made it clear to Mr. Khrushchev that the security of Western Europe and therefore our own security are deeply involved in our presence and our access rights to West Berlin, that those rights are based on law and not on sufferance, and that we are determined to maintain those rights at any risk, and thus meet our obligation to the people of West Berlin, and their right to choose their own future.

Mr. Khrushchev, in turn, presented his views in detail, and his presentation will be the subject of further communications. But we are not seeking to change the present situation. A binding German peace treaty is a matter for all who were at war with Germany, and we and our allies cannot abandon our obligations to the people of West Berlin.

Generally, Mr. Khrushchev did not talk in terms of war. He believes the world will move his way without resort to force. He spoke of his nation's achievements in space. He stressed his intention to outdo us in industrial production, to out-trade us, to prove to the world the superiority of his system over ours. Most of all, he predicted the triumph of communism in the new and less developed countries.

He was certain that the tide there was moving his way, that the revolution of rising peoples would eventually be a Communist revolution, and that the so-called wars of liberation, supported by the Kremlin, would replace the old methods of direct aggression and invasion.

In the 1940's and early fifties, the great danger was from Communist armies marching across free borders, which we saw in Korea. Our nuclear monopoly helped to prevent this in other areas. Now we face a new and different threat. We no longer have a nuclear monopoly. Their missiles, they believe, will hold off our missiles, and their troops can match our troops should we intervene in these so-called wars of liberation. Thus, the local conflict they support can turn in their favor through guerrillas or insurgents or subversion. A small group of disciplined Communists could exploit discontent and misery in a country where the average income may be $60 or $70 a year, and seize control, therefore, of an entire country without Communist troops ever crossing any international frontier. This is the Communist theory.

But I believe just as strongly that time will prove it wrong, that liberty and independence and self-determination--not communism-is the future of man, and that free men have the will and the resources to win the struggle for freedom. But it is clear that this struggle in this area of the new and poorer nations will be a continuing crisis of this decade.

Mr. Khrushchev made one point which I wish to pass on. He said there are many disorders throughout the world, and he should not be blamed for them all. He is quite right. It is easy to dismiss as Communist-inspired every anti-government or anti-American riot, every overthrow of a corrupt regime, or every mass protest against misery and despair. These are not all Communist-inspired. The Communists move in to exploit them, to infiltrate their leadership, to ride their crest to victory. But the Communists did not create the conditions which caused them.

In short, the hopes for freedom in these areas which see so much poverty and illiteracy, so many children who are sick, so many children-who die in the first year, so many families without homes, so many families without hope--the future for freedom in these areas rests with the local peoples and their governments.

If they have the will to determine their own future, if their governments have the support of their own people, if their honest and progressive measures--helping their people--have inspired confidence and zeal, then no guerrilla or insurgent action can succeed. But where those conditions do not exist, a military guarantee against external attack from across a border offers little protection against internal decay.

Yet all this does not mean that our Nation and the West and the free world can only sit by. On the contrary, we have an historic opportunity to help these countries build their societies until they are so strong and broadly based that only an outside invasion could topple them, and that threat, we know, can be stopped.

We can train and equip their forces to resist Communist-supplied insurrections. We can help develop the industrial and agricultural base on which new living standards can be built. We can encourage better administration and better education and better tax and land distribution and a better life for the people.

All this and more we can do because we have the talent and the resources to do it, if we will only use and share them. I know that there is a great deal of feeling in the United States that we have carried the burden of economic assistance long enough, but these countries that we are now supporting-stretching all the way along from the top of Europe through the Middle East, down through Saigon--are now subject to great efforts internally, in many of them, to seize control.

If we're not prepared to assist them in making a better life for their people, then I believe that the prospects for freedom in those areas are uncertain. We must, I believe, assist them if we are determined to meet with commitments of assistance our words against the Communist advance. The burden is heavy; we have carried it for many years. But I believe that this fight is not over. This battle goes on, and we have to play our part in it. And therefore I hope again that we will assist these people so that they can remain free.

It was fitting that Congress opened its hearings on our new foreign military and economic aid programs in Washington at the very time that Mr. Khrushchev's words in Vienna were demonstrating as nothing else could the need for that very program. It should be well run, effectively administered, but I believe we must do it, and I hope that you, the American people, will support it again, because I think it's vitally important to the security of these areas. There is no use talking against the Communist advance unless we're willing to meet our responsibilities, however burdensome they may be.

I do not justify this aid merely on the grounds of anti-Communism. It is a recognition of our opportunity and obligation to help these people be free, and we are not alone.

I found that the people of France, for example, were doing far more in Africa in the way of aiding independent nations than our own country was. But I know that foreign aid is a burden that is keenly felt and I can only say that we have no more crucial obligation now.

My stay in England was short but the visit gave me a chance to confer privately again with Prime Minister Macmillan, just as others of our party in Vienna were conferring yesterday with General de Gaulle and Chancellor Adenauer. We all agreed that there is work to be done in the West and from our conversations have come agreed steps to get on with that work. Our day in London, capped by a meeting with Queen Elizabeth and Prince Philip was a strong reminder at the end of a long journey that the West remains united in its determination to hold to its standards.

May I conclude by saying simply that I am glad to be home. We have on this trip admired splendid places and seen stirring sights, but we are glad to be home. No demonstration of support abroad could mean so much as the support which you, the American people, have so generously given to our country. With that support I am not fearful of the future. We must be patient. We must be determined. We must be courageous. We must accept both risks and burdens, but with the will and the work freedom will prevail.

Good night, and thank you very much.

REMARKS TO THE GRADUATING CLASS OF THE US NAVAL ACADEMY

(JUNE 7, 1961)

Admiral, Mr. Secretary, members of the Joint Chiefs of Staff, members of the faculty, members of the Graduating Class and their families:

I am proud as a citizen of the United States to come to this institution and this room where there is concentrated so many men who have committed themselves to the defense of the United States. I am honored to be here.

In the past I have had some slight contact with this Service, though I never did reach the state of professional and physical perfection where I could hope that anyone would ever mistake me for an Annapolis graduate.

I know that you are constantly warned during your days here not to mix, in your Naval career, in politics. I should point out, however, on the other side, that my rather rapid rise from a Reserve Lieutenant, of uncertain standing, to Commander-in-Chief, has been because I did not follow that very good advice.

I trust, however, that those of you who are Regulars will, for a moment, grant a retired civilian officer some measure of fellowship.

Nearly a half century ago, President Woodrow Wilson came here to Annapolis on a similar mission, and addressed the Class of 1914. On that day, the graduating class numbered 154 men. There has been, since that time, a revolution in the size of our military establishment, and that revolution has been reflected in the revolution in the world around us.

When Wilson addressed the class in 1914, the Victorian structure of power was still intact, the world was dominated by Europe, and Europe itself was the scene of an uneasy balance of power between dominant figures and America was a spectator on a remote sideline.

The autumn after Wilson came to Annapolis, the Victorian world began to fall to pieces, and our world one-half a century later is vastly different. Today we are witnesses to the most extraordinary revolution, nearly, in the history of the world, as the emergent nations of Latin America, Africa, and Asia awaken from long centuries of torpor and impatience.

Today the Victorian certitude's which were taken to be so much a part of man's natural existence are under siege by a faith committed to the destruction of liberal civilization, and today the United States is no longer the spectator, but the leader.

This half century, therefore, has not only revolutionized the size of our military establishment, it has brought about also a more striking revolution in the things that the Nation expects from the men in our Service.

Fifty years ago the graduates of the Naval Academy were expected to be seamen and leaders of men. They were reminded of the saying of John Paul Jones, "Give me a fair ship so that I might go into harm's way."

When Captain Mahan began to write in the nineties on the general issues of war and peace and naval strategy, the Navy quickly shipped him to sea duty. Today we expect all of you--in fact, you must, of necessity-be prepared not only to handle a ship in a storm or a landing party on a beach, but to make great determinations which affect the survival of this country.

The revolution in the technology of war makes it necessary in order that you, when you hold positions of command, may make an educated judgment between various techniques, that you also be a scientist and an engineer and a physicist, and your responsibilities go far beyond the classic problems of tactics and strategy.

In the years to come, some of you will serve as your Commandant did last year, as an adviser to foreign governments; some will negotiate as Admiral Burke did, in Korea, with other governments on behalf of the United States; some will go to the far reaches of space and some will go to the bottom of the ocean. Many of you from one time or another, in the positions of command, or as members of staff, will participate in great decisions which go far beyond the narrow reaches of professional competence.

You gentlemen, therefore, have a most important responsibility, to recognize that your education is just beginning, and to be prepared, in the most difficult period in the life of our country, to play the role that the country hopes and needs and expects from you. You must understand not only this country but other countries. You must know something about strategy and tactics and logic--logistics, but also economics and politics and diplomacy and history. You must know everything you can know about military power, and you must also understand the limits of military power. You must understand that few of the important problems of our time have, in the final analysis, been finally solved by military power alone. When I say that officers today must go far beyond the official curriculum, I say it not because I do not believe in the traditional relationship between the civilian and the military, but you must be more than the servants of national policy. You must be prepared to play a constructive role in the development of national policy, a policy which protects our interests and our security and the peace of the world. Woodrow Wilson reminded your predecessors that you were not serving a government or an administration, but a people. In serving the American people, you represent the American people and the best of the ideals of this free society. Your posture and your performance will provide many people far beyond our shores, who know very little of our country, the only evidence they will ever see as to whether America is truly dedicated to the cause of justice and freedom.

In my inaugural address, I said that each citizen should be concerned not with what his country can do for him, but what he can do for his country. What you have chosen to do for your country, by devoting your life to the service of our country, is the greatest contribution that any man could make. It is easy for you, in a moment of exhilaration today, to say that you freely and gladly dedicate your life to the United States. But the life of service is a constant test of your will.

It will be hard at times to face the personal sacrifice and the family inconvenience, to maintain this high resolve, to place the needs of your country above all else. When there is a visible enemy to fight, the tide of patriotism in this country runs strong. But when there is a long, slow struggle, with no immediate visible foe, when you watch your contemporaries indulging the urge for material gain and comfort and personal advancement, your choice will seem hard, and you will recall, I am sure, the lines found in an old sentry box at Gibraltar, "God and the soldier all men adore in time of trouble and no more, for when war is over, and all things righted, God is neglected and the old soldier slighted."

Never forget, however, that the battle for freedom takes many forms. Those who through vigilance and firmness and devotion are the great servants of this country--and let us have no doubt that the United States needs your devoted assistance today.

The answer to those who challenge us so severely in so many parts of the globe lies in our willingness to freely commit ourselves to the maintenance of our country and the things for which it stands.

This ceremony today represents the kind of commitment which you are willing to make. For that reason, I am proud to be here. This nation salutes you as you commence your service to our country in the hazardous days ahead. And on behalf of all of them, I congratulate you and thank you.

REPORT ON THE BERLIN CRISIS

(JULY 25, 1961)

Good evening:

Seven weeks ago tonight I returned from Europe to report on my meeting with Premier Khrushchev and the others. His grim warnings about the future of the world, his aide memoire on Berlin, his subsequent speeches and threats which he and his agents have launched, and the increase in the Soviet military budget that he has announced, have all prompted a series of decisions by the Administration and a series of consultations with the members of the NATO organization. In Berlin, as you recall, he intends to bring to an end, through a stroke of the pen, first our legal rights to be in West Berlin-and secondly our ability to make good on our commitment to the two million free people of that city. That we cannot permit.

We are clear about what must be done-and we intend to do it. I want to talk frankly with you tonight about the first steps that we shall take. These actions will require sacrifice on the part of many of our citizens. More will be required in the future. They will require, from all of us, courage and perseverance in the years to come. But if we and our allies act out of strength and unity of purpose--with calm determination and steady nerves-- using restraint in our words as well as our weapons. I am hopeful that both peace and freedom will be sustained.

The immediate threat to free men is in West Berlin. But that isolated outpost is not an isolated problem. The threat is worldwide. Our effort must be equally wide and strong, and not be obsessed by any single manufactured crisis. We face a challenge in Berlin, but there is also a challenge in Southeast Asia, where the borders are less guarded, the enemy harder to find, and the dangers of communism less apparent to those who have so little. We face a challenge in our own hemisphere, and indeed wherever else the freedom of human beings is at stake.

Let me remind you that the fortunes of war and diplomacy left the free people of West Berlin, in 1945, 110 miles behind the Iron Curtain.

This map makes very clear the problem that we face. The white is West Germany-the East is the area controlled by the Soviet Union, and as you can see from the chart, West Berlin is 110 miles within the area which the Soviets now dominate-which is immediately controlled by the so-called East German regime.

We are there as a result of our victory over Nazi Germany--and our basic rights to be there, deriving from that victory, include both our presence in West Berlin and the enjoyment of access across East Germany. These rights have been repeatedly confirmed and recognized in special agreements with the Soviet Union. Berlin is not a part of East Germany, but a separate territory under the control of the allied powers. Thus our rights there are clear and deep-rooted. But in addition to those rights is our commitment to sustain--and defend, if need be--the opportunity for more than two million people to determine their own future and choose their own way of life.

Thus, our presence in West Berlin, and our access thereto, cannot be ended by any act of the Soviet government. The NATO shield was long ago extended to cover West Berlin--and we have given our word that an attack upon that city will be regarded as an attack upon us all.

For West Berlin lying exposed 110 miles inside East Germany, surrounded by Soviet troops and close to Soviet supply lines, has many roles. It is more than a showcase of liberty, a symbol, an island of freedom in a Communist sea. It is even more than a link with the Free World, a beacon of hope behind the Iron Curtain, an escape hatch for refugees.

West Berlin is all of that. But above all it has now become--as never before--the great testing place of Western courage and will, a focal point where our solemn commitments stretching back over the years since 1945, and Soviet ambitions now meet in basic confrontation.

It would be a mistake for others to look upon Berlin, because of its location, as a tempting target. The United States is there; the United Kingdom and France are there; the pledge of NATO is there--and the people of Berlin are there. It is as secure, in that sense, as the rest of us--for we cannot separate its safety from our own.

I hear it said that West Berlin is militarily untenable. And so was

Bastogne. And so, in fact, was Stalingrad. Any dangerous spot is tenable if men--brave men--will make it so.

We do not want to fight--but we have fought before. And others in earlier times have made the same dangerous mistake of assuming that the West was too selfish and too soft and too divided to resist invasions of freedom in other lands. Those who threaten to unleash the forces of war on a dispute over West Berlin should recall the words of the ancient philosopher: "A man who causes fear cannot be free from fear."

We cannot and will not permit the Communists to drive us out of Berlin, either gradually or by force. For the fulfillment of our pledge to that city is essential to the morale and security of Western Germany, to the unity of Western Europe, and to the faith of the entire Free World. Soviet strategy has long been aimed, not merely at Berlin, but at dividing and neutralizing all of Europe, forcing us back on our own shores. We must meet our oft-stated pledge to the free peoples of West Berlin-and maintain our rights and their safety, even in the face of force--in order to maintain the confidence of other free peoples in our word and our resolve. The strength of the alliance on which our security depends is dependent in turn on our willingness to meet our commitments to them.

So long as the Communists insist that they are preparing to end by themselves unilaterally our rights in West Berlin and our commitments to its people, we must be prepared to defend those rights and those commitments. We will at all times be ready to talk, if talk will help. But we must also be ready to resist with force, if force is used upon us. Either alone would fail. Together, they can serve the cause of freedom and peace.

The new preparations that we shall make to defend the peace are part of the long-term build-up in our strength which has been underway since January. They are based on our needs to meet a world-wide threat, on a basis which stretches far beyond the present Berlin crisis. Our primary purpose is neither propaganda nor provocation--but preparation.

A first need is to hasten progress toward the military goals which the North Atlantic allies have set for themselves. In Europe today nothing less will suffice. We will put even greater resources into fulfilling those goals, and we look to our allies to do the same.

The supplementary defense build-ups that I asked from the Congress in March and May have already started moving us toward these and our other defense goals. They included an increase in the size of the Marine Corps, improved readiness of our reserves, expansion of our air and sea lift, and stepped-up procurement of needed weapons, ammunition, and other items. To insure a continuing invulnerable capacity to deter or destroy any aggressor, they provided for the strengthening of our missile power and for putting 50% of our B-52 and B-47 bombers on a ground alert which would send them on their way with 15 minutes' warning.

These measures must be speeded up, and still others must now be taken. We must have sea and air lift capable of moving our forces quickly and in large numbers to any part of the world.

But even more importantly, we need the capability of placing in any critical area at the appropriate time a force which, combined with those of our allies, is large enough to make clear our determination and our ability to defend our rights at all costs--and to meet all levels of aggressor pressure with whatever levels of force are required. We intend to have a wider choice than humiliation or all-out nuclear action. While it is unwise at this time either to call up or send abroad excessive numbers of these troops before they are needed, let me make it clear that I intend to take, as time goes on, whatever steps are necessary to make certain that such forces can be deployed at the appropriate time without lessening our ability to meet our commitments elsewhere.

Thus, in the days and months ahead, I shall not hesitate to ask the Congress for additional measures, or exercise any of the executive powers that I possess to meet this threat to peace. Everything essential to the security of freedom must be done; and if that should require more men, or more taxes, or more controls, or other new powers, I shall not hesitate to ask them. The measures proposed today will be constantly studied, and altered as necessary. But while we will not let panic shape our policy, neither will we permit timidity to direct our program.

Accordingly, I am now taking the following steps:

(1) I am tomorrow requesting the Congress for the current fiscal year an additional $3,247,000,000 of appropriations for the Armed Forces.

(2) To fill out our present Army Divisions, and to make more men available for prompt deployment, I am requesting an increase in the Army's total authorized strength from 875,000 to approximately 1 million men.

(3) I am requesting an increase of 29,000 and 63,000 men respectively in the active duty strength of the Navy and the Air Force.

(4) To fulfill these manpower needs, I am ordering that our draft calls be doubled and tripled in the coming months; I am asking the Congress for authority to order to active duty certain ready reserve units and individual reservists, and to extend tours of duty;2 and, under that authority, I am planning to order to active duty a number of air transport squadrons and Air National Guard tactical air squadrons, to give us the airlift capacity and protection that we need. Other reserve forces will be called up when needed.

(5) Many ships and planes once headed for retirement are to be retained or reactivated, increasing our airpower tactically and our sealift, airlift, and anti-submarine warfare capability. In addition, our strategic air power will be increased by delaying the deactivation of B-47 bombers.

(6) Finally, some $1.8 billion--about half of the total sum--is needed for the procurement of non-nuclear weapons, ammunition and equipment.

The details on all these requests will be presented to the Congress tomorrow. Subsequent steps will be taken to suit subsequent needs. Comparable efforts for the common defense are being discussed with our NATO allies. For their commitment and interest are as precise as our own.

And let me add that I am well aware of the fact that many American families will bear the burden of these requests. Studies or careers will be interrupted; husbands and sons will be called away; incomes in some cases will be reduced. But these are burdens which must be borne if freedom is to be defended--Americans have willingly borne them before--and they will not flinch from the task now.

We have another sober responsibility. To recognize the possibilities of nuclear war in the missile age, without our citizens knowing what they should do and where they should go if bombs begin to fall, would be a failure of responsibility. In May, I pledged a new start on Civil Defense. Last week, I assigned, on the recommendation of the Civil Defense Director, basic responsibility for this program to the Secretary of Defense, to make certain it is administered and coordinated with our continental defense efforts at the highest civilian level. Tomorrow, I am requesting of the Congress new funds for the following immediate objectives: to identify and mark space in existing structures--public and private--that could be used for fall-out shelters in case of attack; to stock those shelters with food, water, first-aid kits and other minimum essentials for survival; to increase their capacity; to improve our air-raid warning and fall-out detection systems, including a new household warning system which is now under development; and to take other measures that will be effective at an early date to save millions of lives if needed.

In the event of an attack, the lives of those families which are not hit in a nuclear blast and fire can still be saved--if they can be warned to take shelter and if that shelter is available. We owe that kind of insurance to our families--and to our country. In contrast to our friends in Europe, the need for this kind of protection is new to our shores. But the time to start is now. In the coming months, I hope to let every citizen know what steps he can take without delay to protect his family in case of attack. I know that you will want to do no less.

The addition of $207 million in Civil Defense appropriations brings our total new defense budget requests to $3.454 billion, and a total of $47-5 billion for the year. This is an increase in the defense budget of $6 billion since January, and has resulted in official estimates of a budget deficit of over $5 billion. The Secretary of the Treasury and other economic advisers assure me, however, that our economy has the capacity to bear this new request.

We are recovering strongly from this year's recession. The increase in this last quarter of our year of our total national output was greater than that for any postwar period of initial recovery. And yet, wholesale prices are actually lower than they were during the recession, and consumer prices are only 1/4 of 1% higher than they were last October. In fact, this last quarter was the first in eight years in which our production has increased without an increase in the overall-price index. And for the first time since the fall of 1959, our gold position has improved and the dollar is more respected abroad. These gains, it should be stressed, are being accomplished with Budget deficits far smaller than those of the 1958 recession.

This improved business outlook means improved revenues; and I intend to submit to the Congress in January a budget for the next fiscal year which will be strictly in balance. Nevertheless, should an increase in taxes be needed--because of events in the next few months--to achieve that balance, or because of subsequent defense rises, those increased taxes will be requested in January.

Meanwhile, to help make certain that the current deficit is held to a safe level, we must keep down all expenditures not thoroughly justified in budget requests. The luxury of our current post-office deficit must be ended. Costs in military procurement will be closely scrutinized--and in this effort I welcome the cooperation of the Congress. The tax loopholes I have specified--on expense accounts, overseas income, dividends, interest, coo operatives and others--must be closed.

I realize that no public revenue measure is welcomed by everyone. But I am certain that every American wants to pay his fair share, and not leave the burden of defending freedom entirely to those who bear arms. For we have mortgaged our very future on this defense--and we cannot fail to meet our responsibilities.

But I must emphasize again that the choice is not merely between resistance and retreat, between atomic holocaust and surrender. Our peace-time military posture is traditionally defensive; but our diplomatic posture need not be. Our response to the Berlin crisis will not be merely military or negative. It will be more than merely standing firm. For we do not intend to leave it to others to choose and monopolize the forum and the framework of discussion. We do not intend to abandon our duty to mankind to seek a peaceful solution.

As signers of the UN Charter, we shall always be prepared to discuss international problems with any and all nations that are willing to talk--and listen--with reason. If they have proposals--not demands--we shall hear them. If they seek genuine understanding-not concessions of our rights-we shall meet with them. We have previously indicated our readiness to remove any actual irritants in West Berlin, but the freedom of that city is not negotiable. We cannot negotiate with those who say "What's mine is mine and what's yours is negotiable." But we are willing to consider any arrangement or treaty in Germany consistent with the maintenance of peace and freedom, and with the legitimate security interests of all nations.

We recognize the Soviet Union's historical concern about their security in Central and Eastern Europe, after a series of ravaging invasions, and we believe arrangements can be worked out which will help to meet those concerns, and make it possible for both security and freedom to exist in this troubled area.

For it is not the freedom of West Berlin which is "abnormal" in Germany today, but the situation in that entire divided country. If anyone doubts the legality of our rights in Berlin, we are ready to have it submitted to international adjudication. If anyone doubts the extent to which our presence is desired by the people of West Berlin, compared to East German feelings about their regime, we are ready to have that question submitted to a free vote in Berlin and, if possible, among all the German people. And let us hear at that time from the two and one-half million refugees who have fled the Communist regime in East Germany-voting for Western-type freedom with their feet.

The world is not deceived by the Communist attempt to label Berlin as a hot-bed of war. There is peace in Berlin today. The source of world trouble and tension is Moscow, not Berlin. And if war begins, it will have begun in Moscow and not Berlin.

For the choice of peace or war is largely theirs, not ours. It is the Soviets who have stirred up this crisis. It is they who are trying to force a change. It is they who have opposed free elections. It is they who have rejected an all-German peace treaty, and the rulings of international law. And as Americans know from our history on our own old frontier, gun battles are caused by outlaws, and not by officers of the peace.

In short, while we are ready to defend our interests, we shall also be ready to search for peace--in quiet exploratory talks--in formal or informal meetings. We do not want military considerations to dominate the thinking of either East or West. And Mr. Khrushchev may find that his invitation to other nations to join in a meaningless treaty may lead to their inviting him to join in the community of peaceful men, in abandoning the use of force, and in respecting the sanctity of agreements.

While all of these efforts go on, we must not be diverted from our total responsibilities, from other dangers, from other tasks. If new threats in Berlin or elsewhere should cause us to weaken our program of assistance to the developing nations who are also under heavy pressure from the same source, or to halt our efforts for realistic disarmament, or to disrupt or slow down our economy, or to neglect the education of our children, then those threats will surely be the most successful and least costly maneuver in Communist history. For we can afford all these efforts, and more but we cannot afford not to meet this challenge.

And the challenge is not to us alone. It is a challenge to every nation which asserts its sovereignty under a system of liberty. It is a challenge to all those who want a world of free choice. It is a special challenge to the Atlantic Community--the heartland of human freedom.

We in the West must move together in building military strength. We must consult one another more closely than ever before. We must together design our proposals for peace, and labor together as they are pressed at the conference table. And together we must share the burdens and the risks of this effort.

The Atlantic Community, as we know it, has been built in response to challenge: the challenge of European chaos in 1947, of the Berlin blockade in 1948, the challenge of Communist aggression in Korea in 1950. Now, standing strong and prosperous, after an unprecedented decade of progress, the Atlantic Community will not forget either its history or the principles which gave it meaning.

The solemn vow each of us gave to West Berlin in time of peace will not be broken in time of danger. If we do not meet our commitments to Berlin, where will we later stand? If we are not true to our word there, all that we have achieved in collective security, which relies on these words, will mean nothing. And if there is one path above all others to war, it is the path of weakness and disunity.

Today, the endangered frontier of freedom runs through divided Berlin. We want it to remain a frontier of peace. This is the hope of every citizen of the Atlantic Community; every citizen of Eastern Europe; and, I am confident, every citizen of the Soviet Union. For I cannot believe that the Russian people--who bravely suffered enormous losses in the Second World War-would now wish to see the peace upset once more in Germany. The Soviet government alone can convert Berlin's frontier of peace into a pretext for war.

The steps I have indicated tonight are aimed at avoiding that war. To sum it all up: we seek peace--but we shall not surrender. That is the central meaning of this crisis, and the meaning of your government's policy.

With your help, and the help of other free men, this crisis can be surmounted. Freedom can prevail--and peace can endure.

I would like to close with a personal word. When I ran for the Presidency of the United States, I knew that this country faced serious challenges, but I could not realize--nor could any man realize who does not bear the burdens of this office--how heavy and constant would be those burdens.

Three times in my life-time our country and Europe have been involved in major wars. In each case serious misjudgments were made on both sides of the intentions of others, which brought about great devastation.

Now, in the thermonuclear age, any misjudgment on either side about the intentions of the other could rain more devastation in several hours than has been wrought in all the wars of human history.

Therefore I, as President and Commander-in-Chief, and all of us as Americans, are moving through serious days. I shall bear this responsibility under our Constitution for the next three and one-half years, but I am sure that we all, regardless of our occupations, will do our very best for our country, and for our cause. For all of us want to see our children grow up in a country at peace, and in a world where freedom endures.

I know that sometimes we get impatient, we wish for some immediate action that would end our perils. But I must tell you that there is no quick and easy solution. The Communists control over a billion people, and they recognize that if we should falter, their success would be imminent.

We must look to long days ahead, which if we are courageous and persevering can bring us what we all desire.

In these days and weeks I ask for your help, and your advice. I ask for your suggestions, when you think we could do better.

All of us, I know, love our country, and we shall all do our best to serve it.

In meeting my responsibilities in these coming months as President, I need your good will, and your support--and above all, your prayers.

Thank you, and good night.

ADDRESS TO THE UN GENERAL ASSEMBLY

(SEPTEMBER 25, 1961)

Mr. President, honored delegates, ladies and gentlemen:

We meet in an hour of grief and challenge. Dag Hammarskjold is dead. But the United Nations lives. His tragedy is deep in our hearts, but the task for which he died is at the top of our agenda. A noble servant of peace is gone. But the quest for peace lies before us.

The problem is not the death of one man--the problem is the life of this organization. It will either grow to meet the challenges of our age, or it will be gone with the wind, without influence, without force, without respect. Were we to let it die, to enfeeble its vigor, to cripple its powers, we would condemn our future.

For in the development of this organization rests the only true alternative to war--and war appeals no longer as a rational alternative. Unconditional war can no longer lead to unconditional victory. It can no longer serve to settle disputes. It can no longer concern the great powers alone. For a nuclear disaster, spread by wind and water and fear, could well engulf the great and the small, the rich and the poor, the committed and the uncommitted alike. Mankind must put an end to war--or war will put an end to mankind.

So let us here resolve that Dag Hammarskjold did not live, or die, in vain. Let us call a truce to terror. Let us invoke the blessings of peace. And, as we build an international capacity to keep peace, let us join in dismantling the national capacity to wage war.

This will require new strength and new roles for the United Nations. For disarmament without checks is but a shadow-and a community without law is but a shell. Already the United Nations has become both the measure and the vehicle of man's most generous impulses. Already it has provided-- in the Middle East, in Asia, in Africa this year in the Congo--a means of holding man's violence within bounds.

But the great question which confronted this body in 1945 is still before us: whether man's cherished hopes for progress and peace are to be destroyed by terror and disruption, whether the "foul winds of war" can be tamed in time to free the cooling winds of reason, and whether the pledges of our Charter are to be fulfilled or defied-pledges to secure peace, progress, human rights and world law.

In this Hall, there are not three forces, but two. One is composed of those who are trying to build the kind of world described in Articles I and II of the Charter. The other, seeking a far different world, would undermine this organization in the process.

Today of all days our dedication to the Charter must be maintained. It must be strengthened first of all by the selection of an outstanding civil servant to carry forward the responsibilities of the Secretary General--a man endowed with both the wisdom and the power to make meaningful the moral force of the world community. The late Secretary General nurtured and sharpened the United Nations' obligation to act. But he did not invent it. It was there in the Charter. It is still there in the Charter.

However difficult it may be to fill Mr. Hammarskjold's place, it can better be filled by one man rather than by three. Even the three horses of the Troika did not have three drivers, all going in different directions. They had only one--and so must the United Nations executive. To install a triumvirate, or any panel, or any rotating authority, in the United Nations administrative offices would replace order with anarchy, action with paralysis, confidence with confusion.

The Secretary General, in a very real sense, is the servant of the General Assembly. Diminish his authority and you diminish the authority of the only body where all nations, regardless of power, are equal and sovereign. Until all the powerful are just, the weak will be secure only in the strength of this Assembly.

Effective and independent executive action is not the same question as balanced representation. In view of the enormous change in membership in this body since its founding, the American delegation will join in any effort for the prompt review and revision of the composition of United Nations bodies.

But to give this organization three drivers-to permit each great power to decide its own case, would entrench the Cold War in the headquarters of peace. Whatever advantages such a plan may hold out to my own country, as one of the great powers, we reject it. For we far prefer world law, in the age of self-determination, to world war, in the age of mass extermination.

Today, every inhabitant of this planet must contemplate the day when this planet may no longer be habitable. Every man, woman and child lives under a nuclear sword of Damocles, hanging by the slenderest of threads, capable of being cut at any moment by accident or miscalculation or by madness. The weapons of war must be abolished before they abolish us.

Men no longer debate whether armaments are a symptom or a cause of tension. The mere existence of modern weapons--ten million times more powerful than any that the world has ever seen, and only minutes away from any target on earth--is a source of horror, and discord and distrust. Men no longer maintain that disarmament must await the settlement of all disputes--for disarmament must be a part of any permanent settlement. And men may no longer pretend that the quest for disarmament is a sign of weakness--for in a spiraling arms race, a nation's security may well be shrinking even as its arms increase.

For 15 years this organization has sought the reduction and destruction of arms. Now that goal is no longer a dream--it is a practical matter of life or death. The risks inherent in disarmament pale in comparison to the risks inherent in an unlimited arms race.

It is in this spirit that the recent Belgrade Conference--recognizing that this is no longer a Soviet problem or an American problem, but a human problem--endorsed a program of "general, complete and strictly an internationally controlled disarmament." It is in this same spirit that we in the United States have labored this year, with a new urgency, and with a new, now statutory agency fully endorsed by the Congress, to find an approach to disarmament which would be so far-reaching yet realistic, so mutually balanced and beneficial, that it could be accepted by every nation. And it is in this spirit that we have presented with the agreement of the Soviet Union--under the label both nations now accept of "general and complete disarmament"--a new statement of newly-agreed principles for negotiation.

But we are well aware that all issues of principle are not settled, and that principles alone are not enough. It is therefore our intention to challenge the Soviet Union, not to an arms race, but to a peace race--to advance together step by step, stage by stage, until general and complete disarmament has been achieved. We invite them now to go beyond agreement in principle to reach agreement on actual plans.

The program to be presented to this assembly--for general and complete disarmament under effective international control-moves to bridge the gap between those who insist on a gradual approach and those who talk only of the final and total achievement. It would create machinery to keep the peace as it destroys the machinery Of war. It would proceed through balanced and safeguarded stages designed to give no state a military advantage over another. It would place the final responsibility for verification and control where it belongs, not with the big powers alone, not with one's adversary or one's self, but in an international organization within the framework of the United Nations. It would assure that indispensable condition of disarmament-true inspection--and apply it in stages proportionate to the stage of disarmament. It would cover delivery systems as well as weapons. It would ultimately halt their production as well as their testing, 'their transfer as well as their possession. It would achieve, under the eyes of an international disarmament organization, a steady reduction in force, both nuclear and conventional, until it has abolished all armies and all weapons except those needed for internal order and a new United Nations Peace Force. And it starts that process now, today, even as the talks begin.

In short, general and complete disarmament must no longer be a slogan, used to resist the first steps. It is no longer to be a goal without means of achieving it, without means of verifying its progress, without means of keeping the peace. It is now a realistic plan, and a test--a test of those only willing to talk and a test of those willing to act.

Such a plan would not bring a world free from conflict and greed--but it would bring a world free from the terrors of mass destruction It would not usher in the era of the super state--but it would usher in an era in which no state could annihilate or be annihilated by another.

In 1945, this Nation proposed the Baruch Plan to internationalize the atom before other nations even possessed the bomb or demilitarized their troops. We proposed with our allies the Disarmament Plan of 1951 while still at war in Korea. And we make our proposals today, while building up our defenses over Berlin, not because we are inconsistent or insincere or intimidated, but because we know the rights of free men will prevail-- because while we are compelled against our will to rearm, we look confidently beyond Berlin to the kind of disarmed world we all prefer.

I therefore propose, on the basis of this Plan, that disarmament negotiations resume promptly, and continue without interruption until an entire program for general and complete disarmament has not only been agreed but has been actually achieved.

The logical place to begin is a treaty assuring the end of nuclear tests of all kinds, in every environment, under workable controls. The United States and the United Kingdom have proposed such a treaty that is both reasonable, effective and ready for signature. We are still prepared to sign that treaty today.

We also proposed a mutual ban on atmospheric testing, without inspection or controls, in order to save the human race from the poison of radioactive fallout. We regret that that offer has not been accepted.

For 15 years we have sought to make the atom an instrument of peaceful growth rather than of war. But for 15 years our concessions have been matched by obstruction, our patience by intransigence. And the pleas of mankind for peace have met with disregard.

Finally, as the explosions of others beclouded the skies, my country was left with no alternative but to act in the interests of its own and the free world's security. We cannot endanger that security by refraining from testing while others improve their arsenals. Nor can we endanger it by another long, un-inspected ban on testing. For three years we accepted those risks in our open society while seeking agreement on inspection. But this year, while we were negotiating in good faith in Geneva, others were secretly preparing new experiments in destruction.

Our tests are not polluting the atmosphere. Our deterrent weapons are guarded against accidental explosion or use. Our doctors and scientists stand ready to help any nation measure and meet the hazards to health which inevitably result from the tests in the atmosphere.

But to halt the spread of these terrible weapons, to halt the contamination of the air, to halt the spiraling nuclear arms race, we remain ready to seek new avenues of agreement, our new Disarmament Program thus includes the following proposals:

--First, signing the test-ban treaty by all nations. This can be done now. Test ban negotiations need not and should not await general disarmament.

--Second, stopping the production of fissionable materials for use in weapons, and preventing their transfer to any nation now lacking in nuclear weapons.

--Third, prohibiting the transfer of control over nuclear weapons to states that do not own them.

--Fourth, keeping nuclear weapons from seeding new battlegrounds in outer space.

--Fifth, gradually destroying existing nuclear weapons and converting their materials to peaceful uses; and

--Finally, halting the unlimited testing and production of strategic nuclear delivery vehicles, and gradually destroying them as well.

To destroy arms, however, is not enough. We must create even as we destroy--creating worldwide law and law enforcement as we outlaw worldwide war and weapons. In the world we seek, the United Nations Emergency Forces which have been hastily assembled, uncertainly supplied, and inadequately financed, will never be enough.

Therefore, the United States recommends the Presidents that all member nations earmark special peace-keeping units in their armed forces-to be on call of the United Nations, to be specially trained and quickly available, and with advance provision for financial and logistic support.

In addition, the American delegation will suggest a series of steps to improve the United Nations' machinery for the peaceful settlement of disputes--for on-the-spot fact-finding, mediation and adjudication--for extending the rule of international law. For peace is not solely a matter of military or technical problems--it is primarily a problem of politics and people. And unless man can match his strides in weaponry and technology with equal strides in social and political development, our great strength, like that of the dinosaur, will become incapable of proper control--and like the dinosaur vanish from the earth.

As we extend the rule of law on earth, so must we also extend it to man's new domain--outer space.

All of us salute the brave cosmonauts of the Soviet Union. The new horizons of outer space must not be driven by the old bitter concepts of imperialism and sovereign claims. The cold reaches of the universe must not become the new arena of an even colder war.

To this end, we shall urge proposals extending the United Nations Charter to the limits of man's exploration in the universe, reserving outer space for peaceful use, prohibiting weapons of mass destruction in space or on celestial bodies, and opening the mysteries and benefits of space to every nation. We shall propose further cooperative efforts between all nations in weather prediction and eventually in weather control. We shall propose, finally, a global system of communications satellites linking the whole world in telegraph and telephone and radio and television. The day need not be fat away when such a system will televise the proceedings of this body to every corner of the world for the benefit of peace.

But the mysteries of outer space must not divert our eyes or our energies from the harsh realities that face our fellow men. Political sovereignty is but a mockery without the means of meeting poverty and literacy and disease. Self-determination is but a slogan if the future holds no hope.

That is why my Nation, which has freely shared its capital and its technology to help others help themselves, now proposes officially designating this decade of the 1960's as the United Nations Decade of Development. Under the framework of that Resolution, the United Nations' existing efforts in promoting economic growth can be expanded and coordinated. Regional surveys and training institutes can now pool the talents of many. New research, technical assistance and pilot projects can unlock the wealth of less developed lands and untapped waters. And development can become a cooperative and not a competitive enterprise-to enable all nations, however diverse in their systems and beliefs, to become in fact as well as in law free and equal nations.

My Country favors a world of free and equal states. We agree with those who say that colonialism is a key issue in this Assembly But let the full facts of that issue be discussed in full.

On the one hand is the fact that, since the close of World War II, a worldwide declaration of independence has transformed nearly 1 billion people and 9 million square miles into 42 free and independent states. Less than 2 percent of the world's population now lives in "dependent" territories.

I do not ignore the remaining problems of traditional colonialism which still confront this body. Those problems will be solved, with patience, good will, and determination. Within the limits of our responsibility in such matters, my Country intends to be a participant and not merely an observer, in the peaceful, expeditious movement of nations from the status of colonies to the partnership of equals. That continuing tide of self-determination, which runs so strong, has our sympathy and our support.

But colonialism in its harshest forms is not only the exploitation of new nations by old, of dark skins by light, or the subjugation of the poor by the rich. My Nation was once a colony, and we know what colonialism means; the exploitation and subjugation of the weak by the powerful, of the many by the few, of the governed who have given no consent to be governed, whatever their continent, their class, or their color.

And that is why there is no ignoring the fact that the tide of self-determination has not reached the Communist empire where a population far larger than that officially termed "dependent" lives under governments installed by foreign troops instead of free institutions--under a system which knows only one party and one belief--which suppresses free debate, and free elections, and free newspapers, and free books and free trade unions--and which builds a wall to keep truth a stranger and its own citizens prisoners. Let us debate colonialism in full--and apply the principle of free choice and the practice of free plebiscites in every corner of the globe.

Finally, as President of the United States, I consider it my duty to report to this Assembly on two threats to the peace which are not on your crowded agenda, but which causes us, and most of you, the deepest concern.

The first threat on which I wish to report is widely misunderstood: the smoldering coals of war in Southeast Asia. South Viet-Nam is already under attack--sometimes by a single assassin, sometimes by a band of guerrillas, recently by full battalions. The peaceful borders of Burma, Cambodia, and India have been repeatedly violated. And the peaceful people of Laos are in danger of losing the independence they gained not so long ago.

No one can call these "wars of liberation." For these are free countries living under their own governments. Nor are these aggressions any less real because men are knifed in their homes and not shot in the fields of battle.

The very simple question confronting the world community is whether measures can be devised to protect the small and the weak from such tactics. For if they are successful in Laos and South Viet-Nam, the gates will be opened wide.

The United States seeks for itself no base, no territory, no special position in this area of any kind. We support a truly neutral and independent Laos, its people free from outside interference, living at peace with themselves and with their neighbors, assured that their territory will not be used for attacks on others, and under a government comparable (as Mr. Khrushchev and I agreed at Vienna) to Cambodia and Burma.

But now the negotiations over Laos are reaching a crucial stage. The cease-fire is at best precarious. The rainy season is coming to an end. Laotian territory is being used to infiltrate South Viet-Nam. The world community must recognize--and all those who are involved--that this potent threat to Laotian peace and freedom is indivisible from all other threats to their own.

Secondly, I wish to report to you on the crisis over Germany and Berlin. This is not the time or the place for immoderate tones, but the world community is entitled to know the very simple issues as we see them. If there is a crisis' it is because an existing peace is under threat, because an existing island of free people is under pressure, because solemn agreements are being treated with indifference. Established international rights are being threatened with unilateral usurpation. Peaceful circulation has been interrupted by barbed wire and concrete blocks.

One recalls the order of the Czar in Pushkin's "Boris Godunov": "Take steps at this very hour that our frontiers be fenced in by barriers .... That not a single soul pass o'er the border, that not a hare be able to run or a crow to fly."

It is absurd to allege that we are threatening a war merely to prevent the Soviet Union and East Germany from signing a so-called "treaty" of peace. The Western Allies are not concerned with any paper arrangement the Soviets may wish to make with a regime of their own creation, on territory occupied by their own troops and governed by their own agents. No such action can affect either our rights or our responsibilities.

If there is a dangerous crisis in Berlin-and there is--it is because of threats against the vital interests and the deep commitments of the Western Powers, and the freedom of West Berlin. We cannot yield these interests. We cannot fail these commitments. We cannot surrender the freedom of these people for whom we are responsible. A "peace treaty" which carried with it the provisions which destroy the peace would be a fraud. A "free city" which was not genuinely free would suffocate freedom and would be an infamy.

For a city or a people to be truly free, they must have the secure right, without economic, political or police pressure, to make their own choice and to live their own lives. And as I have said before, if anyone doubts the extent to which our presence is desired by the people of West Berlin, we are ready to have that question submitted to a free vote in all Berlin and, if possible, among all the German people.

The elementary fact about this crisis is that it is unnecessary. The elementary tools for a peaceful settlement are to be found in the charter. Under its law, agreements are to be kept, unless changed by all those who made them. Established rights are to be respected. The political disposition of peoples should rest upon their own wishes, freely expressed in plebiscites or free elections. If there are legal problems, they can be solved by legal means. If there is a threat of force, it must be rejected. If there is desire for change, it must be a subject for negotiation and if there is negotiation, it must be rooted in mutual respect and concern for the rights of others.

The Western Powers have calmly resolved to defend, by whatever means are forced upon them, their obligations and their access to the free citizens of West Berlin and the self-determination of those citizens. This generation learned from bitter experience that either brandishing or yielding to threats can only lead to war. But firmness and reason can lead to the kind of peaceful solution in which my country profoundly believes.

We are committed to no rigid formula. We see no perfect solution. We recognize that troops and tanks can, for a time, keep a nation divided against its will, however unwise that policy may seem to us. But we believe a peaceful agreement is possible which protects the freedom of West Berlin and allied presence and access, while recognizing the historic and legitimate interests of others in assuring European security.

The possibilities of negotiation are now being explored; it is too early to report what the prospects may be. For our part, we would be glad to report at the appropriate time that a solution has been found. For there is no need for a crisis over Berlin, threatening the peace--and if those who created this crisis desire peace, there will be peace and freedom in Berlin.

The events and decisions of the next ten months may well decide the fate of man for the next ten thousand years. There will be no avoiding those events. There will be no appeal from these decisions. And we in this hall shall be remembered either as part of the generation that turned this planet into a flaming funeral pyre or the generation that met its vow "to save succeeding generations from the scourge of war."

In the endeavor to meet that vow, I pledge you every effort this Nation possesses. I pledge you that we shall neither commit nor provoke aggression, that we shall neither flee nor invoke the threat of force, that we shall never negotiate out of fear, we shall never fear to negotiate.

Terror is not a new weapon. Throughout history it has been used by those who could not prevail, either by persuasion or example. But inevitably they fail, either because men are not afraid to die for a life worth living, or because the terrorists themselves came to realize that free men cannot be frightened by threats, and that aggression would meet its own response. And it is in the light of that history that every nation today should know, be he friend or foe, that the United States has both the will and the weapons to join free men in standing up to their responsibilities.

But I come here today to look across this world of threats to a world of peace. In that search we cannot expect any final triumph-for new problems will always arise. We cannot expect that all nations will adopt like systems-- for conformity is the jailer of freedom, and the enemy of growth. Nor can we expect to reach our goal by contrivance, by fiat or even by the wishes of all. But however close we sometimes seem to that dark and final abyss, let no man of peace and freedom despair. For he does not stand alone. If we all can persevere, if we can in every land and office look beyond our own shores and ambitions, then surely the age will dawn in which the strong are just and the weak secure and the peace preserved.

Ladies and gentlemen of this Assembly, the decision is ours. Never have the nations of the world had so much to lose, or so much to gain. Together we shall save our planet, or together we shall perish in its flames. Save it we can--and save it we must--and then shall we earn the eternal thanks of mankind and, as peacemakers, the eternal blessing of God.

ADDRESS AT THE UNIVERSITY
OF NORTH CAROLINA

(OCTOBER 12, 1961)

Mr. Chancellor, Governor Sanford, members of the faculty, ladies and gentlemen:

I am honored today to be admitted to the fellowship of this ancient and distinguished university, and I am pleased to receive in the short space of 1 or 2 minutes the honor for which you spend over 4 years of your lives. But whether the degree be honorary or earned, it is a proud symbol of this university and this State.

North Carolina has long been identified with enlightened and progressive leaders and people, and I can think of no more important reason for that reputation than this university, which year after year has sent educated men and women who have had a recognition of their public responsibility as well as in their private interests.

Distinguished Presidents like President Graham and Gray, distinguished leaders like the Secretary of Commerce, Governor Hodges, distinguished members of the congressional delegation, carry out a tradition which stretches back to the beginning of this school, and that is that the graduate of this university is a man of his Nation as well as a man of his time. And it is my hope, in a changing world, when untold possibilities lie before North Carolina, and indeed the entire South and country, that this university will still hew to the old line of the responsibility that its graduates owe to the community at large--that in your time, too, you will be willing to give to the State and country a portion of your lives and all of your knowledge and all of your loyalty.

I want to emphasize, in the great concentration which we now place upon scientists and engineers, how much we still need the men and women educated in the liberal traditions, willing to take the long look, undisturbed by prejudices and slogans of the moment, who attempt to make an honest judgment on difficult events.

This university has a more important function today than ever before, and therefore I am proud as President of the United States, and as a graduate of a small land grant college in Massachusetts, Harvard University, to come to this center of education.

Those of you who regard my profession of political life with some disdain should remember that it made it possible for me to move from being an obscure lieutenant in the United States Navy to Commander-in-Chief in 14 years, with very little technical competence.

But more than that, I hope that you will realize that from the beginning of this country, and especially in North Carolina, there has been the closest link between educated men and women and politics and government. And also to remember that our nation's first great leaders were also our first great scholars.

A contemporary described Thomas Jefferson as "a gentleman of 32 who could calculate an eclipse, survey an estate, tie an artery, plan an edifice, try a cause, break a horse, dance the minuet, and play the violin." John Quincy Adams, after being summarily dismissed by the Massachusetts Legislature from the United States Senate for supporting Thomas Jefferson, could then become Boylston Professor of Rhetoric and Oratory at Harvard University, and then become a great Secretary of State.

And Senator Daniel Webster could stroll down the corridors of the Congress a few steps, after making some of the greatest speeches in the history of this country, and dominate the Supreme Court as the foremost lawyer of his day.

This versatility, this vitality, this intellectual energy, put to the service of our country, represents our great resource in these difficult days.

I would urge you, therefore, regardless of your specialty, and regardless of your chosen field or occupation, and regardless of whether you bear office or not, that you recognize the contribution which you can make as educated men and women to intellectual and political leadership in these difficult days, when the problems are infinitely more complicated and come with increasing speed, with increasing significance, in our lives than they were a century ago when so many gifted men dominated our political life. The United States Senate had more able men serving in it, from the period of 1830 to 1850, than probably any time in our history, and yet they dealt with three or four problems which they had dealt with for over a generation.

Now they come day by day, from all parts of the world. Even the experts find themselves confused, and therefore in a free society such as this, where the people must make an educated judgment, they depend upon those of you who have had the advantage of the scholar's education.

I ask you to give to the service of our country the critical faculties which society has helped develop in you here. I ask you to decide, as Goethe put it, "whether you will be an anvil or a hammer," whether you will give the United States, in which you were reared and educated, the broadest possible benefits of that education.

It's not enough to lend your talents to deploring present solutions. Most educated men and women on occasions prefer to discuss what is wrong, rather than to suggest alternative courses of action. But, "would you have counted him a friend of ancient Greece," as George William Curtis asked a body of educators a century ago, "would you have counted him a friend of ancient Greece who quietly discussed the theory of patriotism on that hot summer day through whose hopeless and immortal hours Leonidas and the three hundred stood at Thermopylae for liberty? Was John Milton to conjugate Greek verbs in his library when the liberty of Englishmen was imperiled?"

This is a great institution with a great tradition and with devoted alumni, and with the support of the people of this State. Its establishment and continued functioning, like that of all great universities, has required great sacrifice by the people of North Carolina. I cannot believe that all of this is undertaken merely to give this school's graduates an economic advantage in the lifestruggle.

"A university," said Professor Woodrow Wilson, "should be an organ of memory for the State, for the transmission of its best traditions." And Prince Bismarck was even more specific. "One third of the students of German universities," he once said, "'broke down from over-work, another third broke down from dissipation, and the other third ruled Germany." I leave it to each of you to decide in which category you will fall.

I do not suggest that our political and public life should be turned over to college trained experts, nor would I give this university a seat in the Congress, as William and Mary was once represented in the Virginia House of Burgesses, nor would I adopt from the Belgian constitution a provision giving three votes instead of one to college graduates--at least not until more Democrats go to college. But I do hope that you join us.

This university produces trained men and women, and what this country needs are those who look, as the motto of your State says, at things as they are and not at things as they seem to be.

For this meeting is held at an extraordinary time. Angola and Algeria, Brazil and Bizerte, Syria and South Viet-Nam, Korea or Kuwait, the Dominican Republic, Berlin, the United Nations itself--all problems which 20 years ago we could not even dream of.

Our task in this country is to do our best, to serve our Nation's interest as we see 'it, and not to be swayed from our course by the faint-hearted or the unknowing, or the threats of those who would make themselves our foes.

This is not a simple task in a democracy. We cannot open all our books in advance to an adversary who operates in the night, the decisions we make, the weapons we possess, the bargains we will accept--nor can we always see reflected overnight the success or failure of the actions that we may take.

In times past, a simple slogan described our policy: "Fifty-four-forty or fight." "To make the world safe for democracy." "No entangling alliances." But the times, issues, and the weapons, all have changed--and complicate and endanger our lives. It is a dangerous illusion to believe that the policies of the United States, stretching as they do world-wide, under varying and different conditions, can be encompassed in one slogan or one adjective, hard or soft or otherwise-or to believe that we shall soon meet total victory or total defeat.

Peace and freedom do not come cheap, and we are destined, all of us here today, to live out most if not all of our lives in uncertainty and challenge and peril. Our policy must therefore blend whatever degree of firmness and flexibility which is necessary to protect our vital interests, by peaceful means if possible, by resolute action if necessary.

There is, of course, no place in America where reason and firmness are more clearly pointed out than here in North Carolina. All Americans can profit from what happened in this State a century ago. It was this State, firmly fixed in the traditions of the South, which sought a way of reason in a troubled and dangerous world. Yet when the War came, North Carolina provided a fourth of all of the Confederate soldiers who made the supreme sacrifice in those years. And it won the right to the slogan, "First at Bethel. Farthest to the front at Gettysburg and Chickamauga. Last at Appomattox."

Its quest for a peaceful resolution of our problems was never identified in the minds of its people, of people today, with anything but a desire for peace and a preparation to meet their responsibilities.

We move for the first time in our history through an age in which two opposing powers have the capacity to destroy each other, and while we do not intend to see the free world give up, we shall make every effort to prevent the world from being blown up.

The American Eagle on our official seal emphasizes both peace and freedom, and as I said in the State of the Union Address, we in this country give equal attention to its claws when it in its left hand holds the arrows and in its right the olive branch.

This is a time of national maturity, understanding, and willingness to face issues as they are, not as we would like them to be. It is a test of our ability to be far-seeing and calm, as well as resolute, to keep an eye on both our dangers and our opportunities, and not to be diverted by momentary gains, or setbacks, or pressures. And it is the long view of the educated citizen to which the graduates of this university can best contribute.

We must distinguish the real from the illusory, the long-range from the temporary, the significant from the petty, but if we can be purposeful, if we can face up to our risks and live up to our word, if we can do our duty undeterred by fanatics or frenzy at home or abroad, then surely peace and freedom can prevail. We shall be neither Red nor dead, but alive and free-- and worthy of the traditions and responsibilities of North Carolina and the United States of America..

REMARKS AT THE VETERANS DAY CEREMONY

(NOVEMBER 11, 1961)

General Gavan, Mr. Gleason, members of the military forces, veterans, fellow Americans:

Today we are here to celebrate and to honor and to commemorate the dead and the living, the young men who in every war since this country began have given testimony to their loyalty to their country and their own great courage.

I do not believe that any nation in the history of the world has buried its soldiers farther from its native soil than we Americans--or buried them closer to the towns in which they grew up.

We celebrate this Veterans Day for a very few minutes, a few seconds of silence and then this country's life goes on. But I think it most appropriate that we recall on this occasion, and on every other moment when we are faced with great responsibilities, the contribution and the sacrifice which so many men and their families have made in order to permit this country to now occupy its present position of responsibility and freedom, and in order to permit us to gather here together.

Bruce Catton, after totaling the casualties which took place in the battle of Antietam, not so very far from this cemetery, when he looked at statistics which showed that in the short space of a few minutes whole regiments lost 50 to 75 percent of their numbers, then wrote that life perhaps isn't the most precious gift of all, that men died for the possession of a few feet of a corn field or a rocky hill, or for almost nothing at all. But in a very larger sense, they died that this country might be permitted to go on, and that it might permit to be fulfilled the great hopes of its founders.

In a world tormented by tension and the possibilities of conflict, we meet in a quiet commemoration of an historic day of peace. In an age that threatens the survival of freedom, we join together to honor those who made our freedom possible. The resolution of the Congress which first proclaimed Armistice Day, described November 11, 1918, as the end of "the most destructive, sanguinary and far-reaching war in the history of human annals." That resolution expressed the hope that the First World War would be, in truth, the war to end all wars. It suggested that those men who had died had therefore not given their lives in vain.

It is a tragic fact that these hopes have not been fulfilled, that wars still more destructive and still more sanguinary followed, that man's capacity to devise new ways of killing his fellow men have far outstripped his capacity to live in peace with his fellow men.

Some might say, therefore, that this day has lost its meaning, that the shadow of the new and deadly weapons have robbed this day of its great value, that whatever name we now give this day, whatever flags we fly or prayers we utter, it is too late to honor those who died before, and too soon to promise the living an end to organized death.

But let us not forget that November 11, 1918, signified a beginning, as well as an end. "The purpose of all war," said Augustine, "is peace." The First World War produced man's first great effort in recent times to solve by international cooperation the problems of war. That experiment continues in our present day--still imperfect, still short of its responsibilities, but it does offer a hope that some day nations can live in harmony.

For our part, we shall achieve that peace only with patience and perseverance and courage--the patience and perseverance necessary to work with allies of diverse interests but common goals, the courage necessary over a long period of time to overcome an adversary skilled in the arts of harassment and obstruction.

There is no way to maintain the frontiers of freedom without cost and commitment and risk. There is no swift and easy path to peace in our generation. No man who witnessed the tragedies of the last war, no man who can imagine the unimaginable possibilities of the next war, can advocate war out of irritability or frustration or impatience.

But let no nation confuse our perseverance and patience with fear of war or unwillingness to meet our responsibilities. We cannot save ourselves by abandoning those who are associated with us, or rejecting our responsibilities.

In the end, the only way to maintain the peace is to be prepared in the final extreme to fight for our country--and to mean it.

As a nation, we have little capacity for deception. We can convince friend and foe alike that we are in earnest about the defense of freedom only if we are in earnest-and I can assure the world that we are.

This cemetery was first established 97 years ago. In this hill were first buried men who died in an earlier war, a savage war here in our own country. Ninety-seven years ago today, the men in Gray were retiring from Antietam, where thousands of their comrades had fallen between dawn and dusk in one terrible day. And the men in Blue were moving towards Fredericksburg, where thousands would soon lie by a stone wall in heroic and sometimes miserable death.

It was a crucial moment in our Nation's history, but these memories, sad and proud, these quiet grounds, this Cemetery and others like it all around the world, remind us with pride of our obligation and our opportunity.

On this Veterans Day of 1961, on this day of remembrance, let us pray in the name of those who have fought in this country's wars, and most especially who have fought in the First World War and in the Second World War, that there will be no veterans of any further war--not because all shall have perished but because all shall have learned to live together in peace.

And to the dead here in this cemetery we say:
They are the race--

they are the race immortal,
Whose beams make broad

the common light of day!
Though Time may dim,

though Death has barred their portal,
These we salute,
which nameless passed away.

UNIVERSITY OF WASHINGTON'S
100TH ANNIVERSARY

(NOVEMBER 16, 1961)

President Odegaard, members o/the regents, members of the faculty, students, ladies and gentlemen:

It is a great honor on behalf of the people of the United States to extend to you congratulations on the Centennial Anniversary of this University, which represents 100 years of service to this State and country.

This nation in two of the most critical times in the life of our country, once in the days after the Revolution in the Northwest ordinance to which Doctor Odegaard referred, and again during the most difficult days of the Civil War, in the Morrill Act which established our land grant colleges, this nation made a basic commitment to the maintenance of education, for the very reasons which Thomas Jefferson gave, that if this nation were to remain free it could not remain ignorant. The basis of self-government and freedom requires the development of character and self-restraint and perseverance and the long view. And these are qualities which require many years of training and education. So that I think this University and others like it across the country, and its graduates, have recognized that these schools are not maintained by the people of the various States in order to merely give the graduates of these schools an economic advantage in the life struggle. Rather, these schools are supported by our people because our people realize that this country has needed in the past, and needs today as never before, educated men and women who are committed to the cause of freedom. So for what this University has done in the past, and what its graduates can do now and in the future, I salute you.

This University was rounded when the Civil War was already on, and no one could be sure in 1861 whether this country would survive. But the picture which the student of 1961 has of the world, and indeed the picture which our citizens have of the world, is infinitely more complicated and infinitely more dangerous.

In 1961 the world relations of this country have become tangled and complex. One of our former allies has become our adversary—and he has his own adversaries who are not our allies. Heroes are removed from their tombs—history rewritten—the names of cities changed overnight.

We increase our arms at a heavy cost, primarily to make certain that we will not have to use them. We must face up to the chance of war, if we are to maintain the peace. We must work with certain countries lacking in freedom in order to strengthen the cause of freedom. We find some who call themselves neutral who are our friends and sympathetic to us, and others who call themselves neutral who are unremittingly hostile to us. And as the most powerful defender of freedom on earth, we find ourselves unable to escape the responsibilities of freedom, and yet unable to exercise it without restraints imposed by the very freedoms we seek to protect.

We cannot, as a free nation, compete with our adversaries in tactics of terror, assassination, false promises, counterfeit mobs and crises.

We cannot, under the scrutiny of a free press and public, tell different stories to different audiences, foreign and domestic, friendly and hostile.

We cannot abandon the slow processes of consulting with our allies to match the swift expediencies of those who merely dictate to their satellites.

We can neither abandon nor control the international organization in which we now cast less than 1 percent of the vote in the General Assembly.

We possess weapons of tremendous power—but they are least effective in combating the weapons most often used by freedom's foes: subversion, infiltration, guerrilla warfare, civil disorder.

We send arms to other peoples—just as we send them the ideals of democracy in which we believe—but we cannot send them the will to use those arms or to abide by those ideals.

And while we believe not only in the force of arms but in the force of right and reason, we have learned that reason does not always appeal to unreasonable men—that it is not always true that "a soft answer turneth away wrath"—and that right does not always make might.

In short, we must face problems which do not lend themselves to easy or quick or permanent solutions. And we must face the fact that the United States is neither omnipotent or omniscient—that we are only 6 percent of the world's population—that we cannot impose our will upon the other 94 percent of mankind—that we cannot right every wrong or reverse each adversity—and that therefore there cannot be an American solution to every world problem.

These burdens and frustrations are accepted by most Americans with maturity and understanding. They may long for the days when war meant charging up San Juan Hill—or when our isolation was guarded by two oceans—or when the atomic bomb was ours alone—or when much of the industrialized world depended upon our resources and our aid. But they now know that those days are gone—and that gone with them are the old policies and the old complacency's. And they know, too, that we must make the best of our new problems and our new opportunities, whatever the risk and the cost.

But there are others who cannot bear the burden of a long twilight struggle. They lack confidence in our long-run capacity to survive and succeed. Hating communism, yet they see communism in the long run, perhaps, as the wave of the future. And they want some quick and easy and final and cheap solution—now.

There are two groups of these frustrated citizens, far apart in their views yet very much alike in their approach. On the one hand are those who urge upon us what I regard to be the pathway of surrender—appeasing our enemies, compromising our commitments, purchasing peace at any price, disavowing our arms, our friends, our obligations. If their view had prevailed, the world of free choice would be smaller today.

On the other hand are those who urge upon us what I regard to be the pathway of war: equating negotiations with appeasement and substituting rigidity for firmness. If their view had prevailed, we would be at war today, and in more than one place.

It is a curious fact that each of these extreme opposites resembles the other. Each believes that we have only two choices: appeasement or war, suicide or surrender, humiliation or holocaust, to be either Red or dead. Each side sees only "hard" and "soft" nations, hard and soft policies, hard and soft men. Each believes that any departure from its own course inevitably leads to the other: one group believes that any peaceful solution means appeasement; the other believes that any arms build-up means war. One group regards everyone else as warmongers, the other regards everyone else as appeasers. Neither side admits that its path will lead to disaster—but neither can tell us how or where to draw the line once we descend the slippery slopes of appeasement or constant intervention.

In short, while both extremes profess to be the true realists of our time, neither could be more unrealistic. While both claim to be doing the nation a service, they could do it no greater disservice. This kind of talk and easy solutions to difficult problems, if believed, could inspire a lack of confidence among our people when they must all—above all else—be united in recognizing the long and difficult days that lie ahead. It could inspire uncertainty among our allies when above all else they must be confident in us. And even more dangerously, it could, if believed, inspire doubt among our adversaries when they must above all be convinced that we will defend our vital interests.

The essential fact that both of these groups fail to grasp is that diplomacy and defense are not substitutes for one another. Either alone would fail. A willingness to resist force, unaccompanied by a willingness to talk, could provoke belligerence—while a willingness to talk, unaccompanied by a willingness to resist force, could invite disaster.

But as long as we know what comprises our vital interests and our long-range goals, we have nothing to fear from negotiations at the appropriate time, and nothing to gain by refusing to take part in them. At a time when a single clash could escalate overnight into a holocaust of mushroom clouds, a great power does not prove its firmness by leaving the task of exploring the other's intentions to sentries or those without full responsibility. Nor can ultimate weapons rightfully be employed, or the ultimate sacrifice rightfully demanded of our citizens, until every reasonable solution has been explored. "How many wars," Winston Churchill has written, "have been averted by patience and persisting good will! .... How many wars have been precipitated by firebrands!"

If vital interests under duress can be preserved by peaceful means, negotiations will find that out. If our adversary will accept nothing-less than a concession of our rights, negotiations will find that out. And if negotiations are to take place, this nation cannot abdicate to its adversaries the task of choosing the forum and the framework and the time.

For there are carefully defined limits within which any serious negotiations must take place. With respect to any future talks on Germany and Berlin, for example, we cannot, on the one hand, confine our proposals to a list of concessions we are willing to make, nor can we, on the other hand, advance any proposals which compromise the security of free Germans and West Berliners, or endanger their ties with the West.

No one should be under the illusion that negotiations for the sake of negotiations always advance the cause of peace. If for lack of preparation they break up in bitterness, the prospects of peace have been endangered. If they are made a forum for propaganda or a cover for aggression, the processes of peace have been abused.

But it is a test of our national maturity to accept the fact that negotiations are not a contest spelling victory or defeat. They may succeed—they may fail. They are likely to be successful only if both sides reach an agreement which both regard as preferable to the status quo—an agreement in which each side can consider its own situation to be improved. And this is most difficult to obtain.

But, while we shall negotiate freely, we shall not negotiate freedom. Our answer to the classic question of Patrick Henry is still no—life is not so dear, and peace is not so precious, "as to be purchased at the price of chains and slavery." And that is our answer even though, for the first time since the ancient battles between Greek city-states, war entails the threat of total annihilation, of everything we know, of society itself. For to save mankind's future freedom, we must face up to any risk that is necessary. We will always seek peace—but we will never surrender.

In short, we are neither "warmongers" nor "appeasers," neither "hard" nor "soft." We are Americans, determined to defend the frontiers of freedom, by an honorable peace if peace is possible, but by arms if arms are used against us.

And if we are to move forward in that spirit, we shall need all the calm and thoughtful citizens that this great University can produce, all the light they can shed, all the wisdom they can bring to bear. It is customary, both here and around the world, to regard life in the United States as easy. Our advantages are many. But more than any other people on earth, we bear burdens and accept risks unprecedented in their size and their duration, not for ourselves alone but for all who wish to be free. No other generation of free men in any country has ever faced so many and such difficult challenges—not even those who lived in the days when this University was founded in 1861.

This nation was then torn by war. This territory had only the simplest elements of civilization. And this city had barely begun to function. But a university was one of their earliest thoughts—and they summed it up in the motto that they adopted: "Let there be light." What more can be said today, regarding all the dark and tangled problems we face than: Let there be light.

And to accomplish that illumination, the University of Washington shall still hold high the torch.

ADDRESS TO THE NATIONAL
ASSOCIATION OF MANUFACTURERS

(DECEMBER 6, 1961)

But if American industry cannot increase its sales to the Common Market, and increase this nation's surplus of exports over imports, our international payments position and our commitments to the defense of freedom will be endangered.

If American businessmen cannot increase or even maintain their exports to the Common Market, they will surely step up their investment in new American-owned plants behind those tariff walls so they can compete on an equal basis--thereby taking capital away from us, as well as jobs from our own shores, and worsening still further our balance of payments position.

If American industry cannot increase its outlets in the Common Market, our own expansion will be stifled--the growth target of 50% in the sixties, adopted last month by the 20 nations of OECD for their combined gross national product, will not be reached-and our business-community will lack the incentives to lower prices and improve technology which greater competition would otherwise inspire. The industries which would benefit the most from increased trade are our most efficient--even though in many cases they pay our highest wages, their goods can compete with the goods of any other nation. Those who would benefit the least, and are unwilling to adjust to competition, are standing in the way, as the NAM Economic Advisory Committee pointed out last year, of greater growth and a higher standard of living. They are endangering the profits and jobs of others, our efforts against inflation, our balance of payments position, and in the long run their own economic wellbeing because they will suffer from competition in the U.S. inevitably, if not from abroad--for, in order to avoid exertion, they accept paralysis.

Finally, let me add, if we cannot increase our sales abroad, we will diminish our stature in the Free World. Economic isolation and political leadership are wholly incompatible. The United Kingdom, faced with even more serious problems in her efforts to achieve both higher growth and reasonable balance of payments, is moving with boldness, welcoming, in the Prime Minister's words, "the brisk shower of competition." We cannot do less. For if the nations of the West can weld together on these problems a common program of action as extraordinary in economic history as NATO was unprecedented in military history, the long-range Communist aim of dividing and encircling us all is doomed to failure.

In every sense of the word, therefore, Capitalism is on trial as we debate these issues. For many years in many lands, we have boasted of the virtues of the marketplace under free competitive enterprise, of America's ability to compete and sell, of the vitality of our system in keeping abreast with the times. Now the world will see whether we mean it or not--whether America will remain the foremost economic power in the world--or whether we will evacuate the field of power before a shot is fired, or go forth to meet new risks and tests of our ability.

The hour of decision has arrived. We cannot afford to "wait and see what happens," while the tide of events sweeps over and beyond us. We must use time as a tool, not as a couch. We must carve out our own destiny. This is what Americans have always done--and this, I have every confidence, is what we will continue to do in each new trial and opportunity that lies ahead. Address to the National Association of Manufacturers (December 6, 1961)

But if American industry cannot increase its sales to the Common Market, and increase this nation's surplus of exports over imports, our international payments position and our commitments to the defense of freedom will be endangered.

If American businessmen cannot increase or even maintain their exports to the Common Market, they will surely step up their investment in new American-owned plants behind those tariff walls so they can compete on an equal basis--thereby taking capital away from us, as well as jobs from our own shores, and worsening still further our balance of payments position.

If American industry cannot increase its outlets in the Common Market, our own expansion will be stifled--the growth target of 50% in the sixties, adopted last month by the 20 nations of OECD for their combined gross national product, will not be reached-and our business-community will lack the incentives to lower prices and improve technology which greater competition would otherwise inspire. The industries which would benefit the most from increased trade are our most efficient--even though in many cases they pay our highest wages, their goods can compete with the goods of any other nation. Those who would benefit the least, and are unwilling to adjust to competition, are standing in the way, as the NAM Economic Advisory Committee pointed out last year, of greater growth and a higher standard of living. They are endangering the profits and jobs of others, our efforts against inflation, our balance of payments position, and in the long run their own economic wellbeing because they will suffer from competition in the U.S. inevitably, if not from abroad--for, in order to avoid exertion, they accept paralysis.

Finally, let me add, if we cannot increase our sales abroad, we will diminish our stature in the Free World. Economic isolation and political leadership are wholly incompatible. The United Kingdom, faced with even more serious problems in her efforts to achieve both higher growth and reasonable balance of payments, is moving with boldness, welcoming, in the Prime Minister's words, "the brisk shower of competition." We cannot do less. For if the nations of the West can weld together on these problems a common program of action as extraordinary in economic history as NATO was unprecedented in military history, the long-range Communist aim of dividing and encircling us all is doomed to failure.

In every sense of the word, therefore, Capitalism is on trial as we debate these issues. For many years in many lands, we have boasted of the virtues of the marketplace under free competitive enterprise, of America's ability to compete and sell, of the vitality of our system in keeping abreast with the times. Now the world will see whether we mean it or not--whether America will remain the foremost economic power in the world--or whether we will evacuate the field of power before a shot is fired, or go forth to meet new risks and tests of our ability.

The hour of decision has arrived. We cannot afford to "wait and see what happens," while the tide of events sweeps over and beyond us. We must use time as a tool, not as a couch. We must carve out our own destiny. This is what Americans have always done--and this, I have every confidence, is what we will continue to do in each new trial and opportunity that lies ahead.

ADDRESS IN MIAMI AT THE OPENING OF THE AFL-CIO CONVENTION

(DECEMBER 7, 1961)

Mr. Meany, Reverend Clergy, Governor Bryant, gentlemen, ladies:

It's warmer here today than it was yesterday!

I want to express my pleasure at this invitation. As one whose work and continuity of employment has depended in part upon the union movement, I want to say that I have been on the job, training for about 11 months, and feel that I have some seniority rights in the matter.

I'm delighted to be here with you and with Secretary of Labor Arthur Goldberg. I was up in New York stressing physical fitness, and in line with that Arthur went over with a group to Switzerland to climb some of the mountains there. They all got up about 5 and he was in bed--got up to join them later--and when they all came back at 4 o'clock in the afternoon, he didn't come back with them. They sent out search parties and there was no sign of him that afternoon or night. Next day the Red Cross went out and they went around calling "Goldberg--Goldberg--it's the Red Cross." And this voice came down the mountain, "I gave at the office."

Those are the liberties you can take with members of the Cabinet. But I want to say it's a pleasure to be here. This is an important anniversary for all of us, the 20th anniversary of Pearl Harbor.

I suppose, really, the only two dates that most people remember where they were, were Pearl Harbor and the death of President Franklin Roosevelt. We face entirely different challenges on this Pearl Harbor. In many ways the challenges are more serious, and in a sense long-reaching, because I don't think that any of us had any doubt in those days that the United States would survive and prevail and our strength increase.

Now we are face to face in a most critical time with challenges all around the world, and you in the labor movement bear a heavy responsibility. Occasionally I read articles by those who say that the labor movement has fallen into dark days. I don't believe that, and I would be very distressed if it were true.

One of the great qualities about the United States which I don't think people realize who are not in the labor movement, is what a great asset for freedom the American labor movement represents, not only here but all around the world. It's no accident that Communists concentrate their attention on the trade union movement. They know that people--the working people-are frequently left out, that in many areas of the world they have no one to speak for them, and the Communists mislead them and say that they will protect their rights. So many go along.

But in the United States, because we have had a strong, free labor movement, the working people of this country have not felt that they were left out. And as long as the labor movement is strong and as long as it is committed to freedom, then I think that freedom in this country is strengthened. So I would hope that every American, whether he was on one side of the bargaining table or the other or whether he was in a wholly different sphere of life, would recognize that the strength of a free American labor movement is vital to the maintenance of freedom in this country and all around the world.

And I am delighted that there are here today, I understand, nearly 150 trade union leaders from nearly 32 countries around the world. I believe--and I say this as President-that one of the great assets that this country has is the influence which this labor movement can promote around the world in demonstrating what a free trade union can do.

I hope that they will go back from this meeting recognizing that in the long run a strong labor movement is essential to the maintenance of democracy in their country. It's no accident that there has not been a strike in the Soviet Union for 30, or 35, or 40 years. The Communists who in Latin America, or Africa, or Asia say that they represent the people, cannot possibly--under any rule of reason or debate--say that a labor movement is free when it is not able to express its rights, not only in relationship to the employer but also to speak out and recognize the limitations of governmental power. We are not omniscient--we are not all-powerful--this is a free society, and management and labor, and the farmer and the citizen have their rights. We did not give them their rights in government. And I hope that those who go from this hall to Latin America, to Europe, to Africa, will recognize that we believe in freedom and in progress in this country, that we believe that freedom is not an end in itself, but we believe that freedom can bring material abundance and prosperity. And I want you to know that I consider this meeting and the house of labor vital to the interests of this country and the cause of freedom in the coming days.

What unites labor, what unites this country, is far more important than those things on which we may disagree. So, gentlemen and ladies, you are not only leaders of your unions but you occupy a .position of responsibility as citizens of the United States; and therefore I felt it most appropriate to come here today and talk with you.

First, I want to express my appreciation to you for several things. For example, I appreciate the effort that those of you who represent the interests of the men and women who work at our missile plants have made. The fact that you have given and that the men and women who work there have lived up to the no-strike pledge at our missile and space sites has made an appreciable difference in the progress that we are making in these areas-- and the country appreciates the effort you are making.

Secondly, we have for the first time a Presidential Advisory Committee on Labor-Management Policy which for once did not break up on the passage of the Wagner Act in 1935, but instead meets month by month in an attempt to work out and develop economic policies which will permit this country to go forward under conditions of full employment. And I want to thank you for the participation you have given that.

Third, as I said, I want to thank the labor movement for what it is doing abroad in strengthening the free labor movement, and I urge you to redouble your efforts. The hope, as I have said, of freedom in these countries rests in many parts with the labor movement. We do not want to leave the people of some countries a choice between placing their destiny in the hands of a few who hold in their hands most of the property and on the other side the Communist movement. We do not give them that choice. We want them to have the instruments of freedom to protect themselves and provide for progress in their country, and a strong, free labor movement can do it--and I hope you will concentrate your attention in the next 12 months in that area--in Latin America and all around the world.

The fact is that the head of the Congo-Adoula--who has been a strong figure for freedom, came out of the labor movement. And that's happening in country after country. And this is a great opportunity and responsibility for all of us to continue to work together.

And finally, I want to take this opportunity to express my thanks to the AFLCIO for the support that it gave in the passage of our legislative program in the long session of the Congress. We did not always agree on every tactic. We may not have achieved every goal, but we can take some satisfaction in the fact that we did make progress toward a $1.25 minimum wage, that we did expand the coverage for the first time in 20 years; that we did pass the best housing act since 1949; that we did, finally, after two Presidential vetoes in the last 4 years, pass a bill providing assistance to those areas suffering from chronic unemployment; that we did pass a long-range water pollution bill; that we did pass increased Social Security benefits, a lowering of the retirement age in Social Security from 65 to 62 for men, temporary unemployment compensation, and aid to dependent children.

And we are coming back in January and we are going to start again.

The Gross National Product has climbed since January from $500 billion to an estimated $540 billion in the last quarter, and it's a pleasure for me to say that the November employment figures received this morning show not only two million more people than were working in February, but we have now an all-time high for November, 67,349,000 people working. But, more importantly, unlike the usual seasonal run in November, which ordinarily provides for an increase in unemployment of about a half a million, we have now brought the figure for the first time below the 7 percent where it's hovered down to 6.1 percent, and we're going to have to get it lower.

I would not claim we've achieved full .recovery or the permanently high growth rate of which we are capable. Since the recession of '58, from which we only partially recovered, and going into the recession of 1960, too many men and women have been idle for too long a time and our first concern must still be with those unable to get work. Unemployment compensation must be placed on a permanent, rational basis of nationwide standards, and even more importantly those who are older and retired must be permitted under a system of Social Security to get assistance and relief from the staggering cost of their medical bills.

The time has come in the next session of the Congress to face the fact that our eider citizens do need these benefits, that their needs cannot be adequately met in any other way, and that every Member of the Congress should have the opportunity to go on the record, up or down, on this question-and I believe when it comes to the floor--as I believe it must--they are going to vote it up and through before they adjourn in July or August.

172

Now there are six areas that I believe that we need to give our attention to if the manpower budget is to be balanced. First, we must give special attention to the problems of our younger people. Dr. Conant's recent book only highlighted a fact which all of you are familiar with, and that is the problem of those who drop out of school before they have finished, because of hardships in their home, inadequate motivation or counseling or whatever it may be, and then drift without being able to find a decent job.

And this falls particularly heavily upon the young men and women who are in our minority groups. In addition to that, 26 million young people will be crowding into the labor market in the next 10 years. This can be a tremendous asset because we have many tasks that require their talent. But today there are one million young Americans under the age of 25 who are out of school and out of work. Millions of others leave school early, destined to fall for life into a pattern of being untrained, unskilled, and frequently unemployed.

It's for this reason that I have asked the Congress to pass a Youth Employment Opportunities Act to guide these hands so that they can make a life for themselves. Equally important, if our young people are to be well trained and skilled labor is going to be needed in the next years, and if they are to be inspired to finish their studies, the Federal Government must meet its responsibility in the field of education. I'm not satisfied if my particular community has a good school. I want to make sure that every child in this country has an adequate opportunity for a good education.

Thomas Jefferson once said, "If you expect a country to be ignorant and free, you expect what never was and never will be." It's not enough that our own home town has a good school, we want the United States as a country to be among the best educated in the world. And I believe that we must invest in our youth.

Secondly, we need a program of retraining our unemployed workers. All of you who live so close to this problem know what happens when technology changes and industries move out and men are left. And I've seen it in my own State of Massachusetts where textile workers were unemployed, unable to find work even with new electronic plants going up all around them. We want to make sure that our workers are able to take advantage of the new jobs that must inevitably come as technology changes in the 1960's. And I believe, therefore, that retraining deserves the attention of this Congress in the coming days.

And the third group requiring our attention consists of our minority citizens. All of you know the statistics of those who are first discharged and the last to be rehired too often are among those who are members of our minority groups. We want everyone to have a chance, regardless of their race or color, to have an opportunity to make a life for themselves and their families, to get a decent education so they have a fair chance to compete, and then be judged on what's in here and not on what's on the outside. And the American labor movement has been identified with this cause, and I know that you will be in the future.

And we are making a great effort to make sure that all those who secure Federal contracts--and there are billions of dollars spent each year by the Federal Government--will give fair opportunity to all of our citizens to participate in that work.

Fourth, we want to provide opportunities for plant re-investment. One of the matters which is of concern in maintaining our economy now is the fact that we do not have as much re-investment in our plants as we did, for example, in 1955, '56 and '57.' And we want this economy and this rise to be continuous. And I believe we have to give as much incentive as is possible to provide reinvestment in plants which makes work and will keep our economy moving ahead.

And therefore I have suggested a tax credit, which I'm hopeful the American labor movement has not placed on its list of those matters yet that it has not supported, but it will consider this proposal as a method of stimulating the economy so that this recovery does not run out of gas in 12 months or 18 months from now, as the 1958-59 recovery, after the recession of 1958, ran out in

Fifth, to add to our arsenals of built-in stabilizers so we can keep our economy moving ahead, it's my intention to ask the Congress at its next session for stand-by authority somewhat along the lines of the bill introduced by Senator Clark of Pennsylvania, to make grants-in-aid to communities for needed public works when our unemployment begins to mount and our economy to slow down.

Sixth and finally, we must expand our job opportunities by stimulating our trade abroad. I know that this is a matter to which the labor movement has given a good deal of attention. Mr. Meany made an outstanding speech on this matter several weeks ago, and it's a matter which is of concern to this administration. I'm sure you wonder, perhaps, why we're placing so much emphasis on it, and I would like to say why we are, very briefly.

The first is, this country must maintain a favorable balance of trade or suffer severely from the point of view of our national security. We sell abroad now nearly $5 billion more than we import. But unfortunately that $5 billion goes abroad in order to maintain the national security requirements of the United States.

We spend $3 billion of that in order to keep our troops overseas. It costs us nearly $700 to $800 million to keep our divisions in Western Germany, and $300 million to keep our troop establishments in France. And what is true in France and Germany, which are outposts of our commitments, is true in other areas.

So that if we're not able to maintain a favorable balance of trade, then of course we will have to do as the British have had to do, which is begin to bring our troops back and lay the way open for other actions. So that this is a matter which involves very greatly our security, and unless you believe that the United States should retreat to our own hemisphere and forget our commitments abroad, then you can share with me my concern about what will happen if that balance of trade begins to drop.

Now the problems that we face have been intensified by the development of the Common Market. This is our best market for manufactured products. What I am concerned about is that we shall be able to keep moving our trade into those areas; otherwise what we will find is that American capital which cannot place its goods in that market will decide, as they are doing now, to build their plants in Western Europe, and then they hire Western European workers-and you suffer, and the country suffers, and the balance of payments suffers.

So this is a matter of the greatest importance to you--in fact, to all Americans. It is, for example, of the greatest importance to American farmers. They sell $2 billion of agricultural commodities to Western Europe. We bring in $80 million of agricultural commodities from Western Europe. In other words, we make almost $2 billion of our foreign exchange from that sale of agricultural commodities, and yet Western Europe has great agricultural resources which are increasing, and we are going to find it increasingly difficult unless we are able to negotiate from a position of strength with them. So this matter is important.

The purpose of this discussion is to increase employment. The purpose of this discussion is to strengthen the United States, and it is a matter which deserves our most profound attention.

Are we going to export our goods and our crops or, are we going to export our capital? That's the question that we're now facing.

And I know that those of you who have been concerned about this know this to be a major problem. Last year, 1960, we invested abroad $1,700 million, and we took in from our investments abroad $2,300 million-which sounded like it was a pretty good exchange. But if you analyze these figures you will see that we took in, from the underdeveloped world, which needs capital, we took in $1,300 million and we sent out in capital for investment $200 million. And yet this is the area that needs our investment. While in Western Europe we sent out $1,500 million and took in $1 billion. So that if this trend should continue and more and more Western Europe became the object of American investment, it affects us all and affects the people who work with you.

We are attempting to repeal those tax privileges which make it particularly attractive for American capital to invest in Western Europe. We passed laws in the days of the Marshall Plan when we wanted American capital over there, and as the result of that, there are provisions on the tax book which make it good business to go over there.

Now we want it all to be fair, and we have stated we are not putting in exchange controls, which we will not. But we recommended in January the passage of a bill which would lessen the tax privileges of investing in Western Europe and which would have given us $250 million in revenue and in balance of payments.

The tax privileges or the attractions should be in the underdeveloped world, where we have been taking capital out rather than putting it in, and not in Western Europe where the capital is sufficient and which does not serve that great national purpose. So this is a matter of concern for all of us and it is a matter which we must consider in the coming months.

The Common Market is a tremendous market. It has more people than we do. Its rate of growth is twice ours. Its income is about three-fifths of ours, and may some day be equal to ours. This can be a great asset not only to them but to us--a great strength tying Western Europe, the United States, and Latin America and Japan together as a great area of freedom. And I think that it represents one of the most hopeful signs since 1945. It is one place where the Free World can be on the offensive. And I'm anxious that the United States play its proper role to protect the interests of our people and to advance the cause of freedom. And I ask the careful consideration of the American labor movement in this area.

One of the problems which we have is to recognize that those who have been affected by imports have received no protection at all for a number of years from the United States Government. When I was a Senator in 1954, I introduced legislation to provide assistance to those industries which are hard-hit by imports. I am going to recommend in January a program which I hope the Congress will pass, which will provide a recognition of the national responsibility in the period of transition for those industries and people who may be adversely affected.

I am optimistic about the future of this country. This is a great country, with an energetic people, and I believe over the. long period the people of .this country and of the world really want freedom and wish to solve their own lives and their own destiny. I'm hopeful that we can be associated with that movement. I'm hopeful that you will continue to meet your responsibilities to your people as well as to the country. I hope that we can maintain a viable economy here with full employment. I'm hopeful we can be competitive here and around the world. I'm hopeful that management and labor will recognize their responsibility to permit us to compete, that those of you who are in the area of wage negotiations will recognize the desirability of us maintaining as stable prices as possible, and that the area of productivity and stable prices--that your negotiations will take adequate calculation and account of this need for us to maintain a balance of trade in our favor. In the long run it's in the interests of your own workers.

Let me repeat: If we cannot maintain the balance of trade in our favor, which it now is, of $5 billion, and indeed increase it, then this country is going to face most serious problems. In the last 3 years, even though the balance of trade in our favor has been $5 billion, we have lost $5 billion in gold; and if this trend should go on year after year then the United States, as I have said, would have to make adjustments which would be extremely adverse to the cause of freedom around the world.

The solution rests with increasing our export trade, with remaining competitive, with our businesses selling abroad, finding new markets, and keeping our people working at home and around the world.

And it is a fact that the six countries of the Common Market who faced the problems that we now face, have had in the last 4 years full employment and an economic growth twice ours. Even a country which faced staggering economic problems a decade ago--Italy--has been steadily building its gold balance, cutting down its unemployment and moving ahead twice what we have over the last 4 years.

So what I am talking about is an opportunity, not a burden. This is a chance to move the United States forward in the 1960's, not only in the economic sphere but also to make a contribution to the cause of freedom.

And I come to Miami today and ask your help, as on other occasions other Presidents of the United States, stretching back to the time of Woodrow Wilson and Roosevelt and Truman, have come to the AF of L and the CIO--and each time this organization has said yes.

Thank you.

REMARKS TO A U.N. DELEGATION OF WOMEN

(DECEMBER 11, 1961)

LADIES, I want to express my great satisfaction in welcoming you to the White House. And also as a citizen not merely of the United States but also as an inhabitant of the globe in difficult times I want to express my appreciation to you and the appreciation of the people of this country for your efforts in the United Nations.

I was present in 1945 at San Francisco, as a member of the press, at the time that the United Nations was born. I know that at different times in the last 15 or 16 years this organization has come under criticism in many countries--I am sure all of yours, and my own here in the United States.

But recalling what Robert Frost, one of our poets, once said, "Don't take down the fence until you know why it was put up," I have a strong conviction that we should seek to strengthen the United Nations and make it the kind of instrument which all of us hope it will be.

I don't think, really, in any sense, the United Nations has failed as a concept. I think occasionally we fail it. And the more that we can do to strengthen the idea of a community of the world, to seek to develop manners by which the tensions of the world and the problems of the world can be solved in an orderly and peaceful way, I think that's in the common interest of all.

The United Nations has survived 16 difficult years. Countries once unknown have come into existence and are playing important parts in the United Nations. It has come to the present day and plays a most important part in the lives of all of us.

So I congratulate you for the work that you have done. We want you to know that you are very welcome to this country. We are glad that you are seeing something-however much we all admire New York, we are glad you are seeing something of the United States besides New York. And we hope that while you are visiting here you will come not only to Washington and New York, which in a sense are rather special parts of this country, but also go perhaps even to Boston and even further West.

I want to thank you very much indeed.

I want to say that I had not expected that the standard of revolt would be raised in the royal pavilion here, but I'm always rather nervous about how you talk about women who are active in politics, whether they want to be talked about as women or as politicians, but I want you to know that we are grateful to have you as both today. Thank you very much.

STATE OF THE UNION ADDRESS

(JANUARY 11, 1962)

Mr. Vice President, my old colleague from Massachusetts and your new Speaker, John McCormack, Members of the 87th Congress, ladies and gentlemen:

This week we begin anew our joint and separate efforts to build the American future. But, sadly, we build without a man who linked a long past with the present and looked strongly to the future. "Mister Sam" Rayburn is gone. Neither this House nor the Nation is the same without him.

Members of the Congress, the Constitution makes us not rivals for power but partners for progress. We are all trustees for the American people, custodians of the American heritage. It is my task to report the State of the Union--to improve it is the task of us all.

In the past year, I have traveled not only across our own land but to other lands-to the North and the South, and across the seas. And I have found--as I am sure you have, in your travels--that people everywhere, in spite of occasional disappointments, look to us--not to our wealth or power, but to the splendor of our ideals. For our Nation is commissioned by history to be either an observer of freedom's failure or the cause of its success. Our overriding obligation in the months ahead is to fulfill the world's hopes by fulfilling our own faith.

That task must begin at home. For if we cannot fulfill our own ideals here, we cannot expect others to accept them. And when the youngest child alive today has grown to the cares of manhood, our position in the world will be determined first of all by what provisions we make today--for his education, his health, and his opportunities for a good home and a good job and a good life.

At home, we began the year in the valley of recession--we completed it on the high road of recovery and growth. With the help of new congressionally approved or administratively increased stimulants to our economy, the number of major surplus labor u areas has declined from 101 to 60; nonagricultural employment has increased by more than a million jobs; and the average factory work-week has risen to well over 40 hours. At year's end the economy which Mr. Khrushchev once called a "stumbling horse" was racing to new records in consumer spending, labor income, and industrial production.

We are gratified--but we are not satisfied. Too many unemployed are still looking for the blessings of prosperity- As those who leave our schools and farms demand new jobs, automation takes old jobs away. To expand our growth and job opportunities, I urge on the Congress three measures:

First, the Manpower Training and Development Act, to stop the waste of able-bodied men and women who want to work, but whose only skill has been replaced by a machine, or moved with a mill, or shut down with a mine;

Second, the Youth Employment Opportunities Act, to help train and place not only the one million young Americans who are both out of school and out of work, but the twenty-six million young Americans entering the labor market in this decade; and

Third, the 8 percent tax credit for investment in machinery and equipment, which, combined with planned revisions of depreciation allowances, will spur our modernization, our growth, and our ability to compete abroad.

Moreover--pleasant as it may be to bask in the warmth of recovery--let us not forget that we have suffered three recessions in the last 7 years. The time to repair the roof is when the sun is shining--by filling three basic gaps in our anti-recession protection. We need:

First, presidential standby authority, subject to congressional veto, to adjust personal income tax rates downward within a specified range and time, to slow down an economic decline before it has dragged us all down;

Second, presidential standby authority, upon a given rise in the rate of unemployment, to accelerate Federal and federally-aided capital improvement programs; and

Third, a permanent strengthening of our unemployment compensation system--to maintain for our fellow citizens searching for a job who cannot find it, their purchasing power and their living standards without constant resort--as we have seen in recent years by the Congress and the administrations-to temporary supplements.

If we enact this six-part program, we can show the whole world that a free economy need not be an unstable economy--that a free system need not leave men unemployed--and that a free society is not only the most productive but the most stable form of organization yet fashioned by man.

But recession is only one enemy of a free economy--inflation is another. Last year, 1961, despite rising production and demand, consumer prices held almost steady--and wholesale prices declined. This is the best record of overall price stability of any comparable period of recovery since the end of World War II.

Inflation too often follows in the shadow of growth--while price stability is made easy by stagnation or controls. But we mean to maintain both stability and growth in a climate of freedom.

Our first line of defense against inflation is the good sense and public spirit of business and labor--keeping their total increases in wages and profits in step with productivity. There is no single statistical test to guide each company and each union. But I strongly urge them--for their country's interest, and for their own--to apply the test of the public interest to these transactions.

Within this same framework of growth and wage-price stability:

--This administration has helped keep our economy competitive by widening the access of small business to credit and Government contracts, and by stepping up the drive against monopoly, price-fixing, and racketeering;

--We will submit a Federal Pay Reform bill aimed at giving our classified, postal, and other employees new pay scales more comparable to those of private industry;

--We are holding the fiscal 1962 budget deficit far below the level incurred after the last recession in 1958; and, finally,

--I am submitting for fiscal 1963 a balanced Federal Budget.

This is a joint responsibility, requiring Congressional cooperation on appropriations, and on three sources of income in particular:

First, an increase in postal rates, to end the postal deficit;

Secondly, passage of the tax reforms previously urged, to remove unwarranted tax preferences, and to apply to dividends and to interest the same withholding requirements we have long applied to wages; and

Third, extension of the present excise and corporation tax rates, except for those changes--which will be recommended in a message--affecting transportation.

But a stronger nation and economy require more than a balanced Budget. They require progress in those programs that spur our growth and fortify our strength.

A strong America depends on its cities-America's glory, and sometimes America's shame. To substitute sunlight for congestion and progress for decay, we have stepped up existing urban renewal and housing programs, and launched new ones--redoubled the attack on water pollution--speeded aid to airports, hospitals, highways, and our declining mass transit systems-- and secured new weapons to combat organized crime, racketeering, and youth delinquency, assisted by the coordinated and hard-hitting efforts of our investigative services: the FBI, the Internal Revenue, the Bureau of Narcotics, and many others. We shall need further anti-crime, mass transit, and transportation legislation--and new tools to fight air pollution. And with all this effort under way, both equity and commonsense require that our nation's urban areas--containing three-fourths of our population--sit as equals at the Cabinet table. I urge a new Department of Urban Affairs and Housing.

A strong America also depends on its farms and natural resources. American farmers took heart in 1961--from a billion dollar rise in farm income--and from a hopeful start on reducing the farm surpluses. But we are still operating under a patchwork accumulation of old laws, which cost us $1 billion a year in CCC carrying charges alone, yet fail to halt rural poverty or boost farm earnings.

Our task is to master and turn to fully fruitful ends the magnificent productivity of our farms and farmers. The revolution on our own countryside stands in the sharpest contrast to the repeated farm failures of the Communist nations and is a source of pride to us all. Since 1950 our agricultural output per man-hour has actually doubled! Without new, realistic measures, it will someday swamp our farmers and our taxpayers in a national scandal or a farm depression.

I will, therefore, submit to the Congress a new comprehensive farm program--tailored to fit the use of our land and the supplies of each crop to the long-range needs of the sixties--and designed to prevent chaos in the sixties with a program of commonsense.

We also need for the sixties--if we are to bequeath our full national estate to our heirs--a new long-range conservation and recreation program-- expansion of our superb national parks and forests--preservation of our authentic wilderness areas-new starts on water and power projects as our population steadily increases--and expanded REA generation and transmission loans.

But America stands for progress in human rights as well as economic affairs, and a strong America requires the assurance of full and equal rights to all its citizens, of any race or of any color. This administration has shown as never before how much could be done through the full use of Executive powers--through the enforcement of laws already passed by the Congress- through persuasion, negotiation, and litigation, to secure the constitutional rights of all: the right to vote, the right to travel Without hindrance across State lines, and the right to free public education.

I issued last March a comprehensive order to guarantee the right to equal employment opportunity in all Federal agencies and contractors. The Vice President's Committee thus created has done much, including the voluntary "Plans for progress" which, in all sections of the country, are achieving a quiet but striking success in opening up to all races new professional, supervisory, and other job opportunities.

But there is much more to be done--by the Executive, by the courts, and by the Congress. Among the bills now pending before you, on which the executive departments will comment in detail, are appropriate methods of strengthening these basic rights which have our full support. The right to vote, for example, should no longer be denied through such arbitrary devices on a local level, sometimes abused, such as literacy tests and poll taxes. As we approach the 100th anniversary, next January, of the Emancipation Proclamation, let the acts of every branch of the Government--and every citizen--portray that "righteousness does exalt a nation."

Finally, a strong America cannot neglect the aspirations of its citizens-- the welfare of the needy, the health care of the elderly, the education of the young. For we are not developing the Nation's wealth for its own sake. Wealth is the means--and people arc the ends. All our material riches will avail us little if we do not use them to expand the opportunities of our people.

Last year, we improved the diet of needy people--provided more hot lunches and fresh milk to school children built more college dormitories-- and, for the elderly, expanded private housing, nursing homes, heath services, and social security. But we have just begun.

To help those least fortunate of all, I am recommending a new public welfare program, stressing services instead of support, rehabilitation instead of relief, and training for useful work instead of prolonged dependency.

To relieve the critical shortage of doctors and dentists--and this is a matter which should concern us all--and expand research, I urge action to aid medical and dental colleges and scholarships and to establish new National Institutes of Health.

To take advantage of modern vaccination achievements, I am proposing a mass immunization program, aimed at the virtual elimination of such ancient enemies of our children as polio, diphtheria, whooping cough, and tetanus.

To protect our consumers from the careless and the unscrupulous, I shall recommend improvements in the Food and Drug laws-strengthening inspection and standards, halting unsafe and worthless products, preventing misleading labels, and cracking down on the illicit sale of habit-forming drugs.

But in matters of health, no piece of unfinished business is more important or more urgent than the enactment under the social security system of health insurance for the aged.

For our older citizens have longer and more frequent illnesses, higher hospital and medical bills and too little income to pay them. Private health insurance helps very few--for its cost is high and its coverage limited. Public welfare cannot help those too proud to seek relief but hard-pressed to pay their own bills. Nor can their children or grandchildren always sacrifice their own health budgets to meet this constant drain.

Social security has long helped to meet the hardships of retirement, death, and disability. I now urge that its coverage be extended without further delay to provide health insurance for the elderly.

Equally important to our strength is the quality of our education. Eight million adult Americans are classified as functionally illiterate. This is a disturbing figure--reflected in Selective Service rejection rates-reflected in welfare rolls and crime rates. And I shall recommend plans for a massive attack to end this adult illiteracy.

I shall also recommend bills to improve educational quality, to stimulate the arts, and, at the college level, to provide Federal loans for the construction of academic facilities and federally financed scholarships.

If this Nation is to grow in wisdom and strength, then every able high school graduate should have the opportunity to develop his talents. Yet nearly half lack either the funds or the facilities to attend college. Enrollments are going to double in our colleges in the short space of 10 years. The annual cost per student is skyrocketing to astronomical levels-- now averaging $1,650 a year, although almost half of our families earn less than $5,000. They cannot afford such costs--but this Nation cannot afford to maintain its military power and neglect its brainpower.

But excellence in education must begin at the elementary level. I sent to the Congress last year a proposal for Federal aid to public school construction and teachers' salaries. I believe that bill, which passed the Senate and received House Committee approval, offered the minimum amount required by our needs and--in terms of across-the-board aid--the maximum scope permitted by our Constitution. I therefore see no reason to weaken or withdraw that bill: and I urge its passage at this session.

"Civilization," said H. G. Wells, "is a race between education and catastrophe." It is up to you in this Congress to determine the winner of that race.

These are not unrelated measures addressed to specific gaps or grievances in our national life. They are the pattern of our intentions and the foundation of our hopes. "I believe in democracy," said Woodrow Wilson, "because it releases the energy of every human being." The dynamic of democracy is the power and the purpose of the individual, and the policy of this administration is to give to the individual the opportunity to realize his own highest possibilities.

Our program is to open to all the opportunity for steady and productive employment, to remove from all the handicap of arbitrary or irrational exclusion, to offer to all the facilities for education and health and welfare, to make society the servant of the individual and the individual the source of progress, and thus to realize for all the full promise of American life.

All of these efforts at home give meaning to our efforts abroad. Since the close of the Second World War, a global civil war has divided and tormented mankind. But it is not our military might, or our higher standard of living, that has most distinguished us from our adversaries. It is our belief that the state is the servant of the citizen and not his master.

This basic clash of ideas and wills is but one of the forces reshaping our globe--swept as it is by the tides of hope and fear, by crises in the headlines today that become mere footnotes tomorrow. Both the successes and the setbacks of the past year remain on our agenda of unfinished business. For every apparent blessing contains the seeds of danger--every area of trouble gives out a ray of hope--and the one unchangeable certainty is that nothing is certain or unchangeable.

Yet our basic goal remains the same: a peaceful world community of free and independent states--free to choose their own future and their own system, so long as it does not threaten the freedom of others.

Some may choose forms and ways that we would not choose for ourselves--but it is not for us that they are choosing. We can welcome diversity--the Communists cannot. For we offer a world of choice--they offer the world of coercion. And the way of the past shows clearly that freedom, not coercion, is the wave of the future. At times our goal has been obscured by crisis or endangered by conflict--but it draws sustenance from five basic sources of strength:

--the moral and physical strength of the United States;

--the united strength of the Atlantic Community;

--the regional strength of our Hemispheric relations;

--the creative strength of our efforts in the new and developing nations; and

--the peace-keeping strength of the United Nations.

Our moral and physical strength begins at home as already discussed. But it includes our military strength as well. So long as fanaticism and fear brood over the affairs of men, we must arm to deter others from aggression.

In the past 12 months our military posture has steadily improved. We increased the previous defense budget by 15 percent--not in the expectation of war but for the preservation of peace. We more than doubled our acquisition rate of Polaris submarines--we doubled the production capacity for Minuteman missiles--and increased by 50 percent the number of manned bombers standing ready on a 15 minute alert. This year the combined force levels planned under our new Defense budget--including nearly three hundred additional Polaris and Minuteman missiles--have been precisely calculated to insure the continuing strength of our nuclear deterrent.

But our strength may be tested at many levels. We intend to have at all times the capacity to resist non-nuclear or limited attacks--as a complement to our nuclear capacity, not as a substitute. We have rejected any all-or-nothing posture which would leave no choice but inglorious retreat or unlimited retaliation.

Thus we have doubled the number of ready combat divisions in the Army's strategic reserve--increased our troops in Europe--built up the Marines--added new sealift and airlift capacity--modernized our weapons and ammunition--expanded our anti-guerrilla forces--and increased the active fleet by more than 70 vessels and our tactical air forces by nearly a dozen wings.

Because we needed to reach this higher long-term level of readiness more quickly, 155,000 members of the Reserve and National Guard were activated under the Act of this Congress. Some disruptions and distress were inevitable. But the overwhelming majority bear their burdens--and their Nation's burdens--with admirable and traditional devotion.

In the coming year, our reserve programs will be revised--two Army Divisions will, I hope, replace those Guard Divisions on duty--and substantial other increases will boost our Air Force fighter units, the procurement of equipment, and our continental defense and warning efforts. The Nation's first serious civil defense shelter program is under way, identifying, marking, and stocking 50 million spaces; and I urge your approval of Federal incentives for the construction of public fall-out shelters in schools and hospitals and similar centers.

But arms alone are not enough to keep the peace--it must be kept by men. Our instrument and our hope is the United Nations-and I see little merit in the impatience of those who would abandon this imperfect world instrument because they dislike our imperfect world. For the troubles of a world organization merely reflect the troubles of the world itself. And if the organization is weakened, these troubles can only increase. We may not always agree with every detailed action taken by every officer of the United Nations, or with every voting majority. But as an institution, it should have in the future, as it has had in the past since its inception, no stronger or more faithful member than the United States of America.

In 1961 the peace-keeping strength of the United Nations was reinforced. And those who preferred or predicted its demise, envisioning a troika in the seat of Hammarskiold--or Red China inside the Assembly-have seen instead a new vigor, under a new Secretary General and a fully independent Secretariat. In making plans for a new forum and principles on disarmament for peace-keeping in outer space--for a decade of development effort--the UN fulfilled its Charter's lofty aim.

Eighteen months ago the tangled and turbulent Congo presented the UN with its gravest challenge. The prospect was one of chaos--or certain big-power confrontation, with all of its hazards and all of its risks, to us and to others. Today the hopes have improved for peaceful conciliation within a united Congo. This is the objective of our policy in this important area.

No policeman is universally popular-particularly when he uses his stick to restore law and order on his beat. Those members who are willing to contribute their votes and their views--but very little else--have created a serious deficit by refusing to pay their share of special UN assessments. Yet they do pay their annual assessments to retain their votes--and a new UN Bond issue, financing special operations for the next 18 months, is to be repaid with interest from these regular assessments. This is clearly in our interest. It will not only keep the UN solvent, but require all voting members to pay their fair share of its activities. Our share of special operations has long been much higher than our share of the annual assessment--and the bond issue will in effect reduce our disproportionate obligation, and for these reasons, I am urging Congress to approve our participation.

With the approval of this Congress, we have undertaken in the past year a great new effort in outer space. Our aim is not simply to be first on the moon, any more than Charles Lindbergh's real aim was to be the first to Paris. His aim was to develop the techniques of our own country and other countries in the field of air and the atmosphere, and our objective in making this effort, which we hope will place one of our citizens on the moon, is to develop in a new frontier of science, commerce and cooperation, the position of the United States and the Free World.

This Nation belongs among the first to explore it, and among the first-- if not the first--we shall be. We are offering our know-how and our cooperation to the United Nations. Our satellites will soon be providing other nations with improved weather observations. And I shall soon send to the Congress a measure to govern the financing and operation of an International Communications Satellite system, in a manner consistent with the public interest and our foreign policy.

But peace in space will help us naught once peace on earth is gone. World order will be secured only when the whole world has laid down these weapons which seem to offer us present security but threaten the future survival of the human race. That armistice day seems very far away. The vast resources of this planet are being devoted more and more to the means of destroying, instead of enriching, human life.

But the world was not meant to be a prison in which man awaits his execution. Nor has mankind survived the tests and trials of thousands of years to surrender everything-including its existence--now. This Nation has the will and the faith to make a supreme effort to break the log jam on disarmament and nuclear tests--and we will persist until we prevail, until the rule of law has replaced the ever dangerous use of force.

I turn now to a prospect of great promise: our Hemispheric relations. The Alliance for Progress is being rapidly transformed from proposal to program. Last month in Latin America I saw for myself the quickening of hope, the revival of confidence, the new trust in our country--among workers and farmers as well as diplomats. We have pledged our help in speeding their economic, educational, and social progress. The Latin American Republics have in turn pledged a new and strenuous effort of self-help and self-reform.

To support this historic undertaking, I am proposing--under the authority contained in the bills of the last session of the Congress--a special long-term Alliance for Progress fund of $3 billion. Combined with our Food for Peace, Export-Import Bank, and other resources, this will provide more than $1 billion a year in new support for the Alliance. In addition, we have increased twelve-fold our Spanish and Portuguese language broadcasting in Latin America, .and improved Hemispheric trade and defense. And while the blight of communism has been increasingly exposed and isolated in the Americas, liberty has scored a gain. The people of the Dominican Republic, with our firm encouragement and help, and those of our sister Republics of this Hemisphere are safely passing through the treacherous course from dictatorship through disorder towards democracy.

Our efforts to help other new or developing nations, and to strengthen their stand for freedom, have also made progress. A newly unified Agency for International Development is reorienting our foreign assistance to emphasize long-term development loans instead of grants, more economic aid instead of military, individual plans to meet the individual needs of the nations, and new standards on what they must do to marshal their own resources.

A newly conceived Peace Corps is winning friends and helping people in fourteen countries--supplying trained and dedicated young men and women, to give these new nations a hand in building a society, and a glimpse of the best that is in our country. If there is a problem here, it is that we cannot supply the spontaneous and mounting demand.

A newly-expanded Food for Peace Pro-. gram is feeding the hungry of many lands with the abundance of our productive farms--providing lunches for children in school, wages for economic development, relief for the victims of flood and famine, and a better diet for millions whose daily bread is their chief concern.

These programs help people; and, by helping people, they help freedom. The views of their governments may sometimes be very different from ours--but events in Africa, the Middle East, and Eastern Europe teach us never to write off any nation as lost to the Communists- That is the lesson of our time. We support the independence of those newer or weaker states whose history, geography, economy or lack of power impels them to remain outside "entangling alliances"--as we did for more than a century. For the independence of nations is a bar to the Communists' "grand design"-it is the basis of our own.

In the past year, for example, we have urged a neutral and independent Laos-regained there a common policy with our major allies--and insisted that a cease-fire precede negotiations. While a workable formula for supervising its independence is still to be achieved, both the spread of war-which might have involved this country also--and a Communist occupation have thus far been prevented.

A satisfactory settlement in Laos would also help to achieve and safeguard the peace in Viet-Nam--where the foe is increasing his tactics of terror--where our own efforts have been stepped up--and where the local government has initiated new programs and reforms to broaden the base of resistance. The systematic aggression now bleeding that country is not a "war of liberation"--for Viet-Nam is already free. It is a war of attempted subjugation--and it will be resisted.

Finally, the united strength of the Atlantic Community has flourished in the last year under severe tests. NATO has increased both the number and the readiness of its air, ground, and naval units--both its nuclear and non-nuclear capabilities. Even greater efforts by all its members are still required. Nevertheless our unity of purpose and will has been, I believe, immeasurably strengthened.

The threat to the brave city of Berlin remains. In these last 6 months the Allies have made it unmistakably clear that our presence in Berlin, our free access thereto, and the freedom of two million West Berliners would not be surrendered either to force or through appeasement--and to maintain those rights and obligations, we are prepared to talk, when appropriate, and to fight, if necessary. Every member of NATO stands with us in a common commitment to preserve this symbol of free man's will to remain free.

I cannot now predict the course of future negotiations over Berlin. I can only say that we are sparing no honorable effort to find a peaceful and mutually acceptable resolution of this problem. I believe such a resolution can be found, and with it an improvement in our relations with the Soviet Union, if only the leaders in the Kremlin will recognize the basic rights and interests involved, and the interest of all mankind in peace.

But the Atlantic Community is no longer concerned with purely military aims. As its common undertakings grow at an ever-increasing pace, we are, and increasingly will be, partners in aid, trade, defense, diplomacy, and monetary affairs.

The emergence of the new Europe is being matched by the emergence of new ties across the Atlantic. It is a matter of undramatic daily cooperation in hundreds of workaday tasks: of currencies kept in effective relation, of development loans meshed together, of standardized weapons, and concerted diplomatic positions. The Atlantic Community grows, not like a volcanic mountain, by one mighty explosion, but like a coral reef, from the accumulating activity of all.

Thus, we in the free world are moving steadily toward unity and cooperation, in the teeth of that old Bolshevik prophecy, and at the very time when extraordinary rumbles of discord can be heard across the Iron Curtain. It is not free societies which bear within them the seeds of inevitable disunity.

On one special problem, of great concern to our friends, and to us, I am proud to give the Congress an encouraging report. Our efforts to safeguard the dollar are progressing. In the 11 months preceding last February 1, we suffered a net loss of nearly $2 billion in gold. In the 11 months that followed, the loss was just over half a billion dollars. And our deficit in our basic transactions with the rest of the world--trade, defense, foreign aid, and capital, excluding volatile short-term flows--has been reduced from $2 billion for 1960 to about one-third that amount for 1961. Speculative fever against the dollar is ending--and confidence in the dollar has been restored.

We did not--and could not--achieve these gains through import restrictions, troop withdrawals, exchange controls, dollar devaluation or choking off domestic recovery. We acted not in panic but in perspective. But the problem is not yet solved. Persistently large deficits would endanger our economic growth and our military and defense commitments abroad. Our goal must be a reasonable equilibrium in our balance of payments. With the cooperation of the Congress, business, labor, and our major allies, that goal can be reached.

We shall continue to attract foreign tourists and investments to our shores, to seek increased military purchases here by our allies, to maximize foreign aid procurement from American firms, to urge increased aid from other fortunate nations to the less fortunate, to seek tax laws which do not favor investment in other industrialized nations or tax havens, and to urge coordination of allied fiscal and monetary policies So as to discourage large and disturbing capital movements.

Above all, if we are to pay for our commitments abroad, we must expand our exports. Our businessmen must be export conscious and export competitive. Our tax policies must spur modernization of our plants--our wage and price gains must be consistent with productivity to hold the line on prices--our export credit . and promotion campaigns for American industries must continue to expand.

But the greatest challenge of all is posed by the growth of the European Common Market. Assuming the accession of the United Kingdom, there will arise across the Atlantic a trading partner behind a single external tariff similar to ours with an economy which nearly equals our own. Will we in this country adapt our thinking to these new prospects and patterns--or will we wait until events have passed us by?

This is the year to decide. The Reciprocal Trade Act is expiring. We need a new law--a wholly new approach--a bold new instrument of American trade policy. Our decision could well affect the unity of the West, the course of the Cold War, and the economic growth of our Nation for a generation to come.

If we move decisively, our factories and farms can increase their sales to their richest, fastest-growing market. Our exports will increase. Our balance of payments position will improve. And we will have forged across the Atlantic a trading partnership with vast resources for freedom.

If, on the other hand, we hang back in deference to local economic pressures, we will find ourselves cut off from our major allies. Industries-- and I believe this is most vital--industries will move their plants and jobs and capital inside the walls of the Common Market, and jobs, therefore, will be lost here in the United States if they cannot otherwise compete for its consumers. Our farm surpluses--our balance of trade, as you all know, to Europe, the Common Market, in farm products, is nearly three or four to one in our favor, amounting to one of the best earners of dollars in our balance of payments structure, and without entrance to this Market, without the ability to enter it, our farm surpluses will pile up in the Middle West, tobacco in the South, and other commodities, which have gone through Western Europe for 15 years. Our balance of payments position will worsen. Our consumers, will lack a wider choice of goods at lower prices. And millions of American workers-whose jobs depend on the sale or the transportation or the distribution of exports or imports, or whose jobs will be endangered by the movement of our capital to Europe, or whose jobs can be maintained only in. an expanding economy--these millions of workers in your home States and mine will see their real interests sacrificed.

Members of the Congress: The United States did not rise to greatness by waiting for others to lead. This Nation is the world's foremost manufacturer, farmer, banker, consumer, and exporter. The Common Market is moving ahead at an economic growth rate twice ours. The Communist economic offensive is under way. The opportunity is ours--the initiative is up to us--and I believe that 1962 is the time.

To seize that initiative, I shall shortly send to the Congress a new five-year Trade Expansion Action, far-reaching in scope but designed with great care to make certain that its benefits to our people far outweigh any risks.

The bill will permit the gradual elimination of tariffs here in the United States and in the Common Market on those items in which we together supply 80 percent of the world's trade--mostly items in which our own ability to compete is demonstrated by the fact that we sell abroad, in these items, substantially more than we import. This step will make it possible for our major industries to compete with their counterparts in Western Europe for access to European consumers.

On other goods the bill will permit a gradual reduction of duties up to 50 percent-permitting bargaining by major categories-and provide for appropriate and tested forms of assistance to firms and employees adjusting to import competition. We are not neglecting the safeguards provided by peril points, an escape clause, or the National Security Amendment. Nor are we abandoning our non-European friends or our traditional "most-favored nation" principle. On the contrary, the bill will provide new encouragement for their sale of tropical agricultural products, so important to our friends in Latin America, who have long depended upon the European market, who now find themselves faced with new challenges which we must join with them in overcoming.

Concessions, in this bargaining, must of course be reciprocal, not unilateral. The Common Market will not fulfill its own high promise unless its outside tariff walls are low. The dangers of restriction or timidity in our own policy have counterparts for our friends in Europe. For together we face a common challenge: to enlarge the prosperity of free men everywhere--to build in partnership a new trading community in which all free nations may gain from the productive energy of free competitive effort.

These various elements in our foreign policy lead, as I have said, to a single goal--the goal of a peaceful world of free and independent states. This is our guide for the present and our vision for the future--a free community of nations, independent but interdependent, uniting north and south, east and west, in one great family of man, outgrowing and transcending the hates and fears that rend our age.

We will not reach that goal today, or tomorrow. We may not reach it in our own lifetime. But the quest is the greatest adventure of our century. We sometimes chafe at the burden of our obligations, the complexity of our decisions, the agony of our choices. But there is no comfort or security for us in evasion, no solution in abdication, no relief in irresponsibility.

A year ago, in assuming the tasks of the Presidency, I said that few generations, in all history, had been granted the role of being the great defender of freedom in its hour of maximum danger. This is our good fortune; and I welcome it now as I did a year ago. For it is the fate of this generation-of you in the Congress and of me as President--to live with a struggle we did not start, in a world we did not make. But the pressures of life are not always distributed by choice. And while no nation has ever faced such a challenge, no nation has ever been so ready to seize the burden and the glory of freedom.

And in this high endeavor, may God watch over the United States of America.

President John F. Kennedy

ADDRESS AT THE UNIVERSITY OF CALIFORNIA BERKLEY

(MARCH 23, 1962)

Mr. President, Governor Brown, Dr. Pauley, Chancellor, members of the Board of Regents, members of the faculty and fellow students, ladies and gentlemen:

The last time that I came to this Stadium was 22 years ago, when I visited it in November of 1940 as a student at a nearby small school for the game with Stanford. And we got a--I must say I had a much warmer reception today than I did from my Coast friends here on that occasion. In those days we used to fill these universities for football, and now we do it for academic events, and I'm not sure that this doesn't represent a rather dangerous trend for the future of our country.

I am delighted to be here on this occasion for though it is the 94th anniversary of the Charter, in a sense this is the hundredth anniversary. For this university and so many other universities across our country owe their birth to the most extraordinary piece of legislation which this country has ever adopted, and that is the Morrill Act, signed by President Abraham Lincoln in the darkest and most uncertain days of the Civil War, which set before the country the opportunity to build the great land-grant colleges, of which this is so distinguished a part. Six years later, this university obtained its Charter.

In its first graduating class it included a future Governor of California, a future Congressman, a judge, a State assemblyman, a clergyman, a lawyer, a doctor--all in a graduating class of 12 students!

This college, therefore, from its earliest beginnings, has recognized, and its graduates have recognized, that the purpose of education is not merely to advance the economic self-interest of its graduates. The people of California, as much if not more than the people of any other State, have supported their colleges and their universities and their schools, because they recognize how important it is to the maintenance of a free society that its citizens be well educated.

"Every man," said Professor Woodrow Wilson, "sent out from a university should be a man of his nation as well as a man of his time."

And Prince Bismarck was even more specific. One third, he said, of the students of German universities broke down from overwork, another third broke down from dissipation, and the other third ruled Germany.

I do not know which third of students are here today, but I am confident that I am talking to the future leaders of this State and country who recognize their responsibilities to the public interest.

Today you carry on that tradition. Our distinguished and courageous Secretary of Defense, our distinguished Secretary of State, the Chairman of the Atomic Energy Commission, the Director of the CIA and others, all are graduates of this University. It is a disturbing fact to me, and it may be to some of you, that the New frontier owes as much to Berkeley as it does to Harvard University.

This has been a week of momentous events around the world. The long and painful struggle in Algeria which comes to an end. Both nuclear powers and neutrals labored at Geneva for a solution to the problem of a spiraling arms race, and also to the problems that so vex our relations with the Soviet Union. The Congress opened hearings on a trade bill, which is far more than a trade bill, but an opportunity to build a stronger and closer Atlantic Community. And my wife had her first and last ride on an elephant!

But history may well remember this as a week for an act of lesser immediate impact, and that is the decision by the United States and the Soviet Union to seek concrete agreements on the joint exploration of space. Experience has taught us that an agreement to negotiate does not always mean a negotiated agreement. But should such a joint effort be realized, its significance could well be tremendous for us all. In terms of space science, our combined knowledge and efforts can benefit the people of all the nations: joint weather satellites to provide more ample warnings against destructive storms-joint communications systems to draw the world more closely together--and cooperation in space medicine research and space tracking operations to speed the day when man will go to the moon and beyond.

But the scientific gains from such a joint effort would offer, I believe, less realized return than the gains for world peace. For a cooperative Soviet-American effort in space science and exploration would emphasize the interests that must unite us, rather than those that always divide us. It offers us an area in which the stale and sterile dogmas of the cold war could be literally left a quarter of a million miles behind. And it would remind us on both sides that knowledge, not hate, is the passkey to the future--that knowledge transcends national antagonisms-that it speaks a universal language-that it is the possession, not of a single class, or of a single nation or a single ideology, but of all mankind.

I need hardly emphasize the happy pursuit of knowledge in this place. Your faculty includes more Nobel laureates than any other faculty in the world--more in this one community than our principal adversary has received since the awards began in 1901. And we take pride in that, only from a national point of view, because it indicates, as the Chancellor pointed out, the great intellectual benefits of a free society. This University of California will continue to grow as an intellectual center because your presidents and your chancellors and your professors have rigorously defended that unhampered freedom of discussion and inquiry which is the soul of the intellectual enterprise and the heart of a free university.

We may be proud as a nation of our record in scientific achievement--but at the same time we must be impressed by the interdependence of all knowledge. I am certain that every scholar and scientist here today would agree that his own work has benefited immeasurably from the work of the men and women in other countries. The prospect of a partnership with Soviet scientists in the exploration of space opens up exciting prospects of collaboration in other areas of learning. And cooperation in the pursuit of knowledge can hopefully lead to cooperation in the pursuit of peace.

Yet the pursuit of knowledge itself implies a world where men are free to follow out the logic of their own ideas. It implies a world where nations are free to solve their own problems and to realize their own ideals. It implies, in short, a world where collaboration emerges from the voluntary decisions of nations strong in their own independence and their own self-respect. It implies, I believe, the kind of world which is emerging before our eyes--the world produced by the revolution of national independence which has today, and has been since 1945, sweeping across the face of the world.

I sometimes think that we are too much impressed by the clamor of daily events. The newspaper headlines and the television screens give us a short view. They so flood us with the stop-press details of daily stories that we lose sight of one of the great movements of history. Yet it is the profound tendencies of history and not the passing excitements, that will shape our future.

The short view gives us the impression as a nation of being shoved and harried, everywhere on the defense. But this impression is surely an optical illusion. From the perspective of Moscow, the world today may seem ever more troublesome, more intractable, more frustrating than it does to us. The leaders of the Communist world are confronted not only by acute internal problems in each Communist country--the failure of agriculture, the rising discontent of the youth and the intellectuals, the demands of technical and managerial groups for status and security. They are confronted in addition by profound divisions within the Communist world itself--divisions which have already shattered the image of Communism as a universal system guaranteed to abolish all social and international conflicts-- the most valuable asset the Communists had for many years.

Wisdom requires the long view. And the long view shows us that the revolution of national independence is a fundamental fact of our era. This revolution will not be stopped. As new nations emerge from the oblivion of centuries, their first aspiration is to affirm their national identity. Their deepest hope is for a world where, within a framework of international cooperation, every country can solve its own problems according to its own traditions and ideals.

It is in the interests of the pursuit of .knowledge--and it is in our own national interest--that this revolution of national independence succeed. For the Communists rest everything on the idea of a monolithic world--a world where all knowledge has a single pattern, all societies move toward a single model, and all problems and roads have a single solution and a single destination. The pursuit of knowledge, on the other hand, rests everything on the opposite idea--on the idea of a world based on diversity, self-determination, freedom. And that is the kind of world to which we Americans, as a nation, are committed by the principles upon which the great Republic was founded.

As men conduct the pursuit of knowledge, they create a world which freely unites national diversity and international partnership. This emerging world is incompatible with the Communist world order. It will irresistibly burst the bonds of the Communist organization and the Communist ideology. And diversity and independence, far from being opposed to the American conception of world order, represent the very essence of our view of the future of the world.

There used to be so much talk a few years ago about the inevitable triumph of communism. We hear such talk much less now. No one who examines the modern world can doubt that the great currents of history are carrying the world away from the monolithic idea towards the pluralistic idea--away from communism and towards national independence and freedom. No one can doubt that the wave of the future is not the conquest of the world by a single dogmatic creed but the liberation of the diverse energies of free nations and free men. No one can doubt that cooperation in the pursuit of knowledge must lead to freedom of the mind and freedom of the soul.

Beyond the drumfire of daily crisis, therefore, there is arising the outlines of a robust and vital world community, founded on nations secure in their own independence, and united by allegiance to world peace. It would be foolish to say that this world will be won tomorrow, or the day after. The processes of history are fitful and uncertain and aggravating. There will be frustrations and setbacks. There will be times of anxiety and gloom. The specter of thermonuclear war will continue to hang over mankind; and we must heed the advice of Oliver Wendell Holmes of "freedom leaning on her spear" until all nations are wise enough to disarm safely and effectively.

Yet we can have a new confidence today in the direction in which history is moving. Nothing is more stirring than the recognition of great public purpose. Every great age is marked by innovation and daring-by the ability to meet unprecedented problems with intelligent solutions. In a time of turbulence and change, it is more true than ever that knowledge is power; for only by true understanding and steadfast judgment are we able to master the challenge of history.

If this is so, we must strive to acquire knowledge--and to apply it with wisdom. We must reject over-simplified theories of international life--the theory that American power is unlimited, or that the American mission is to remake the world in the American image. We must seize the vision of a free and diverse world--and shape our policies to speed progress toward a more flexible world order.

This is the unifying spirit of our policies in the world today. The purpose of our aid programs must be to help developing countries move forward as rapidly as possible on the road to genuine national independence. Our military policies must assist nations to protect the processes of democratic reform and development against disruption and intervention. Our diplomatic policies must strengthen our relations with the whole world, with our several alliances and within the United Nations.

As we press forward on every front to realize a flexible world order, the role of the university becomes ever more important, both as a reservoir of ideas and as a repository of the long view of the shore dimly seen.

"Knowledge is the great sun of the firmament," said Senator Daniel Webster. "Life and power are scattered with all its beams."

In its light, we must think and act not only for the moment but for our time. I am reminded of the story of the great French Marshal Lyautey, who once asked his gardener to plant a tree. The gardener objected that the tree was slow-growing and would not reach maturity for a hundred years. The Marshal replied, "In that case, there is no time to lose, plant it this afternoon."

Today a world of knowledge--a world of cooperation--a just and lasting peace--may be years away. But we have no time to lose. Let us plant our trees this afternoon.

REMARKS AT WEST POINT

(JUNE 6, 1962)

General Westmoreland, General Lemnitzer, Mr. Secretary, General Decker, General Taylor, members of the graduating class and their parents, gentlemen:

I want to express my appreciation for your generous invitation to come to this graduating class. I am sure that all of you who sit here today realize, particularly in view of the song we have just heard, that you are part of a long tradition stretching back to the earliest days of this country's history, and that where you sit sat once some of the most celebrated names in our Nation's history, and also some who are not so well known, but who, on 100 different battlefields in many wars involving every generation of this country's history, have given very clear evidence of their commitment to their country.

So that I know you feel a sense of pride in being part of that tradition, and as a citizen of the United States, as well as President, I want to express our high regard to all of you in appreciation for what you are doing and what you will do for our country in the days ahead.

I would also like to announce at this time that as Commander in Chief I am exercising my privilege of directing the Secretary of the Army and the Superintendent of West Point to remit all existing confinements and other cadet punishments, and I hope that it will be possible to carry this out today.

General Westmoreland was slightly pained to hear that this was impending in view of the fact that one cadet, who I am confident will some day be the head of the Army, has just been remitted for 8 months, and is about to be released. But I am glad to have the opportunity to participate in the advancement of his military career.

My own confinement goes for another two and a half years, and I may

205

ask for it to be extended instead of remitted.

I want to say that I wish all of you, the graduates, success. While I say that, I am not unmindful of the fact that two graduates of this Academy have reached the White House, and neither was a member of my party. Until I am more certain that this trend will be broken, I wish that all of you may be generals and not Commanders in Chief.

I want to say that I am sure you recognize that your schooling is only interrupted by today's occasion and not ended because the demands that will be made upon you in the service of your country in the coming months and years will be really more pressing, and in many ways more burdensome, as well as more challenging, than ever before in our history. I know that many of you may feel, and many of our citizens may feel that in these days of the nuclear age, when war may last in its final form a day or two or three days before much of the world is burned up, that your service to your country will be only standing and waiting. Nothing, of course, could be further from the truth. I am sure that many Americans believe that the days before World War II were the golden age when the stars were falling on all the graduates of West Point, that that was the golden time of service, and that you have moved into a period where military service, while vital, is not as challenging as it was then. Nothing could be further from the truth.

The fact of the matter is that the period just ahead in the next decade will offer more opportunities for service to the graduates of this Academy than ever before in the history of the United States, because all around the world, in countries which are heavily engaged in the maintenance of their freedom, graduates of this Academy are heavily involved. Whether it is in Viet-Nam or in Laos or in Thailand, whether it is a military advisory group in Iran, whether it is a military attach? in some Latin American country during a difficult and challenging period, whether it is the commander of our troops in South Korea--the burdens that will be placed upon you when you fill those positions as you must inevitably, will require more from you than ever before in our history. The graduates of West Point, the Naval Academy, and the Air Academy in the next 10 years will have the greatest opportunity for the defense of freedom that this Academy's graduates have ever had. And I am sure that the Joint Chiefs of Staff endorse that view, knowing as they do and I do, the heavy burdens that are required of this Academy's graduates every day-General Tucker in Laos, or General Harkins in Viet-Nam, and a dozen others who hold key and significant positions involving the security of the United States and the defense of freedom. You are going to follow in their footsteps and I must say that I think that you will be privileged in the years ahead to find yourselves so heavily involved in the great interests of this country.

Therefore, I hope that you realize--and I hope every American realizes--how much we depend upon you. Your strictly military responsibilities, therefore, will require a versatility and an adaptability never before required in either war or in peace. They may involve the command and control of modern nuclear weapons and modern delivery systems, so complex that only a few scientists can understand their operation, so devastating that their inadvertent use would be of worldwide concern, but so new that their employment and their effects have never been tested in combat conditions.

On the other hand, your responsibilities may involve the command of more traditional forces, but in less traditional roles. Men risking their lives, not as combatants, but as instructors or advisers, or as symbols of our Nation's commitments. The fact that the United States is not directly at war in these areas in no way diminishes the skill and the courage that will be required, the service to our country which is rendered, or the pain of the casualties which are suffered.

To cite one final example of the range of responsibilities that will fall upon you: you may hold a position of command with our special forces, forces which are too unconventional to be called conventional, forces which are growing in number and importance and significance, for we now know that it is wholly misleading to call this "the nuclear age," or to say that our security rests only on the doctrine of massive retaliation.

Korea has not been the only battleground since the end of the Second World War. Men have fought and died in Malaya, in Greece, in the Philippines, in Algeria and Cuba and Cyprus, and almost continuously on the Indo-Chinese Peninsula. No nuclear weapons have been fired. No massive nuclear retaliation has been considered appropriate. This is another type of war, new in its intensity, ancient in its origin--war by guerrillas, subversives, insurgents, assassins, war by ambush instead of by combat; by infiltration, instead of aggression, seeking victory by eroding and exhausting the enemy instead of engaging him. It is a form of warfare uniquely adapted to what has been strangely called "wars of liberation," to undermine the efforts of new and poor countries to maintain the freedom that they have finally achieved. It preys on economic unrest and ethnic conflicts. It requires in those situations where we must counter it, and these are the kinds of challenges that will be before us in the next decade if freedom is to be saved, a whole new kind of strategy, a wholly different kind of force, and therefore a new and wholly different kind of military training.

But I have spoken thus far only of the military challenges which your education must prepare you for. The nonmilitary problems which you will face will also be most demanding, diplomatic, political, and economic. In the years ahead, some of you will serve as advisers to foreign aid missions or even to foreign governments. Some will negotiate terms of a cease-fire with broad political as well as military ramifications. Some of you will go to the far corners of the earth, and to the far reaches of space. Some of you will sit in the highest councils of the Pentagon. Others will hold delicate command posts which are international in character. Still others will advise on plans to abolish arms instead of using them to abolish others. Whatever your position, the scope of your decisions will not be confined to the traditional tenets of military competence and training. You will need to know and understand not only the foreign policy of the United States but the foreign policy of all countries scattered around the world who 20 years ago were the most distant names to us. You will need to give orders in different tongues and read maps by different systems. You will be involved in economic judgments which most economists would hesitate to make. At what point, for example, does military aid become burdensome to a country and make its freedom endangered rather than helping to secure it? To what extent can the gold and dollar cost of our overseas deployments be offset by foreign procurement? Or at what stage can a new weapons system be considered sufficiently advanced to justify large dollar appropriations?

In many countries, your posture and performance will provide the local population with the only evidence of what our country is really like. In other countries, your military mission, its advice and action, will play a key role in determining whether those people will remain free. You will need to understand the importance of military power and also the limits of military power, to decide what arms should be used to fight and when they should be used to prevent a fight, to determine what represents our vital interests and what interests are only marginal.

Above all, you will have a responsibility to deter war as well as to fight it. For the basic problems facing the world today are not susceptible of a final military solution. While we will long require the services and admire the dedication and commitment of the fighting men of this country, neither our strategy nor our psychology as a nation, and certainly not our economy, must become permanently dependent upon an ever-increasing military establishment.

Our forces, therefore, must fulfill a broader role as a complement to our diplomacy, as an arm of our diplomacy, as a deterrent to our adversaries, and as a symbol to our allies of our determination to support them.

That is why this Academy has seen its curriculum grow and expand in dimension, in substance, and in difficulty. That is why you cannot possibly have crowded into these 4 busy years all of the knowledge and all of the range of experience which you must bring to these subtle and delicate tasks which I have described. And that is why go to school year after year so you can serve this country to the best of your ability and your talent.

To talk of such talent and effort raises in the minds, I am sure, of everyone, and the minds of all of our countrymen, why--why should men such as you, able to master the complex arts of science, mathematics, language, economy, and all the rest devote their lives to a military career, with all of its risks and hardships? Why should their families be expected to make the personal and financial sacrifices that a military career inevitably brings with it? When there is a visible enemy to fight in open combat, the answer is not so difficult. Many serve, all applaud, and the tide of patriotism runs high. But when there is a long, slow struggle, with no immediate visible foe, your choice will seem hard indeed. And you will recall, I am sure, the lines found in an old sentry box in Gibraltar:

God and the soldier all men adore

In time of trouble--and no more,

For when war is over, and all things righted,

God is neglected--and the old soldier slighted.

But you have one satisfaction, however difficult those days may be: when you are asked by a President of the United States or by any other American what you are doing for your country, no man's answer will be clearer than your own. And that moral motivation which brought you here in the first place is part of your training here as well. West Point was not built to produce technical experts alone. It was built to produce men committed to the defense of their country, leaders of men who understand the great stakes which are involved, leaders who can be entrusted with the heavy responsibility which modern weapons and the fight for freedom entail, leaders who can inspire in their men the same sense of obligation to duty which you bring to it.

There is no single slogan that you can repeat to yourself in hard days or give to those who may be associated with you. In times past, a simple phrase, "54-40 or fight" or "to make the world safe for democracy"-that was enough. But the times, the weapons, and the issues are now more complicated than ever.

Eighteen years ago today, Ernie Pyle, describing those tens of thousands of young men who crossed the "ageless and indifferent" sea of the English Channel, searched in vain for a word to describe what they were fighting for. And finally he concluded that they were at least fighting for each other.

You and I leave here today to meet our separate responsibilities, to protect our Nation's vital interests by peaceful means if possible, by resolute action if necessary. And we go forth confident of support and success because we know that we are working and fighting for each other and for all those men and women all over the globe who are determined to be free.

YALE UNIVERSITY COMMENCEMENT

(JUNE 11, 1962)

President Griswold, members of the faculty, graduates and their families, ladies and gentlemen:

Let me begin by expressing my appreciation for the very deep honor that you have conferred upon me. As General de Gaulle occasionally acknowledges America to be the daughter of Europe, so I am pleased to come to Yale, the daughter of Harvard. It might be said now that I have the best of both worlds, a Harvard education and a Yale degree.

I am particularly glad to become a Yale man because as I think about my troubles, I find that a lot of them have come from other Yale men. Among businessmen, I have had a minor disagreement with Roger Blough, of the law school class of 1931, and I have had some complaints, too, from my friend Henry ford, of the class of 1940. In journalism I seem to have a difference with John Hay Whitney, of the class of 1926 and sometimes I also displease Henry Luce of the class of 1920, not to mention also William F. Buckley, Jr., of the class of 1950. I even have some trouble with my Yale advisers. I get along with them, but I am not always sure how they get along with each other.

I have the warmest feelings for Chester Bowles of the class of 1924, and for Dean Acheson of the class of 1915, and my assistant, McGeorge Bundy, of the class of 1940. But I am not 100 percent sure that these three wise and experienced Yale men wholly agree with each other on every issue.

So this administration which aims at peaceful cooperation among all Americans has been the victim of a certain natural pugnacity developed in this city among Yale men. Now that I, too, am a Yale man, it is time for peace. Last week at West Point, in the historic tradition of that Academy, I availed myself of the powers of Commander in Chief to remit all sentences of offending cadets. In that same spirit, and in the historic tradition of Yale, let me now offer to smoke the clay pipe of friendship with all of my brother

Ells, and I hope that they may be friends not only with me but even with each other.

In any event, I am very glad to be here and as a new member of the club, I have been checking to see what earlier links existed between the institution of the Presidency and Yale. I found that a member of the class of 1878, William Howard Taft, served one term in the White House as preparation for becoming a member of this faculty. And a graduate of 1804, John C. Calhoun, regarded the Vice Presidency, quite naturally, as too lowly a status for a Yale alumnus and became the only man in history to ever resign that office.

Calhoun in 1804 and Taft in 1878 graduated into a world very different from ours today. They and their contemporaries spent entire careers stretching over 40 years in grappling with a few dramatic issues on which the Nation was sharply and emotionally divided, issues that occupied the attention of a generation at a time: the national bank, the disposal of the public lands, nullification or union, freedom or slavery, gold or silver. Today these old sweeping issues very largely have disappeared. The central domestic issues of our time are more subtle and less simple. They relate not to basic clashes of philosophy or ideology but to ways and means of reaching common goals to research for sophisticated solutions to complex and obstinate issues. The world of Calhoun, the world of Taft had its own hard problems and notable challenges. But its problems are not our problems. Their age is not our age. As every past generation has had to disenthrall itself from an inheritance of truisms and stereotypes, so in our own time we must move on from the reassuring repetition of stale phrases to a new, difficult, but essential confrontation with reality.

For the great enemy of the truth is very often not the lie—deliberate, contrived, and dishonest—but the myth—persistent, persuasive, and unrealistic. Too often we hold fast to the cliches of our forebears. We subject all facts to a prefabricated set of interpretations. We enjoy the comfort of opinion without the discomfort of thought.

Mythology distracts us everywhere—in government as in business, in politics as in economics, in foreign affairs as in domestic affairs. But today I want to particularly consider the myth and reality in our national economy. In recent months many have come to feel, as I do, that the dialog between the parties—between business and government, between the government and the public—is clogged by illusion and platitude and fails to reflect the true realities of contemporary American society.

I speak of these matters here at Yale because of the self-evident truth that a great university is always enlisted against the spread of illusion and on the side of reality. No one has said it more clearly than your President Griswold: "Liberal learning is both a safeguard against false ideas of freedom and a source of true ones." Your role as university men, whatever your calling, will be to increase each new generation's grasp of its duties.

There are three great areas of our domestic affairs in which, today, there is a danger that illusion may prevent effective action. They are, first, the question of the size and the shape of government's responsibilities; second, the question of public fiscal policy; and third, the matter of confidence, business confidence or public confidence, or simply confidence in America. I want to talk about all three, and I want to talk about them carefully and dispassionately—and I emphasize that I am concerned here not with political debate but with finding ways to separate false problems from real ones.

If a contest in angry argument were forced upon it, no administration could shrink from response, and history does not suggest that American Presidents are totally without resources in an engagement forced upon them because of hostility in one sector of society. But in the wider national interest, we need not partisan wrangling but common concentration on common problems. I come here to this distinguished university to ask you to join in this great task.

Let us take first the question of the size and shape of government. The myth here is that government is big, and bad—and steadily getting bigger and worse. Obviously this myth has some excuse for existence. It is true that in recent history each new administration has spent much more money than its predecessor. Thus President Roosevelt outspent President Hoover, and with allowances for the special case of the Second World War, President Truman outspent President Roosevelt. Just to prove that this was not a partisan matter, President Eisenhower then outspent President Truman by the handsome figure of $182 billion. It is even possible, some think, that this trend may continue.

But does it follow from this that big government is growing relatively bigger? It does not—for the fact is for the last 15 years, the Federal Government—and also the Federal debt—and also the Federal bureaucracy—have grown less rapidly than the economy as a whole. If we leave defense and space expenditures aside, the Federal Government since the Second World War has expanded less than any other major sector of our national life—less than industry, less than commerce, less than agriculture, less than higher education, and very much less than the noise about big government.

The truth about big government is the truth about any other great activity—it is complex. Certainly it is true that size brings dangers—but it is also true that size can bring benefits. Here at Yale which has contributed so much to our national progress in science and medicine, it may be proper for me to mention one great and little noticed expansion of government which has brought strength to our whole society—the new role of our Federal Government as the major patron of research in science and in medicine. Few people realize that in 1961, in support of all university research in science and medicine, three dollars out of every four came from the Federal Government. I need hardly point out that this has taken place without undue enlargement of Government control—that American scientists remain second to none in their independence and in their individualism.

I am not suggesting that Federal expenditures cannot bring some measure of control. The whole thrust of Federal expenditures in agriculture have been related by purpose and design to control, as a means of dealing with the problems created by our farmers and our growing productivity. Each sector, my point is, of activity must be approached on its own merits and in terms of specific national needs. Generalities in regard to federal expenditures, therefore, can be misleading—each case, science, urban renewal, education, agriculture, natural resources, each case must be determined on its merits if we are to profit from our unrivaled ability to combine the strength of public and private purpose.

Next, let us turn to the problem of our fiscal policy. Here the myths are legion and the truth hard to find. But let me take as a prime example the problem of the Federal budget. We persist in measuring our federal fiscal integrity today by the conventional or administrative budget—with results which would be regarded as absurd in any business firm—in any country of Europe—or in any careful assessment of the reality of our national finances. The administrative budget has sound administrative uses. But for wider purposes it is less helpful. It omits our special trust funds and the effect that they have on our economy; it neglects changes in assets or inventories. It cannot tell a loan from a straight expenditure—and worst of all it cannot distinguish between operating expenditures and long term investments.

This budget, in relation to the great problems of Federal fiscal policy which are basic to our economy in 1962, is not simply irrelevant; it can be actively misleading. And yet there is a mythology that measures all of our national soundness or unsoundness on the single simple basis of this same annual administrative budget. If our Federal budget is to serve not the debate but the country, we must and will find ways of clarifying this area of discourse.

Still in the area of fiscal policy, let me say a word about deficits. The myth persists that Federal deficits create inflation and budget surpluses prevent it. Yet sizeable budget surpluses after the war did not prevent inflation, and persistent deficits for the last several years have not upset our basic price stability. Obviously deficits are sometimes dangerous—and so are surpluses. But honest assessment plainly requires a more sophisticated view than the old and automatic cliche that deficits automatically bring inflation.

There are myths also about our public debt. It is widely supposed that this debt is growing at a dangerously rapid rate. In fact, both the debt per person and the debt as a proportion of our gross national product have declined sharply since the Second World War. In absolute terms the national debt since the end of World War II has increased only 8 percent, while private debt was increasing 305 percent, and the debts of State and local governments—on whom people frequently suggest we should place additional burdens—the debts of State and local governments have increased 378 percent. Moreover, debts, public and private, are neither good nor bad, in and of themselves. Borrowing can lead to over-extension and collapse—but it can also lead to expansion and strength. There is no single, simple slogan in this field that we can trust.

Finally, I come to the problem of confidence. Confidence is a matter of myth and also a matter of truth—and this time let me take the truth of the matter first.

It is true—and of high importance—that the prosperity of this country depends on the assurance that all major elements within it will live up to their responsibilities. If business were to neglect its obligations to the public, if labor were blind to all public responsibility, above all, if government were to abandon its obvious—and statutory—duty of watchful concern for our economic health-if any of these things should happen, then confidence might well be weakened and the danger of stagnation would increase. This is the true issue of confidence.

But there is also the false issue—and its simplest form is the assertion that any and all unfavorable turns of the speculative wheel—however temporary and however plainly speculative in character—are the result of, and I quote, "a lack of confidence in the national administration." This I must tell you, while comforting, is not wholly true. Worse, it obscures the reality—which is also simple. The solid ground of mutual confidence is the necessary partnership of government with all of the sectors of our society in the steady quest for economic progress.

Corporate plans are not based on a political confidence in party leaders but on an economic confidence in the Nation's ability to invest and produce and consume. Business had full confidence in the administrations in power in 1929, 1954, 1958, and 1960—but this was not enough to prevent recession when business lacked full confidence in the economy. What matters is the capacity of the Nation as a whole to deal with its economic problems and its opportunities.

The stereotypes I have been discussing distract our attention and divide our effort. These stereotypes do our Nation a disservice, not just because they are exhausted and irrelevant, but above all because they are misleading—because they stand in the way of the solution of hard and complicated facts. It is not new that past debates should obscure present realities. But the damage of such a false dialogue is greater today than ever before simply because today the safety of all the world—the very future of freedom—depends as never before upon the sensible and clearheaded management of the domestic affairs of the United States.

The real issues of our time are rarely as dramatic as the issues of Calhoun. The differences today are usually matters of degree. And we cannot understand and attack our contemporary problems in 1962 if we are bound by traditional labels and worn-out slogans of an earlier era. But the unfortunate fact of the matter is that our rhetoric has not kept pace with the speed of social and economic change. Our political debates, our public discourse—on current domestic and economic issues—too often bear little or no relation to the actual problems the United States faces.

What is at stake in our economic decisions today is not some grand warfare of rival ideologies which will sweep the country with passion but the practical management of a modern economy. What we need is not labels and cliches but more basic discussion of the sophisticated and technical questions involved in keeping a great economic machinery moving ahead.

The national interest lies in high employment and steady expansion of output, in stable prices, and a strong dollar. The declaration of such an objective is easy; their attainment in an intricate and interdependent economy and world is a little more difficult. To attain them, we require not some automatic response but hard thought. Let me end by suggesting a few of the real questions on our national agenda.

First, how can our budget and tax policies supply adequate revenues and preserve our balance of payments position without slowing up our economic growth?

Two, how are we to set our interest rates and regulate the flow of money in ways which will stimulate the economy at home, without weakening the dollar abroad? Given the spectrum of our domestic and international responsibilities, what should be the mix between fiscal and monetary policy?

Let me give several examples from my experience of the complexity of these matters and how political labels and ideological approaches are irrelevant to the solution.

Last week, a distinguished graduate of this school, Senator Proxmire, of the class of 1938, who is ordinarily regarded as a liberal Democrat, suggested that we should follow in meeting our economic problems a stiff fiscal policy, with emphasis on budget balance and an easy monetary policy with low interest rates in order to keep our economy going. In the same week, the Bank for International Settlement in Basel, Switzerland, a conservative organization representing the central bankers of Europe suggested that the appropriate economic policy in the United States should be the very opposite; that we should follow a flexible budget policy, as in Europe, with deficits when the economy is down and a high monetary policy on interest rates, as in Europe, in order to control inflation and protect goals. Both may be right or wrong. It will depend on many different factors.

The point is that this is basically an administrative or executive problem in which political labels or cliches do not give us a solution.

A well-known business journal this morning, as I journeyed to New Haven, raised the prospects that a further budget deficit would bring inflation and encourage the flow of gold. We have had several budget deficits beginning with a $12 1/2 billion deficit in 1958, and it is true that in the fall of 1960 we had a gold dollar loss running at $5 billion annually. This would seem to prove the case that a deficit produces inflation and that we lose gold, yet there was no inflation following the deficit of 1958 nor has there been inflation since then.

Our wholesale price index since 1958 has remained completely level in spite of several deficits, because the loss of gold has been due to other reasons: price instability, relative interest rates, relative export-import balances, national security expenditures—all the rest.

Let me give you a third and final example. At the World Bank meeting in September, a number of American bankers attending predicted to their European colleagues that because of the fiscal 1962 budget deficit, there would be a strong inflationary pressure on the dollar and a loss of gold. Their predictions of inflation were shared by many in business and helped push the market up. The recent reality of non-inflation helped bring it down. We have had no inflation because we have had other factors in our economy that have contributed to price stability.

I do not suggest that the Government is right and they are wrong. The fact of the matter is in the Federal Reserve Board and in the administration this fall, a similar view was held by many well-informed and disinterested men that inflation was the major problem that we would face in the winter of 1962. But it was not. What I do suggest is that these problems are endlessly complicated and yet they go to the future of this country and its ability to prove to the world what we believe it must prove.

I am suggesting that the problems of fiscal and monetary policies in the sixties as opposed to the kinds of problems we faced in the thirties demand subtle challenges for which technical answers, not political answers, must be provided. These are matters upon which government and business may and in many cases will disagree. They are certainly matters that government and business should be discussing in the most dispassionate, and careful way if we to maintain the kind of vigorous upon which our country depends.

How can we develop and sustain strong and stable world markets for basic commodities without unfairness to the consumer and without undue stimulus to the producer? How can we generate the buying power which can consume what we produce on our farms and in our factories? How can we take advantage of the miracles of automation with the great demand that it will put upon highly skilled labor and yet offer employment to the half million of unskilled school dropouts each year who enter the labor market, eight million of them in the 1960's?

How do we eradicate the barriers which separate substantial minorities of our citizens from access to education and employment on equal terms with the rest?

How, in sum, can we make our free economy work at full capacity—that is, provide adequate profits for enterprise, adequate wages for labor, adequate utilization of plant, and opportunity for all?

These are the problems that we should be talking about—that the political parties and the various groups in our country should be discussing. They cannot be solved by incantations from the forgotten past. But the example of Western Europe shows that they are capable of solution—that governments, and many of them are conservative governments, prepared to face technical problems without ideological preconceptions, can coordinate the elements of a national economy and bring about growth and prosperity—a decade of it.

Some conversations I have heard in our own country sound like old records, long-playing, left over from the middle thirties. The debate of the thirties had its great significance and produced great results, but it took place in a different world with different needs and different tasks. It is our responsibility today to live in our own world, and to identify the needs and discharge the tasks of the 1960's.

If there is any current trend toward meeting present problems with old cliches, this is the moment to stop it—before it lands us all in a bog of sterile acrimony.

Discussion is essential; and I am hopeful that the debate of recent weeks, though up to now somewhat barren, may represent the start of a serious dialog of the kind which has led in Europe to such fruitful collaboration among all the elements of economic society and to a decade of unrivaled economic progress. But let us not engage in the wrong argument at the wrong time between the wrong people in the wrong country—while the real problems of our own time grow and multiply, fertilized by our neglect.

Nearly 150 years ago Thomas Jefferson wrote, "The new circumstances under which we are placed call for new words, new phrases, and for the transfer of old words to new objects." New words, new phrases, the transfer of old words to new objects-that is truer today than it was in the time of Jefferson, because the role of this country is so vastly more significant. There is a show in England called "Stop the World, I Want to Get Off." You have not chosen to exercise that option. You are part of the world and you must participate in these days of our years in the solution of the problems that pour upon us, requiring the most sophisticated and technical judgment; and as we work in consonance to meet the authentic problems of our times, we will generate a vision and an energy which will demonstrate anew to the world the superior vitality and the strength of the free society.

ADDRESS ON THE SPACE EFFORT

(SEPTEMBER 12, 1962)

President Pitzer, Mr. Vice President, Governor, Congressman Thomas, Senator Wiley, and Congressman Miller, Mr. Webb. Mr. Bell, scientists, distinguished guests, and ladies and gentlemen:

I appreciate your president having made me an honorary visiting professor, and I will assure you that my first lecture will be very brief.

I am delighted to be here and I'm particularly delighted to be here on this occasion.

We meet at a college noted for knowledge, in a city noted for progress, in a State noted for strength, and we stand in need of all three, for we meet in an hour of change and challenge, in a decade of hope and fear, in an age of both knowledge and ignorance. The greater our knowledge increases, the greater our ignorance unfolds.

Despite the striking fact that most of the scientists that the world has ever known are alive and working today, despite the fact that this Nation's own scientific manpower is doubling every 12 years in a rate of growth more than three times that of our population as a whole, despite that, the vast stretches of the unknown and the unanswered and the unfinished still far outstrip our collective comprehension.

No man can fully grasp how far and how fast we have come, but condense, if you will, the 50,000 years of man's recorded history in a time span of but a half-century. Stated in these terms, we know very little about the first 40 years, except at the end of them advanced man had learned to use the skins of animals to cover them. Then about 10 years ago, under this standard, man emerged from his caves to construct other kinds of shelter. Only 5 years ago man learned to write and use a cart with wheels. Christianity began less than 2 years ago. The printing press came this year, and then less than 2 months ago, during this whole 50-year span of human history, the steam engine provided a new source of power.

Newton explored the meaning of gravity. Last month electric lights and telephones and automobiles and airplanes became available. Only last week did we develop penicillin and television and nuclear power, and now if America's new spacecraft succeeds in reaching Venus, we will have literally reached the stars before midnight tonight.

This is a breathtaking pace, and such a pace cannot help but create new ills as it dispels old, new ignorance, new problems, new dangers. Surely the opening vistas of space promise high costs and hardships, as well as high reward.

So it is not surprising that some would have us stay where we are a little longer to rest, to wait. But this city of Houston, this State of Texas, this country of the United States was not built by those who waited and rested and wished to look behind them. This country was conquered by those who moved forward—and so will space.

William Bradford, speaking in 1630 of the founding of the Plymouth Bay Colony, said that all great and honorable actions are accompanied with great difficulties, and both must be enterprised and overcome with answerable courage.

If this capsule history of our progress teaches us anything, it is that man, in his quest for knowledge and progress, is determined and cannot be deterred. The exploration of space will go ahead, whether we join in it or not, and it is one of the great adventures of all time, and no nation which expects to be the leader of other nations can expect to stay behind in this race for space.

Those who came before us made certain that this country rode the first waves of the industrial revolutions, the first waves of modern invention, and the first wave of nuclear power, and this generation does not intend to founder in the backwash of the coming age of space. We mean to be a part of it—we mean to lead it. For the eyes of the world now look into space, to the moon and to the planets beyond, and we have vowed that we shall not see it governed by a hostile flag of conquest, but by a banner of freedom and peace. We have vowed that we shall not see space filled with weapons of mass destruction, but with instruments of knowledge and understanding.

Yet the vows of this Nation can only be fulfilled if we in this Nation are first, and, therefore, we intend to be first. In short, our leadership in science and in industry, our hopes for peace and security, our obligations to ourselves as well as others, all require us to make this effort, to solve these mysteries, to solve them for the good of all men, and to become the world's leading space-faring nation.

We set sail on this new sea because there is new knowledge to be gained, and new rights to be won, and they must be won and used for the progress of all people. For space science, like nuclear science and all technology, has no conscience of its own. Whether it will become a force for good or ill depends on man, and only if the United States occupies a position of pre-eminence can we help decide whether this new ocean will be a sea of peace or a new terrifying theater of war. I do not say that we should or will go unprotected against the hostile misuse of space any more than we go unprotected against the hostile use of land or sea, but I do say that space can be explored and mastered without feeding the fires of war, without repeating the mistakes that man has made in extending his writ around this globe of ours.

There is no strife, no prejudice, no national conflict in outer space as yet. Its hazards are hostile to us all. Its conquest deserves the best of all mankind, and its opportunity for peaceful cooperation may never come again. But why, some say, the moon? Why choose this as our goal? And they may well ask why climb the highest mountain. Why, 35 years ago, fly the Atlantic? Why does Rice play Texas?

We choose to go to the moon. We choose to go to the moon in this decade and do the other things, not because they are easy, but because they are hard, because that goal will serve to organize and measure the best of our energies and skills, because that challenge is one that we are willing to accept, one we are unwilling to postpone, and one which we intend to win, and the others, too.

It is for these reasons that I regard the decision last year to shift our efforts in space from low to high gear as among the most important decisions that will be made during my incumbency in the Office of the Presidency.

In the last 24 hours we have seen facilities now being created for the greatest and most complex exploration in man's history. We have felt the ground shake and the air shattered by the testing of a Saturn C-1 booster rocket, many times as powerful as the Atlas which launched John Glenn, generating power equivalent to 10,000 automobiles with their accelerators on the floor. We have seen the site where five F-1 rocket engines, each one as powerful as all eight engines of the Saturn combined, will be clustered together to make the advanced Saturn missile, assembled in a new building to be built at Cape Canaveral as tall as a 48-story structure, as wide as a city block, and as long as two lengths of this field.

Within these last 19 months at least 45 satellites have circled the earth. Some 40 of them were "made in the United States of America" and they were far more sophisticated and supplied far more knowledge to the people of the world than those of the Soviet Union.

The Mariner spacecraft now on its way to Venus is the most intricate instrument in the history of space science. The accuracy of that shot is comparable to firing a missile from Cape Canaveral and dropping it in this stadium between the 40-yard lines.

Transit satellites are helping our ships at sea to steer a safer course. Tiros satellites have given us unprecedented warnings of hurricanes and storms, and will do the same for forest fires and icebergs.

We have had our failures, but so have others, even if they do not admit them. And they may be less public.

To be sure, we are behind, and will be behind for some time in manned flight. But we do not intend to stay behind, and in this decade we shall make up and move ahead.

The growth of our science and education will be enriched by new knowledge of our universe and environment, by new techniques of learning and mapping and observation, by new tools and computers for industry, medicine, the home as well as the school. Technical institutions, such as Rice, will reap the harvest of these gains.

And finally, the space effort itself, while still in its infancy, has already created a great number of new companies, and tens of thousands of new jobs. Space and related industries are generating new demands in investment and skilled personnel, and this city and this State, and this region, will share greatly in this growth. What was once the furthest outpost on the old frontier of the West will be the furthest outpost on the new frontier of science and space. Houston, your City of Houston, with its Manned Spacecraft Center, will become the heart of a large scientific and engineering community. During the next 5 years the National Aeronautics and Space Administration expects to double the number of scientists and engineers in this area, to increase its outlays for salaries and expenses to $60 million a year; to invest some $200 million in plant and laboratory facilities; and to direct or contract for new space efforts over $1 billion from this Center in this City.

To be sure, all this costs us all a good deal of money. This year's space budget is three times what it was in January 1961, and it is greater than the space budget of the previous 8 years combined. That budget now stands at $5,400 million a year—a staggering sum, though somewhat less than we pay for cigarettes and cigars every year. Space expenditures will soon rise some more, from 40 cents per person per week to more than 50 cents a week for every man, woman, and child in the United States, for we have given this program a high national priority—even though I realize that this is in some measure an act of faith and vision, for we do not now know what benefits await us. But if I were to say, my fellow citizens, that we shall send to the moon, 240,000 miles away from the control station in Houston, a giant rocket more than 300 feet tall, the length of this football field, made of new metal alloys, some of which have not yet been invented, capable of standing heat and stresses several times more than have ever been experienced, fitted together with a precision better than the finest watch, carrying all the equipment needed for propulsion, guidance, control, communications, food and survival, on an untried mission, to an unknown celestial body, and then return it safely to earth, reentering the atmosphere at speeds of over 25,000 miles per hour, causing heat about half that of the temperature of the sun— almost as hot as it is here today—and do all this, and do it right, and do it first before this decade is out, then we must be bold.

I'm the one who is doing all the work, so we just want you to stay cool for a minute. [Laughter]

However, I think we're going to do it, and I think that we must pay what needs to be paid. I don't think we ought to waste any money, but I think we ought to do the job. And this will be done in the decade of the sixties. It may be done while some of you are still here at school at this college and university. It will be done during the terms of office of some of the people who sit here on this platform. But it will be done. And it will be done before the end of this decade.

I am delighted that this university is playing a part in putting a man on the moon as part of a great national effort of the United States of America.

Many years ago the great British explorer George Mallory, who was to die on Mount Everest, was asked why did he want to climb it. He said, "Because it is there."

Well, space is there, and we're going to climb it, and the moon and the planets are there, and new hopes for knowledge and peace are there. And, therefore, as we set sail we ask God's blessing on the most hazardous and dangerous and greatest adventure on which man has ever embarked.

Thank you.

ADDRESS ON THE SITUATION AT THE UNIVERSITY OF MISSISSIPPI

(SEPTEMBER 30, 1962)

The orders of the court in the case of Meredith versus Fair are beginning to be carried out. Mr. James Meredith is now in residence on the campus of the University of Mississippi.

This has been accomplished thus far without the use of National Guard or other troops. And it is to be hoped that the law enforcement officers of the State of Mississippi and the Federal marshals will continue to be sufficient in the future.

All students, members of the faculty, and public officials in both Mississippi and the Nation will be able, it is hoped, to return to their normal activities with full confidence in the integrity of American law.

This is as it should be, for our Nation is founded on the principle that observance of the law is the eternal safeguard of liberty and defiance of the law is the surest road to tyranny. The law which we obey includes the final rulings of the courts, as well as the enactment's of our legislative bodies. Even among law-abiding men few laws are universally loved, but they are uniformly respected and not resisted.

Americans are free, in short, to disagree with the law but not to disobey it. For in a government of laws and not of men, no man, however prominent or powerful, and no mob, however unruly or boisterous, is entitled to defy a court of law. If this country should ever reach the point where any man or group of men by force or threat of force could long defy the commands of our court and our Constitution, then no law would stand free from doubt, no judge would be sure of his writ, and no citizen would be safe from his neighbors.

In this case in which the United States Government was not until recently involved, Mr. Meredith brought a private suit in Federal court against those who were excluding him from the University. A series of Federal courts all the way to the Supreme Court repeatedly ordered Mr. Meredith's admission to the University. When those orders were defied, and those who sought to implement them threatened with arrest and violence, the United States Court of Appeals consisting of Chief Judge Tuttle of Georgia, Judge Hutcheson of Texas, Judge Rives of Alabama, Judge Jones of Florida, Judge Brown of Texas, Judge Wisdom of Louisiana, Judge Gewin of Alabama, and Judge Bell of Georgia, made clear the fact that the enforcement of its order had become an obligation of the United States Government. Even though this Government had not originally been a party to the case, my responsibility as President was therefore inescapable. I accept it. My obligation under the Constitution and the statutes of the United States was and is to implement the orders of the court with whatever means are necessary, and with as little force and civil disorder as the circumstances permit.

It was for this reason that I federalized the Mississippi National Guard as the most appropriate instrument, should any be needed, to preserve law and order while United States marshals carried out the orders of the court and prepared to back them up with whatever other civil or military enforcement might have been required.

I deeply regret the fact that any action by the executive branch was necessary in this case, but all other avenues and alternatives, including persuasion and conciliation, had been tried and exhausted. Had the police powers of Mississippi been used to support the orders of the court, instead of deliberately and unlawfully blocking them, had the University of Mississippi fulfilled its standard of excellence by quietly admitting this applicant ' in conformity with what so many other southern State universities have done for so many years, a peaceable and sensible solution would have been possible without any Federal intervention.

This Nation is proud of the many instances in which Governors, educators, and everyday citizens from the South have shown to the world the gains that can be made by persuasion and good will in a society ruled by law. Specifically, I would like to take this occasion to express the thanks of this Nation to those southerners who have contributed to the progress of our democratic development in the entrance of students regardless of race to such great institutions as the State-supported universities of Virginia, North Carolina, Georgia, Florida, Texas, Louisiana, Tennessee, Arkansas, and Kentucky.

I recognize that the present period of transition and adjustment in our

Nation's Southland is a hard one for many people. Neither Mississippi nor any other southern State deserves to be charged with all the accumulated wrongs of the last 100 years of race relations. To the extent that there has been failure, the responsibility for that failure must be shared by us all, by every State, by every citizen.

Mississippi and her University, moreover, are noted for their courage, for their contribution of talent and thought to the affairs of this Nation. This is the State of Lucius Lamar and many others who have placed the national good ahead of sectional interest. This is the State which had four Medal of Honor winners in the Korean war alone. In fact, the Guard unit federalized this morning, early, is part of the 155th Infantry, one of the 10 oldest regiments in the Union and one of the most decorated for sacrifice and bravery in 6 wars.

In 1945 a Mississippi sergeant, Jake Lindsey, was honored by an unusual joint session of the Congress. I close therefore with this appeal to the students of the University, the people who are most concerned.

You have a great tradition to uphold, a tradition of honor and courage won on the field of battle and on the gridiron as well as the University campus. You have a new opportunity to show that you are men of patriotism and integrity. For the most effective means of upholding the law is not the State policeman or the marshals or the National Guard. It is you. It lies in your courage to accept those laws with which you disagree as well as those with which you agree. The eyes of the Nation and of all the world are upon you and upon all of us, and the honor of your University and State are in the balance. I am certain that the great majority of the students will uphold that honor.

There is in short no reason why the books on this case cannot now be quickly and quietly closed in the manner directed by the court. Let us preserve both the law and the peace and then healing those wounds that are within we can turn to the greater crises that are without and stand united as one people in our pledge to man's freedom. Thank you and good night.

ADDRESS ON THE BUILDUP OF ARMS IN CUBA

(OCTOBER 22, 1962)

Good evening, my fellow citizens:

This Government, as promised, has maintained the closest surveillance of the Soviet military buildup on the island of Cuba. Within the past week, unmistakable evidence has established the fact that a series of offensive missile sites is now in preparation on that imprisoned island. The purpose of these bases can be none other than to provide a nuclear strike capability against the Western Hemisphere.

Upon receiving the first preliminary hard information of this nature last Tuesday morning at 9 a.m., I directed that our surveillance be stepped up. And having now confirmed and completed our evaluation of the evidence and our decision on a course of action, this Government feels obliged to report this new crisis to you in fullest detail.

The characteristics of these new missile sites indicate two distinct types of installations. Several of them include medium range ballistic missiles, capable of carrying a nuclear warhead for a distance of more than 1,000 nautical miles. Each of these missiles, in short, is capable of striking Washington, D.C., the Panama Canal, Cape Canaveral, Mexico City, or any other city in the southeastern part of the United States, in Central America, or in the Caribbean area.

Additional sites not yet completed appear to be designed for intermediate range bailistic missiles--capable of traveling more than twice as far--and thus capable of striking most of the major cities in the Western Hemisphere, ranging as far north as Hudson Bay, Canada, and as far south as Lima, Peru. In addition, jet bombers, capable of carrying nuclear weapons, are now being uncrated and assembled in Cuba, while the necessary air bases are being prepared.

This urgent transformation of Cuba into an important strategic base--by the presence of these large, long-range, and clearly offensive weapons of sudden mass destruction-constitutes an explicit threat to the peace and security of all the Americas, in flagrant and deliberate defiance of the Rio Pact of 1947, the traditions of this Nation and hemisphere, the joint resolution of the 87th Congress, the Charter of the United Nations, and my own public warnings to the Soviets on September 4 and 13. This action also contradicts the repeated assurances of Soviet spokesmen, both publicly and privately delivered, that the arms buildup in Cuba would retain its original defensive character, and that the Soviet Union had no need or desire to station strategic missiles on the territory of any other nation.

The size of this undertaking makes clear that it has been planned for some months. ? Yet only last month, after I had made clear the distinction between any introduction of ground-to-ground missiles and the existence of defensive antiaircraft missiles, the Soviet Government publicly stated on September 11 that, and I quote, "the armaments and military equipment sent to Cuba are designed exclusively for defensive purposes," that, and I quote the Soviet Government, "there is no need for the Soviet Government to shift its weapons . . . For a retaliatory blow to any other country, for instance Cuba," and that, and I quote their government, "the Soviet Union has so powerful rockets to carry these nuclear warheads that there is no need to search for sites for them beyond the boundaries of the Soviet Union." That statement was false.

Only last Thursday, as evidence of this rapid offensive buildup was already in my hand, Soviet Foreign Minister Gromyko told me in my office that he was instructed to make it clear once again, as he said his government had already done, that Soviet assistance to Cuba, and I quote, "pursued solely the purpose of contributing to the defense capabilities of Cuba," that, and I quote him, "training by Soviet specialists of Cuban nationals in handling defensive armaments was by no means offensive, and if it were otherwise," Mr. Gromyko went on, "the Soviet Government would never become involved in rendering such assistance." That statement also was false.

Neither the United States of America nor the world community of nations can tolerate deliberate deception and offensive threats on the part of any nation, large or small. We no longer live in a world where only the actual firing of weapons represents a sufficient challenge to a nation's security to constitute maximum peril. Nuclear weapons are so destructive and ballistic missiles are so swift, that any substantially increased possibility of their use or any sudden change in their deployment may well be regarded as a definite threat to peace.

For many years, both the Soviet Union and the United States, recognizing this fact, have deployed strategic nuclear weapons with great care, never upsetting the precarious status quo which insured that these weapons would not be used in the absence of some vital challenge. Our own strategic missiles have never been transferred to the territory of any other nation under a cloak of secrecy and deception; and our history--unlike that of the Soviets since the end of World War II--demonstrates that we have no desire to dominate or conquer any other nation or impose our system upon its people. Nevertheless, American citizens have become adjusted to living daily on the bull's-eye of Soviet missiles located inside the U.S.S.R. or in submarines.

In that sense, missiles in Cuba add to an already clear and present danger--although it should be noted the nations of Latin America have never previously been subjected to a potential nuclear threat.

But this secret, swift, and extraordinary buildup of Communist missiles--in an area well known to have a special and historical relationship to the United States and the nations of the Western Hemisphere, in violation of Soviet assurances, and in defiance of American and hemispheric policy--this sudden, clandestine decision to station strategic weapons for the first time outside of Soviet soil--is a deliberately provocative and unjustified change in the status quo which cannot be accepted by this country, if our courage and our commitments are ever to be trusted again by either friend or foe.

The 1930's taught us a clear lesson: aggressive conduct, if allowed to go unchecked and unchallenged, ultimately leads to war. This nation is opposed to war. We are also true to our word. Our unswerving objective, therefore, must be to prevent the use of these missiles against this or any other country, and to secure their withdrawal or elimination from the Western Hemisphere.

Our policy has been one of patience and restraint, as befits a peaceful and powerful nation, which leads a worldwide alliance. We have been determined not to be diverted from our central concerns by mere irritants and fanatics. But now further action is required-and it is under way; and these actions may only be the beginning. We will not prematurely or unnecessarily risk the costs of worldwide nuclear war in which even the fruits of victory would be ashes in our mouth--but neither will we shrink from that risk at any time it must be faced.

Acting, therefore, in the defense of our own security and of the entire

Western Hemisphere, and under the authority entrusted to me by the Constitution as endorsed by the resolution of the Congress, I have directed that the following initial steps be taken immediately:

First: To halt this offensive buildup, a strict quarantine on all offensive military equipment under shipment to Cuba is being initiated. All ships of any kind bound for Cuba from whatever nation or port will, if found to contain cargoes of offensive weapons, be turned back. This quarantine will be extended, if needed, to other types of cargo and carriers. We are not at this time, however, denying the necessities of life as the Soviets attempted to do in their Berlin blockade of 1948.

Second: I have directed the continued and increased close surveillance of Cuba and its military buildup. The foreign ministers of the OAS, in their communique of October 6, rejected secrecy on such matters in this hemisphere. Should these offensive military preparations continue, thus increasing the threat to the hemisphere, further action will be justified. I have directed the Armed Forces to prepare for any eventualities; and I trust that in the interest of both the Cuban people and the Soviet technicians at the sites, the hazards to all concerned of continuing this threat will be recognized.

Third: It shall be the policy of this Nation to regard any nuclear missile launched from Cuba against any nation in the Western Hemisphere as an attack by the Soviet Union on the United States, requiring a full retaliatory response upon the Soviet Union.

Fourth: As a necessary military precaution, I have reinforced our base at Guantanamo, evacuated today the dependents of our personnel there, and ordered additional military units to be on a standby alert basis.

Fifth: We are calling tonight for an immediate meeting of the Organ of Consultation under the Organization of American States, to consider this threat to hemispheric security and to invoke articles 6 and 8 of the Rio Treaty in support of all necessary action. The United Nations Charter allows for regional security arrangements--and the nations of this hemisphere decided long ago against the military presence of outside powers. Our other allies around the world have also been alerted.

Sixth: Under the Charter of the United Nations, we are asking tonight that an emergency meeting of the Security Council be convoked without delay to take action against this latest Soviet threat to world peace. Our resolution will call for the prompt dismantling and withdrawal of all offensive weapons in Cuba, under the supervision of U.N. observers, before the quarantine can be lifted.

Seventh and finally: I call upon Chairman Khrushchev to halt and eliminate this clandestine, reckless, and provocative threat to world peace and to stable relations between our two nations. I call upon him further to abandon this course of world domination, and to join in an historic effort to end the perilous arms race and to transform the history of man. He has an opportunity now to move the world back from the abyss of destruction--by returning to his government's own words that it had no need to station missiles outside its own territory, and withdrawing these weapons from Cuba by refraining from any action which will widen or deepen the present crisis--and then by participating in a search for peaceful and permanent solutions.

This Nation is prepared to present its case against the Soviet threat to peace, and our own proposals for a peaceful world, at any time and in any forum--in the OAS, in the United Nations, or in any other meeting that could be useful--without limiting our freedom of action. We have in the past made strenuous efforts to limit the spread of nuclear weapons. We have proposed the elimination of all arms and military bases in a fair and effective disarmament treaty. We are prepared to discuss new proposals for the removal of tensions on both sides--including the possibilities of a genuinely independent Cuba, free to determine its own destiny. We have no wish to war with the Soviet Union-for we are a peaceful people who desire to live in peace with all other peoples.

But it is difficult to settle or even discuss these problems in an atmosphere of intimidation. That is why this latest Soviet threat--or any other threat which is made either independently or in response to our actions this week--must and will be met with determination. Any hostile move anywhere in the world against the safety and freedom of peoples to whom we are committed-including in particular the brave people of West Berlin--will be met by whatever action is needed.

Finally, I want to say a few words to the captive people of Cuba, to whom this speech is being directly carried by special radio facilities. I speak to you as a friend, as one who knows of your deep attachment to your fatherland, as one who shares your aspirations for liberty and justice for all. And I have watched and the American people have watched with deep sorrow how your nationalist revolution was betrayed--and how your fatherland fell under foreign domination. Now your leaders are no longer Cuban leaders inspired by Cuban ideals. They are puppets and agents of an international conspiracy which has turned Cuba against your friends and neighbors in the Americas--and turned it into the first Latin American country to become a target for nuclear war--the first Latin American country to have these weapons on its soil.

These new weapons are not in your interest. They contribute nothing to your peace and well-being. They can only undermine it. But this country has no wish to cause you to suffer or to impose any system upon you. We know that your lives and land are being used as pawns by those who deny your freedom.

Many times in the past, the Cuban people have risen to throw out tyrants who destroyed their liberty. And I have no doubt that most Cubans today look forward to the time when they will be truly free--free from foreign domination, free to choose their own leaders, free to select their own system, free to own their own land, free to speak and write and worship without fear or degradation. And then shall Cuba be welcomed back to the society of free nations and to the associations of this hemisphere.

My fellow citizens: let no one doubt that this is a difficult and dangerous effort on which we have set out. No one can foresee precisely what course it will take or what costs or casualties will be incurred. Many months of sacrifice and self-discipline lie ahead--months in which both our patience and our will be tested--months in which many threats and denunciations will keep us aware of our dangers. But the greatest danger of all would be to do nothing.

The path we have chosen for the present is full of hazards, as all paths are--but it is the one most consistent with our character and courage as a nation and our commitments around the world. The cost of freedom is always high--but Americans have always paid it. And one path we shall never choose, and that is the path of surrender or submission.

Our goal is not the victory of might, but the vindication of right--not peace at the expense of freedom, but both peace and freedom, here in this hemisphere, and, we hope, around the world. God willing, that goal will be achieved.

Thank you and good night.

STATE OF THE UNION ADDRESS

(JANUARY 14, 1963)

Mr. Vice President, Mr. Speaker, Members of the 88th Congress:

I congratulate you all--not merely on your electoral victory but on your selected role in history. For you and I are privileged to serve the great Republic in what could be the most decisive decade in its long history. The choices we make, for good or ill, may well shape the state of the Union for generations yet to come.

Little more than 100 weeks ago I assumed the office of President of the United States. In seeking the help of the Congress and our countrymen, I pledged no easy answers. I pledged--and asked--only toil and dedication. These the Congress and the people have given in good measure. And today, having witnessed in recent months a heightened respect for our national purpose and power--having seen the courageous calm of a united people in a perilous hour-and having observed a steady improvement in the opportunities and well-being of our citizens--I can report to you that the state of this old but youthful Union, in the 175th year of its life, is good.

In the world beyond our borders, steady progress has been made in building a world of order. The people of West Berlin remain both free and secure. A settlement, though still precarious, has been reached in Laos. The spearpoint of aggression has been blunted in Viet-Nam. The end of agony may be in sight in the Congo. The doctrine of troika is dead. And, while danger continues, a deadly threat has been removed in Cuba.

At home, the recession is behind us. Well over a million more men and women are working today than were working 2 years ago. The average factory workweek is once again more than 40 hours; our industries are turning out more goods than ever before; and more than half of the manufacturing capacity that lay silent and wasted 100 weeks ago is humming with activity.

In short, both at home and abroad, there may now be a temptation to relax. For the road has been long, the burden heavy, and the pace consistently urgent.

But we cannot be satisfied to rest here. This is the side of the hill, not the top. The mere absence of war is not peace. The mere absence of recession is not growth. We have made a beginning--but we have only begun.

Now the time has come to make the most of our gains--to translate the renewal of our national strength into the achievement of our national purpose.

America has enjoyed 22 months of uninterrupted economic recovery. But recovery is not enough. If we are to prevail in the long run, we must expand the long-run strength of our economy. We must move along the path to a higher rate of growth and full employment.

For this would mean tens of billions of dollars more each year in production, profits, wages, and public revenues. It would mean an end to the persistent slack which has kept our unemployment at or above 5 percent for 61 out of the past 62 months--and an end to the growing pressures for such restrictive measures as the 35-hour week, which alone could increase hourly labor costs by as much as 14 percent, start a new wage-price spiral of inflation, and undercut our efforts to compete with other nations.

To achieve these greater gains, one step, above all, is essential--the enactment this year of a substantial reduction and revision in Federal income taxes.

For it is increasingly clear--to those in Government, business, and labor who are responsible for our economy's success--that our obsolete tax system exerts too heavy a drag on private purchasing power, profits, and employment. Designed to check inflation in earlier years, it now checks growth instead. It discourages extra effort and risk. It distorts the use of resources. It invites recurrent recessions, depresses our Federal revenues, and causes chronic budget deficits.

Now, when the inflationary pressures of the war and the post-war years no longer threaten, and the dollar commands new respect-now, when no military crisis strains our resources--now is the time to act. We cannot afford to be timid or slow. For this is the most urgent task confronting the

Congress in 1963.

In an early message, I shall propose a permanent reduction in tax rates which will lower liabilities by $13.5 billion. Of this, $11 billion results from reducing individual tax rates, which now range between 20 and 91 percent, to a more sensible range of 14 to 65 percent, with a split in the present first bracket. Two and one-half billion dollars results from reducing corporate tax rates, from 52 percent--which gives the Government today a majority interest in profits-to the permanent pre-Korean level of 47 percent. This is in addition to the more than $2 billion cut in corporate tax liabilities resulting from last year's investment credit and depreciation reform.

To achieve this reduction within the limits of a manageable budgetary deficit, I urge: first, that these cuts be phased over 3 calendar years, beginning in 1963 with a cut of some $6 billion at annual rates; second, that these reductions be coupled with selected structural changes, beginning in 1964, which will broaden the tax base, end unfair or unnecessary preferences, remove or lighten certain hardships, and in the net offset some $3.5 billion of the revenue loss; and third, that budgetary receipts at the outset be increased by $1.5 billion a year, without any change in tax liabilities, by gradually shifting the tax payments of large corporations to a . more current time schedule. This combined program, by increasing the amount of our national income, will in time result in still higher Federal revenues. It is a fiscally responsible program--the surest and the soundest way of achieving in time a balanced budget in a balanced full employment economy.

This net reduction in tax liabilities of $10 billion will increase the purchasing power of American families and business enterprises in every tax bracket, with greatest increase going to our low-income consumers. It will, in addition, encourage the initiative and risk-taking on which our free system depends--induce more investment, production, and capacity use--help provide the 2 million new jobs we need every year--and reinforce the American principle of additional reward for additional effort.

I do not say that a measure for tax reduction and reform is the only way to achieve these goals.

--No doubt a massive increase in Federal spending could also create jobs and growth-but, in today's setting, private consumers, employers, and investors should be given a full opportunity first.

--No doubt a temporary tax cut could provide a spur to our economy--

but a long run problem compels a long-run solution.

--No doubt a reduction in either individual or corporation taxes alone would be of great help--but corporations need customers and job seekers need jobs.

--No doubt tax reduction without reform would sound simpler and more attractive to many--but our growth is also hampered by a host of tax inequities and special preferences which have distorted the flow of investment.

--And, finally, there are no doubt some who would prefer to put off a tax cut in the hope that ultimately an end to the cold war would make possible an equivalent cut in expenditures-but that end is not in view and to wait for it would be costly and self-defeating.

In submitting a tax program which will, of course, temporarily increase the deficit but can ultimately end it--and in recognition of the need to control expenditures--I will shortly submit a fiscal 1964 administrative budget which, while allowing for needed rises in defense, space, and fixed interest charges, holds total expenditures for all other purposes below this year's level.

This requires the reduction or postponement of many desirable programs, the absorption of a large part of last year's Federal pay raise through personnel and other economies, the termination of certain installations and projects, and the substitution in several programs of private for public credit. But I am convinced that the enactment this year of tax reduction and tax reform overshadows all other domestic problems in this Congress. For we cannot for long lead the cause of peace and freedom, if we ever cease to set the pace here at home.

Tax reduction alone, however, is not enough to strengthen our society, to provide opportunities for the four million Americans who are born every year, to improve the lives of 32 million Americans who live on the outskirts of poverty.

The quality of American life must keep pace with the quantity of American goods.

This country cannot afford to be materially rich and spiritually poor.

Therefore, by holding down the budgetary cost of existing programs to keep within the limitations I have set, it is both possible and imperative to adopt other new measures that we cannot afford to postpone.

These measures are based on a series of fundamental premises, grouped under four related headings:

First, we need to strengthen our Nation by investing in our youth:

--The future of any country which is dependent upon the will and wisdom of its citizens is damaged, and irreparably damaged, whenever any of its children is not educated to the full extent of his talent, from grade school through graduate school. Today, an estimated 4 out of every 10 students in the 5th grade will not even finish high school--and that is a waste we cannot afford.

--In addition, there is no reason why one million young Americans, out of school and out of work, should all remain unwanted and often untrained on our city streets when their energies can be put to good use.

--Finally, the overseas success of our Peace Corps volunteers, most of them young men and women carrying skills and ideas to needy people, suggests the merit of a similar corps serving our own community needs: in mental hospitals, on Indian reservations, in centers for the aged or for young delinquents, in schools for the illiterate or the handicapped. As the idealism of our youth has served world peace, so can it serve the domestic tranquility.

Second, we need to strengthen our Nation by safeguarding its health:

--Our working men and women, instead of being forced to beg for help from public charity once they are old and ill, should start contributing now to their own retirement health program through the Social Security System.

--Moreover, all our miracles of medical research will count for little if we cannot reverse the growing nationwide shortage of doctors, dentists, and nurses, and the widespread shortages of nursing homes and modern urban hospital facilities. Merely to keep the present ratio of doctors and dentists from declining any further, we must over the next 10 years increase the capacity of our medical schools by 50 percent and our dental schools by 100 percent.

--Finally, and of deep concern, I believe that the abandonment of the mentally ill and the mentally retarded to the grim mercy of custodial institutions too often inflicts on them and on their families a needless cruelty which this Nation should not endure. The incidence of mental retardation in this country is three times as high as that of Sweden, for example--and that figure can and must be reduced.

Third, we need to strengthen our Nation by protecting the basic rights of its citizens:

--The right to competent counsel must be assured to every man accused of crime in Federal court, regardless of his means.

--And the most precious and powerful right in the world, the right to vote in a free American election, must not be denied to any citizen on grounds of his race or color. I wish that all qualified Americans permitted to vote were willing to vote, but surely in this centennial year of Emancipation all those who are willing to vote should always be permitted.

Fourth, we need to strengthen our Nation by making the best and the most economical use of its resources and facilities:

--Our economic health depends on healthy transportation arteries; and I believe the way to a more modern, economical choice of national transportation service is through increased competition and decreased regulation. Local mass transit, faring even worse, is as essential a community service as hospitals and highways. Nearly three-fourths of our citizens live in urban areas, which occupy only 2 percent of our land-and if local transit is to survive and relieve the congestion of these cities, it needs Federal stimulation and assistance.

--Next, this Government is in the storage and stockpile business to the melancholy tune of more than $ 16 billion. We must continue to support farm income, but we should not pile more farm surpluses on top of the $7.5 billion we already own. We must maintain a stockpile of strategic materials, but the $8.5 billion we have acquired--for reasons both good and bad--is much more than we need; and we should be empowered to dispose of the excess in ways which will not cause market disruption.

--Finally, our already overcrowded national parks and recreation areas will have twice as many visitors 10 years from now as they do today. If we do not plan today for the future growth of these and other great natural assets--not only parks and forests but wildlife and wilderness preserves, and water projects of all kinds--our children and their children will be poorer in every sense of the word.

These are not domestic concerns alone. For upon our achievement of greater vitality and strength here at home hang our fate and future in the world: our ability to sustain and supply the security of free men and nations, our ability to command their respect for our leadership, our ability to expand our trade without threat to our balance of payments, and our ability to adjust to the changing demands of cold war competition and challenge.

We shall be judged more by what we do at home than by what we preach abroad. Nothing we could do to help the developing countries would help them half as much as a booming U.S. economy. And nothing our opponents could do to encourage their own ambitions would encourage them half as much as a chronic lagging U.S. economy. These domestic tasks do not divert energy from our security--they provide the very foundation for freedom's survival and success,

Turning to the world outside, it was only a few years ago--in Southeast Asia, Africa, Eastern Europe, Latin America, even outer space--that communism sought to convey the image of a unified, confident, and expanding empire, closing in on a sluggish America and a free world in disarray. But few people would hold to that picture today.

In these past months we have reaffirmed the scientific and military superiority of freedom. We have doubled our efforts in space, to assure us of being first in the future. We have undertaken the most far-reaching defense improvements in the peacetime history of this country. And we have maintained the frontiers of freedom from Viet-Nam to West Berlin.

But complacency or self-congratulation can imperil our security as much as the weapons of tyranny. A moment of pause is not a promise of peace. Dangerous problems remain from Cuba to the South China Sea. The world's prognosis prescribes, in short, not a year's vacation for us, but a year of obligation and opportunity.

Four special avenues of opportunity stand out: the Atlantic Alliance, the developing nations, the new Sino-Soviet difficulties, and the search for worldwide peace.

First, how fares the grand alliance? Free Europe is entering into a new phase of its long and brilliant history. The era of colonial expansion has passed; the era of national rivalries is fading; and a new era of interdependence and unity is taking shape. Defying the old prophecies of Marx, consenting to what no conqueror could ever compel, the free nations of Europe are moving toward a unity of purpose and power and policy in every sphere of activity.

For 17 years this movement has had our consistent support, both political and economic. Far from resenting the new Europe, we regard her as a welcome partner, not a rival. For the road to world peace and freedom is still long, and there are burdens which only full partners can share--in supporting the common defense, in expanding world trade, in aligning our balance of payments, in aiding the emergent nations, in concerting political and economic policies, and in welcoming to our common effort other industrialized nations, notably Japan, whose remarkable economic and political development of the 1950's permits it now to play on the world scene a major constructive role.

No doubt differences of opinion will continue to get more attention than agreements on action, as Europe moves from independence to more formal interdependence. But these are honest differences among honorable associates--more real and frequent, in fact, among our Western European allies than between them and the United States. For the unity of freedom has never relied on uniformity of opinion. But the basic agreement of this alliance on fundamental issues continues.

The first task of the alliance remains the common defense. Last month Prime Minister Macmillan and I laid plans for a new stage in our long cooperative effort, one which aims to assist in the wider task of framing a common nuclear defense for the whole alliance.

The Nassau agreement recognizes that the security of the West is indivisible, and so must be our defense. But it also recognizes that this is an alliance of proud and sovereign nations, and works best when we do not forget it. It recognizes further that the nuclear defense of the West is not a matter for the present nuclear powers alone--that France will be such a power in the future--and that ways must be found without increasing the hazards of nuclear diffusion, to increase the role of our other partners in planning, manning, and directing a truly multilateral nuclear force within an increasingly intimate NATO alliance. Finally, the Nassau agreement recognizes that nuclear defense is not enough, that the agreed NATO levels of conventional strength must be met, and that the alliance cannot afford to be in a position of having to answer every threat with nuclear weapons or nothing.

We remain too near the Nassau decisions, and too far from their full realization, to know their place in history. But I believe that, for the first time, the door is open for the nuclear defense of the alliance to become a source of confidence, instead of a cause of contention.

The next most pressing concern of the alliance is our common economic goals of trade and growth. This Nation continues to be concerned about its balance-of-payments deficit, which, despite its decline, remains a stubborn and troublesome problem. We believe, moreover, that closer economic ties among all free nations are essential to prosperity and peace. And neither we nor the members of the European Common Market are so affluent that we can long afford to shelter high cost farms or factories from the winds of foreign competition, or to restrict the channels of trade with other nations of the free world. If the Common Market should move toward protectionism and restrictionism, it would undermine its own basic principles. This Government means to use the authority conferred on it last year by the Congress to encourage trade expansion on both sides of the Atlantic and around the world.

Second, what of the developing and nonaligned nations? They were shocked by the Soviets' sudden and secret attempt to transform Cuba into a nuclear striking base-and by Communist China's arrogant invasion of India. They have been reassured by our prompt assistance to India, by our support through the United Nations of the Congo's unification, by our patient search for disarmament, and by the improvement in our treatment of citizens and visitors whose skins do not happen to be white. And as the older colonialism recedes, and the neocolonialism of the Communist powers stands out more starkly than ever, they realize more clearly that the issue in the world struggle is not communism versus capitalism, but coercion versus free choice.

They are beginning to realize that the longing for independence is the same the world over, whether it is the independence of West Berlin or Viet-Nam. They are beginning to realize that such independence runs athwart all Communist ambitions but is in keeping with our own--and that our approach to their diverse needs is resilient and resourceful, while the Communists are still relying on ancient doctrines and dogmas.

Nevertheless it is hard for any nation to focus on an external or subversive threat to its independence when its energies are drained in daily combat with the forces of poverty and despair. It makes little sense for us to assail, in speeches and resolutions, the horrors of communism, to spend $50 billion a year to prevent its military advance-and then to begrudge spending, largely on American products, less than one-tenth of that amount to help other nations strengthen their independence and cure the social chaos in which communism always has thrived.

I am proud--and I think most Americans are proud--of a mutual defense and assistance program, evolved with bipartisan support in three administrations, which has, with all its recognized problems, contributed to the fact that not a single one of the nearly fifty U.N. members to gain independence since the Second World War has succumbed to Communist control.

I am proud of a program that has helped to arm and feed and clothe millions of people who live on the front lines of freedom.

I am especially proud that this country has put forward for the 60's a vast cooperative effort to achieve economic growth and social progress throughout the Americas-the Alliance for Progress.

I do not underestimate the difficulties that we face in this mutual effort among our close neighbors, but the free states of this hemisphere, working in close collaboration, have begun to make this alliance a living reality. Today it is feeding one out of every four school age children in Latin America an extra food ration from our farm surplus. It has distributed 1.5 million school books and is building 17,000 classrooms. It has helped resettle tens of thousands of farm families on land they can call their own. It is stimulating our good neighbors to more self-help and self-reform--fiscal, social, institutional, and land reforms. It is bringing new housing and hope, new health and dignity, to millions who were forgotten. The men and women of this hemisphere know that the alliance cannot Succeed if it is only another name for United States handouts--that it can succeed only as the Latin American nations themselves devote their best effort to fulfilling its goals.

This story is the same in Africa, in the Middle East, and in Asia. Wherever nations are willing to help themselves, we stand ready to help them build new bulwarks of freedom. We are not purchasing votes for the cold war; we have gone to the aid of imperiled nations, neutrals and allies alike. What we do ask--and all that we ask--is that our help be used to best advantage, and that their own efforts not be diverted by needless quarrels with other independent nations.

Despite all its past achievements, the continued progress of the mutual assistance program requires a persistent discontent with present performance. We have been reorganizing this program to make it a more effective, efficient instrument--and that process will continue this year.

But free world development will still be an uphill struggle. Government aid can only supplement the role of private investment, trade expansion, commodity stabilization, and, above all, internal self-improvement. The processes of growth are gradual--bearing fruit in a decade, not a day. Our successes will be neither quick nor dramatic. But if these programs were ever to be ended, our failures in a dozen countries would be sudden and certain.

Neither money nor technical assistance, however, can be our only weapon against poverty. In the end, the crucial effort is one of purpose, requiring the fuel of finance but also a torch of idealism. And nothing carries the spirit of this American idealism more effectively to the far corners of the earth than the American Peace Corps.

A year ago, less than 900 Peace Corps volunteers were on the job. A year from now they will number more than 9,000-men and women, aged 18 to 79, willing to give 2 years of their lives to helping people in other lands.

There are, in fact, nearly a million Americans serving their country and the cause of freedom in overseas posts, a record no other people can match. Surely those of us who stay at home should be glad to help indirectly; by supporting our aid programs; .by opening our doors to foreign visitors and diplomats and students; and by proving, day by day, by deed as well as word, that we are a just and generous people.

Third, what comfort can we take from the increasing strains and tensions within the Communist bloc? Here hope must be tempered with caution. For the Soviet-Chinese disagreement is over means, not ends. A dispute over how best to bury the free world is no grounds for Western rejoicing.

Nevertheless, while a strain is not a fracture, it is clear that the forces of diversity are at work inside the Communist camp, despite all the iron disciplines of regimentation and all the iron dogmatism's of ideology. Marx is proven wrong once again: for it is the closed Communist societies, not the free and open societies which carry within themselves the seeds of internal disintegration.

The disarray of the Communist empire has been heightened by two other formidable forces. One is the historical force of nationalism-and the yearning of all men to be free. The other is the gross inefficiency of their economies. For a closed society is not open to ideas of progress--and a police state finds that it cannot command the grain to grow.

New nations asked to choose between two competing systems need only compare conditions in East and West Germany, Eastern and Western Europe, North and South Viet-Nam. They need only compare the disillusionment of Communist Cuba with the promise of the Alliance for Progress. And all the world knows that no successful system builds a wall to keep its people in and freedom out--and the wall of shame dividing Berlin is a symbol of Communist failure.

Finally, what can we do to move from the present pause toward enduring peace? Again I would counsel caution. I foresee no spectacular reversal in Communist methods or goals. But if all these trends and developments can persuade the Soviet Union to walk the path of peace, then let her know that all free nations will journey with her. But until that choice is made, and until the world can develop a reliable system of international security, the free peoples have no choice but to keep their arms nearby.

This country, therefore, continues to require the best defense in the world--a defense which is suited to the sixties. This means, unfortunately, a rising defense budget-for there is no substitute for adequate defense, and no "bargain basement" way of achieving it. It means the expenditure of more than $15 billion this year on nuclear weapons systems alone, a sum which is about equal to the combined defense budgets of our European Allies.

But it also means improved air and missile defenses, improved civil defense, a strengthened anti-guerrilla capacity and, of prime importance, more powerful and flexible nonnuclear forces. For threats of massive retaliation may not deter piecemeal aggression-and a line of destroyers in a quarantine, or a division of well-equipped men on a border, may be more useful to our real security than the multiplication of awesome weapons beyond all rational need.

But our commitment to national safety is not a commitment to expand our military establishment indefinitely. We do not dismiss disarmament as merely an idle dream. For we believe that, in the end, it is the only way to assure the security of all without impairing the interests of any. Nor do we mistake honorable negotiation for appeasement. While we shall never weary in the defense of freedom, neither shall we ever abandon the pursuit of peace.

In this quest, the United Nations requires our full and continued support. Its value in serving the cause of peace has been shown anew in its role in the West New Guinea settlement, in its use as a forum for the Cuban crisis, and in its task of unification in the Congo. Today the United Nations is primarily the protector of the small and the weak, and a safety valve for the strong. Tomorrow it can form the framework for a world of law--a world in which no nation dictates the destiny of another, and in which the vast resources now devoted to destructive means will serve constructive ends.

In short, let our adversaries choose. If they choose peaceful competition, they shall have it. If they come to realize that their ambitions cannot succeed--if they see their "wars of liberation" and subversion will ultimately fail--if they recognize that there is more security in accepting inspection than in permitting new nations to master the black arts of nuclear war--and if they are willing to turn their energies, as we are, to the great unfinished tasks of our own peoples--then, surely, the areas of agreement can be very wide indeed: a clear understanding about Berlin, stability in Southeast Asia, an end to nuclear testing, new checks on surprise or accidental attack, and, ultimately, general and complete disarmament.

For we seek not the worldwide victory of one nation or system but a worldwide victory of man. The modern globe is too small, its weapons are too destructive, and its disorders are too contagious to permit any other kind of victory.

To achieve this end, the United States will continue to spend a greater portion of its national production than any other people in the free world. For 15 years no other free nation has demanded so much of itself. Through hot wars and cold, through recession and prosperity, through the ages of the atom and outer space, the American people have never faltered and their faith has never flagged. If at times our actions seem to make life difficult for others, it is only because history has made life difficult for us all.

But difficult days need not be dark. I think these are proud and memorable days in the cause of peace and freedom. We are proud, for example, of Major Rudolf Anderson who gave his life over the island of Cuba. We salute Specialist James Allen Johnson who died on the border of South Korea. We pay honor to Sergeant Gerald Pendell who was killed in Viet-Nam. They are among the many who in this century, far from home, have died for our country. Our task now, and the task of all Americans is to live up to their commitment.

My friends: I close on a note of hope. We are not lulled by the momentary calm of the sea or the somewhat clearer skies above. We know the turbulence that lies below, and the storms that are beyond the horizon this year. But now the winds of change appear to be blowing more strongly than ever, in the world of communism as well as our own. For 175 years we have sailed with those winds at our back, and with the tides of human freedom in our favor. We steer our ship with hope, as Thomas Jefferson said, "leaving Fear astern."

Today we still welcome those winds of change--and we have every reason to believe that our tide is running strong. With thanks to Almighty God for seeing us through a perilous passage, we ask His help anew in guiding the "Good Ship Union."

90TH ANNIVERSARY OF VANDERBILT UNIVERSITY

(MAY 18, 1963)

Mr. Chancellor, Mr. Vanderbilt, Senator Kefauver, Senator Gore, Congressman Fulton, Congressman Evins, Congressman Bass, Congressman Everett, Tom Murray, distinguished guests, members of the judiciary, the Army Corps of Engineers of the Tennessee Valley:

I first of all want to express my warm appreciation to the Governor and to the Mayor of this State and city and to the people for a very generous welcome, and particularly to all those young men and women who lined the street and played music for us as we drove into this stadium. We are glad they are here with us, and we feel the musical future of this city and State is assured.

Many things bring us together today. We are saluting the 90th anniversary of Vanderbilt University, which has grown from a small Tennessee university and institution to one of our Nation's greatest, with 7 different colleges, and with more than half of its 4200 students from outside of the State of Tennessee.

And we are saluting the 30th anniversary of the Tennessee Valley Authority, which transformed a parched, depressed, and floodravaged region into a fertile, productive center of industry, science, and agriculture.

We are saluting--by initiating construction of a dam in his name--a great Tennessee statesman, Cordell Hull, the father of reciprocal trade, the grandfather of the United Nations, the Secretary of State who presided over the transformation of this Nation from a life of isolation and almost indifference to a state of responsible world leadership.

And finally, we are saluting--by the recognition of a forthcoming dam in his name-J. Percy Priest, a former colleague of mine in the House of Representatives, who represented this district, this State, and this Nation in

251

the Congress for 16 turbulent years--years which witnessed the crumbling of empires, the splitting of the atom, the conquest of one threat to freedom, and the emergence of still another.

If there is one unchanging theme that runs throughout these separate stories, it is that everything changes but change itself. We live in an age of movement and change, both evolutionary and revolutionary, both good and evil--and in such an age a university has a special obligation to hold fast to the best of the past and move fast to the best of the future.

Nearly 100 years ago Prince Bismarck said that one-third of the students of German universities broke down from overwork, another third broke down from dissipation, and the other third ruled Germany. I do not know which third of the student body of Vanderbilt is here today, but I am confident we are talking to the future rulers of Tennessee and America in the spirit of this university.

The essence of Vanderbilt is still learning, the essence of its outlook is still liberty, and liberty and learning will be and must be the touchstones of Vanderbilt University and of any free university in this country or the world. I say two touchstones, yet they are almost inseparable, inseparable if not indistinguishable, for liberty without learning is always in peril, and learning without liberty is always in vain.

This State, this city, this campus, have stood long for both human rights and human enlightenment--and let that forever be true. This Nation is now engaged in a continuing debate about the rights of a portion of its citizens. That will go on, and those rights will expand until the standard first forged by the Nation's founders has been reached, and all Americans enjoy equal opportunity and liberty under law.

But this Nation was not founded solely on the principle of citizens' rights. Equally important, though too often not discussed, is the citizen's responsibility. For our privileges can be no greater than our obligations. The protection of our rights can endure no longer than the performance of our responsibilities. Each can be neglected only at the peril of the other. I speak to you today, therefore, not of your rights as Americans, but of your responsibilities. They are many in number and different in nature. They do not rest with equal weight upon the shoulders of all. Equality of opportunity does not mean equality of responsibility. All Americans must be responsible citizens, but some must be more responsible than others, by virtue of their public or their private position, their role in the family or community, their prospects for the future, or their legacy from the past.

Increased responsibility goes with increased ability, for "of those to whom much is given, much is required."

Commodore Vanderbilt recognized this responsibility and his recognition made possible the establishment of a great institution of learning for which he will be long remembered after his steamboats and railroads have been forgotten. I speak in particular, therefore, of the responsibility of the educated citizen, including the students, the faculty, and the alumni of this great institution. The creation and maintenance of Vanderbilt University, like that of all great universities, has required considerable effort and expenditure, and I cannot believe that all of this was undertaken merely to give this school's graduates an economic advantage in the life struggle. "Every man sent out from a university," said Professor Woodrow Wilson, "Every man sent out from a university should be a man of his Nation, as well as a man of his time."

You have responsibilities, in short, to use your talents for the benefit of the society which helped develop those talents. You must decide, as Goethe put it, whether you will be an anvil or a hammer, whether you will give to the world in which you were reared and educated the broadest possible benefits of that education. Of the many special obligations incumbent upon an educated citizen, I would cite three as outstanding: your obligation to the pursuit of learning, your obligation to serve the public, your obligation to uphold the law.

If the pursuit of learning is not defended by the educated citizen, it will not be defended at all. For there will always be those who scoff at intellectuals, who cry out against research, who seek to limit our educational system. Modern cynics and skeptics see no more reason for landing a man on the moon, which we shall do, than the cynics and skeptics of half a millennium ago saw for the discovery of this country. They see no harm in paying those to whom they entrust the minds of their children a smaller wage than is paid to those to whom they entrust the care of their plumbing.

But the educated citizen knows how much more there is to know. He knows that "knowledge is power," more so today than ever before. He knows that only an educated and informed people will be a free people, that the ignorance of one voter in a democracy impairs the security of all, and that if we can, as Jefferson put it, "enlighten the people generally ... tyranny and the oppressions of mind and body will vanish, like evil spirits at the dawn of day." And, therefore, the educated citizen has a special obligation to encourage the pursuit of learning, to promote exploration of the unknown, to preserve the freedom of inquiry, to support the advancement of research, and to assist at every level of government the improvement of education for all Americans, from grade school to graduate school.

Secondly, the educated citizen has an obligation to serve the public. He may be a precinct worker or President. He may give his talents at the courthouse, the State house, the White House. He may be a civil servant or a Senator, a candidate or a campaign worker, a winner or a loser. But he must be a participant and not a spectator.

"At the Olympic games," Aristotle wrote, "it is not the finest and strongest men who are crowned, but they who enter the lists-for out of these the prize-men are elected. So, too, in life, of the honorable and the good, it is they who act who rightly win the prizes."

I urge all of you today, especially those who are students, to act, to enter the lists of public service and rightly win or lose the prize. For we can have only one form of aristocracy in this country, as Jefferson wrote long ago in rejecting John Adams' suggestion of an artificial aristocracy of wealth and birth. It is, he wrote, the natural aristocracy of character and talent, and the best form of government, he added, was that which selected these men for positions of responsibility.

I would hope that all educated citizens would fulfill this obligation--in politics, in Government, here in Nashville, here in this State, in the Peace Corps, in the Foreign Service, in the Government Service, in the Tennessee Valley, in the world. You will find the pressures greater than the pay. You may endure more public attacks than support. But you will have the unequaled satisfaction of knowing that your character and talent are contributing to the direction and success of this free society.

Third, and finally, the educated citizen has an obligation to uphold the law. This is the obligation of every citizen in a free and peaceful society--but the educated citizen has a special responsibility by the virtue of his greater understanding. For whether he has ever studied history or current events, ethics or civics, the rules of a profession or the tools of a trade, he knows that only a respect for the law makes it possible for free men to dwell together in peace and progress.

He knows that law is the adhesive force in the cement of society, creating order out of chaos and coherence in place of anarchy. He knows that for one man to defy a law or court order he does not like is to invite others to defy those which they do not like, leading to a breakdown of all justice and all order. He knows, too, that every fellowman is entitled to be regarded with decency and treated with dignity. Any educated citizen who seeks to subvert the law, to suppress freedom, or to subject other human beings to acts that are less than human, degrades his heritage, ignores his learning, and betrays his obligation.

Certain other societies may respect the rule of force--we respect the rule of law.

The Nation, indeed the whole world, has watched recent events in the United States with alarm and dismay. No one can deny the complexity of the problems involved in assuring to all of our citizens their full fights as Americans. But no one can gainsay the fact that the determination to secure these rights is in the highest traditions of American freedom.

In these moments of tragic disorder, a special burden rests on the educated men and women of our country to reject the temptations of prejudice and violence, and to reaffirm the values of freedom and law on which our free society depends.

When Bishop McTyeire, 90 years ago, proposed it to Commodore Vanderbilt, he said, "Commodore, our country has been torn to pieces by a civil war .... We want to repair this damage." And Commodore Vanderbilt reportedly replied, "I want to unite this country, and all sections of it, so that all our people will be one." His response, his recognition of his obligation and opportunity gave Vanderbilt University not only an endowment but also a mission. Now, 90 years later, in a time of tension, it is more important than ever to unite this country and strengthen these ties so that all of our people will be one.

Ninety years from now I have no doubt that Vanderbilt University will still be fulfilling this mission. It will still uphold learning, encourage public service, and teach respect for the law. It will neither turn its back on proven wisdom or turn its face from newborn challenge. It will still pass on to the youth of our land the full meaning of their rights and their responsibilities. And it will still be teaching the truth--the truth that makes us free and will keep us free. Thank you.

REMARKS AT U.S. AIR FORCE ACADEMY

(JUNE 5, 1963)

General, Secretary Zuckert, General LeMay, Members of the Congress, Mr. Fraser, fellow graduates:

I want to express my appreciation for becoming an instant graduate of this academy, and consider it a high honor.

Mr. Salinger, Press Secretary of the White House, received the following letter several days ago:

"Dear Sir:

"Would you desire to become an honorary member of the Air Force Cadet Wing for granting one small favor? Your name, Mr. Salinger, shall become more hallowed and revered than the combined memories of Generals Mitchell, Arnold, and Doolittle.

"My humble desire is that you convey a request from the Cadet Wing to the President. Sir, there are countless numbers of our group who are oppressed by Class 3 punishments, the bane of cadets everywhere. The President is our only hope for salvation. By granting amnesty to our oppressed brethren, he and you could end your anguish and depression.

"Please, sir, help us return to the ranks of the living so that we may work for the New Frontier with enthusiasm and vigor."

It is signed "Sincerely, Cadet Marvin B. Hopkins," who's obviously going to be a future General.

As Mr. Salinger wants to be honored with Generals Mitchell, Arnold, and Doolittle, I therefore take great pleasure in granting amnesty to all those who not only deserve it, but need it.

It is customary for speakers on these occasions to say in graduating addresses that commencement signifies the beginning instead of an end, yet this thought applies with particular force to those of you who are graduating from our Nation's service academies today, for today you receive not only your degrees, but also your commissions, and tomorrow you join with all those in the military service, in the foreign service, the civil service, and elsewhere, and one million of them serve outside our frontiers who have chosen to serve the Great Republic at a turning point in our history. You will have an opportunity to help make that history-an opportunity for a service career more varied and demanding than any that has been opened to any officer corps in the history of any country.

There are some who might be skeptical of that assertion. They claim that the future of the Air Force is mortgaged to an obsolete weapons system, the manned aircraft, or that Air Force officers of the future will be nothing more than "silent silo sitters," but nothing could be further from the truth. It is this very onrush of technology which demands an expanding role for the Nation's Air Force and Air Force officers, and which guarantees that an Air Force career in the next 40 years will be even more changing and more challenging than the careers of the last 40 years.

For some of you will travel where no man has ever traveled before. Some of you will fly the fastest planes that have ever been built, reach the highest altitudes that man has ever gone to, and lift the heaviest payloads of any aviator in history. Some of you will hold in your hands the most awesome destructive power which any nation or any man has conceived. Some of you will work with the leaders of new nations which were not even nations a few years ago. Some of you will support guerrilla and counter-guerrilla operations that combine the newest techniques of warfare with the oldest techniques of the jungle, and some of you will help develop new planes that spread their wings in flight, detect other planes at an unheard of distance, deliver new weapons with unprecedented accuracy, and survey the ground from incredible heights as a testament to our strong faith in the future of air power and the manned airplane.

I am announcing today that the United States will commit itself to an important new program in civilian aviation. Civilian aviation, long both the beneficiary and the benefactor of military aviation, is of necessity equally dynamic. Neither the economics nor the politics of international air competition permits us to stand still in this area. Today the challenging new frontier in commercial aviation and in military aviation is a frontier already crossed by the military-supersonic flight. Leading members of the administration under the chairmanship of the Vice President have been considering carefully the role to be played by the National Government in determining the economic and technical feasibility of an American commercial supersonic aircraft, and in the development of such an aircraft if it be feasible.

Having reviewed their recommendations, it is my judgment that this Government should immediately commence a new program in partnership with private industry to develop at the earliest practical date the prototype of a commercially successful supersonic transport superior to that being built in any other country of the world. An open, preliminary design competition will be initiated immediately among American airframe and powerplant manufacturers with a more detailed design phase to follow. If these initial phases do not produce an aircraft capable of transporting people and goods safely, swiftly, and at prices the traveler can afford and the airlines find profitable, we shall not go further.

But if we can build the best operational plane of this type--and I believe we can--then the Congress and the country should be prepared to invest the funds and effort necessary to maintain this Nation's lead in long-range aircraft, a lead we have held since the end of the Second World War, a lead we should make every responsible effort to maintain. Spurred by competition from across the Atlantic and by the productivity of our own companies, the Federal Government must pledge funds to supplement the risk capital to be contributed by private companies. It must then rely heavily on the flexibility and ingenuity of private enterprise to make the detailed decisions and to introduce successfully this new jet-age transport into worldwide service, and we are talking about a plane in the end of the 60's that will move ahead at a speed faster than Mach 2 to all corners of the globe. This commitment, I believe, is essential to a strong and forward-looking Nation, and indicates the future of the manned aircraft as we move into a missile age as well.

The fact that the greatest value of all of the weapons of massive retaliation lies in their ability to deter war does not diminish their importance, nor will national security in the years ahead be achieved simply by piling up bigger bombs or burying our missiles under bigger loads of concrete. For in an imperfect world where human folly has been the rule and not the exception, the surest way to bring on the war that can never happen is to sit back and assure ourselves it will not happen. The existence of mutual nuclear deterrents cannot be shrugged off as stalemate, for our national security in a period of rapid change will depend on constant reappraisal of our present doctrines, on alertness to new developments, on imagination and resourcefulness, and new ideas. Stalemate is a static term and not one of you would be here today if you believed you were entering an outmoded service requiring only custodial duties in a period of nuclear stalemate.

I am impressed by the extraordinary scholastic record, unmatched by any new college or university in this country, which has been made by the students and graduates of this Academy. Four Rhodes scholarships last year, two this year, and other selected scholarships, and also your record in the graduate record examination makes the people of this country proud of this Academy and the Air Force which made it possible.

This country is proud of the fact that more than one out of five of your all-military faculty has a doctor's degree, and all the rest have master's degrees. This is what we need for leadership in our military services, for the Air Force officer of today and tomorrow requires the broadest kind of scholarship to understand a most complex and changing world. He requires understanding and learning unmatched in the days before World War II. Any graduate of this Academy who serves in our Armed Forces will need to know economics and history, and international affairs, and languages. You will need an appreciation of other societies, and an understanding of our own Nation's purposes and policy.

General Norstad's leadership in NATO, General Smart's outstanding tour of duty as the senior military representative in Japan are examples of Air Force officers who use their broad talents for the benefit of our country. Many of you will have similar opportunities to represent this country in negotiations with our adversaries as well as our friends, working with international organizations, working in every way in the hundred free countries around the globe to help them maintain their freedom. Your major responsibilities, in the final analysis, will relate to military command. Some of you may be members of the Joint Chiefs of Staff and participate as advisers to the President who holds office.

Last October's crisis in the Caribbean amply demonstrated that military policy and power cannot and must not be separated from political and diplomatic decisions. Whatever the military motive and implications of the reckless attempt to put missiles on the island of Cuba, the political and psychological implications were equally important. We needed in October-- and we had them and we shall need them in the future, and we shall have them--military commanders who are conscious of the enormous stakes in the nuclear age of every decision that they take, who are aware of the fact that there are no purely political .decisions or purely military decisions; that .every problem is a mixture of both, men who know the difference between vital interests and peripheral interests, who can maneuver military forces with judgment and precision, as well as courage and determination, and who can foresee the effects of military action on political policy. We need men, in short, who can cope with the challenges of a new political struggle, an armed doctrine which uses every weapon in the struggle around the globe.

We live in a world, in short, where the principal problems that we face are not susceptible to military solutions alone. The role of our military power, in essence, is, therefore, to free ourselves and our allies to pursue the goals of freedom without the danger of enemy attack, but we do not have a separate military policy, and a separate diplomatic policy, and a separate disarmament policy, and a separate foreign aid policy, all unrelated to each other. They are all bound up together in the policy of the United States. Our goal is a coherent, overall, national security policy, one that truly serves the best interests of this country and those who depend upon it. It is worth noting that all of the decisions which we now face today will come in increased numbers in the months and years ahead.

I want to congratulate all of you who have chosen the United States Air Force as a career. As far as any of us can now see in Washington in the days ahead, you will occupy positions of the highest responsibility, and merely because we move into a changing period of weapon technology, as well as political challenge, because, in fact, we move into that period, there is greater need for you than ever before. You, here today on this field, your colleagues at Omaha, Nebraska, or at Eglin in Florida, or who may be stationed in Western Europe, or men who are at sea in ships hundreds of miles from land, or soldiers in camps in Texas, or on the Island of Okinawa, they maintain the freedom by being on the ready. They maintain the freedom, the security, and the peace not only of the United States, but of the dozens of countries who are allied to us who are close to the Communist power and who depend upon us and, in a sense, only upon us for their freedom and security. These distant ships, these distant planes, these distant men keep the peace in a great half-circle stretching all the way from Berlin to South Korea. This is the role which history and our own determination has placed upon a country which lived most of its history in isolation and neutrality, and yet in the last 18 years has carried the burden for free people everywhere. I think that this is a burden which we accept willingly, recognizing that if this country does not accept it, no people will, recognizing that in the most difficult time in the whole life of freedom, the United States is called upon to play its greatest role. This is a role which we are proud to accept, and I am particularly proud to see the United States accept it in the presence of these young men who have committed themselves to the service of our country and to the cause of its freedom. I congratulate you all, and most of all, I congratulate your mothers and fathers who made it possible.

Thank you.

AMERICAN UNIVERSITY COMMENCEMENT

(JUNE 10, 1963)

President Anderson, members of the faculty, board of trustees, distinguished guests, my old colleague, Senator Bob Byrd, who has earned his degree through many years of attending night law school while I am earning mine in the next 30 minutes, ladies and gentlemen:

It is with great pride that I participate in this ceremony of the American University, sponsored by the Methodist Church, founded by Bishop John Fletcher Hurst, and first opened by President Woodrow Wilson in 1914. This is a young and growing university, but it has already fulfilled Bishop Hurst's enlightened hope for the study of history and public affairs in a city devoted to the making of history and to the conduct of the public's business. By sponsoring this institution of higher learning for all who wish to learn, whatever their color or their creed, the Methodists of this area and the Nation deserve the Nation's thanks, and I commend all those who are today graduating.

Professor Woodrow Wilson once said that every man sent out from a university should be a man of his nation as well as a man of his time, and I am confident that the men and women who carry the honor of graduating from this institution will continue to give from their lives, from their talents, a high measure of public service and public support.

"There are few earthly things more beautiful than a university," wrote John Masefield, in his tribute to English universities—and his words are equally true today. He did not refer to spires and towers, to campus greens and ivied walls. He admired the splendid beauty of the university, he said, because it was "a place where those who hate ignorance may strive to know, where those who perceive truth may strive to make others see."

I have, therefore, chosen this time and this place to discuss a topic on which ignorance too often abounds and the truth is too rarely perceived— yet it is the most important topic on earth: world peace.

What kind of peace do I mean? What kind of peace do we seek? Not a Pax Americana enforced on the world by American weapons of war. Not the peace of the grave or the security of the slave. I am talking about genuine peace, the kind of peace that makes life on earth worth living, the kind that enables men and nations to grow and to hope and to build a better life for their children—not merely peace for Americans but peace for all men and women—not merely peace in our time but peace for all time.

I speak of peace because of the new face of war. Total war makes no sense in an age when great powers can maintain large and relatively invulnerable nuclear forces and refuse to surrender without resort to those forces. It makes no sense in an age when a single nuclear weapon contains almost ten times the explosive force delivered by all of the allied air forces in the Second World War. It makes no sense in an age when the deadly poisons produced by a nuclear exchange would be carried by wind and water and soil and seed to the far corners of the globe and to generations yet unborn.

Today the expenditure of billions of dollars every year on weapons acquired for the purpose of making sure we never need to use them is essential to keeping the peace. But surely the acquisition of such idle stockpiles—which can only destroy and never create—is not the only, much less the most efficient, means of assuring peace.

I speak of peace, therefore, as the necessary rational end of rational men. I realize that the pursuit of peace is not as dramatic as the pursuit of war—and frequently the words of the pursuer fall on deaf ears. But we have no more urgent task.

Some say that it is useless to speak of world peace or world law or world disarmament—and that it will be useless until the leaders of the Soviet Union adopt a more enlightened attitude. I hope they do. I believe we can help them do it. But I also believe that we must reexamine our own attitude—as individuals and as a Nation—for our attitude is as essential as theirs. And every graduate of this school, every thoughtful citizen who despairs of war and wishes to bring peace, should begin by looking inward—by examining his own attitude toward the possibilities of peace, toward the Soviet Union, toward the course of the cold war and toward freedom and peace here at home.

First: Let us examine our attitude toward peace itself. Too many of us think it is impossible. Too many think it unreal. But that is a dangerous, defeatist belief. It leads to the conclusion that war is inevitable—that mankind is doomed—that we are gripped by forces we cannot control.

We need not accept that view. Our problems are manmade—therefore, they can be solved by man. And man can be as big as he wants. No problem of human destiny is beyond human beings. Man's reason and spirit have often solved the seemingly unsolvable—and we believe they can do it again.

I am not referring to the absolute, infinite concept of universal peace and good will of which some fantasies and fanatics dream. I do not deny the value of hopes and dreams but we merely invite discouragement and incredulity by making that our only and immediate goal.

Let us focus instead on a more practical, more attainable peace—based not on a sudden revolution in human nature but on a gradual evolution in human institutions—on a series of concrete actions and effective agreements which are in the interest of all concerned. There is no single, simple key to this peace—no grand or magic formula to be adopted by one or two powers. Genuine peace must be the product of many nations, the sum of many acts. It must be dynamic, not static, changing to meet the challenge of each new generation. For peace is a process—a way of solving problems.

With such a peace, there will still be quarrels and conflicting interests, as there are within families and nations. World peace, like community peace, does not require that each man love his neighbor—it requires only that they live together in mutual tolerance, submitting their disputes to a just and peaceful settlement. And history teaches us that enmities between nations, as between individuals, do not last forever. However fixed our likes and dislikes may seem, the tide of time and events will often bring surprising changes in the relations between nations and neighbors.

So let us persevere. Peace need not be impracticable, and war need not be inevitable. By defining our goal more clearly, by making it seem more manageable and less remote, we can help all peoples to see it, to draw hope from it, and to move irresistibly toward it.

Second: Let us reexamine our attitude toward the Soviet Union. It is discouraging to think that their leaders may actually believe what their propagandists write. It is discouraging to read a recent authoritative Soviet text on Military Strategy and find, on page after page, wholly baseless and incredible claims—such as the allegation that "American imperialist circles are preparing to unleash different types of wars ... that there is a very real threat of a preventive war being unleashed by American imperialists against the Soviet Union ... [and that] the political aims of the American imperialists are to enslave economically and politically the European and other capitalist countries... [and] to achieve world domination ... by means of aggressive wars."

Truly, as it was written long ago: "The wicked flee when no man pursueth." Yet it is sad to read these Soviet statements—to realize the extent of the gulf between us. But it is also a warning—a warning to the American people not to fall into the same trap as the Soviets, not to see only a distorted and desperate view of the other side, not to see conflict as inevitable, accommodation as impossible, and communication as nothing more than an exchange of threats.

No government or social system is so evil that its people must be considered as lacking in virtue. As Americans, we find communism profoundly repugnant as a negation of personal freedom and dignity. But we can still hail the Russian people for their many achievements—in science and space, in economic and industrial growth, in culture and in acts of courage.

Among the many traits the peoples of our two countries have in common, none is stronger than our mutual abhorrence of war. Almost unique, among the major world powers, we have never been at war with each other. And no nation in the history of battle ever suffered more than the Soviet Union suffered in the course of the Second World War. At least 20 million lost their lives. Countless millions of homes and farms were burned or sacked. A third of the nation's territory, including nearly two thirds of its industrial base, was turned into a wasteland—a loss equivalent to the devastation of this country east of Chicago.

Today, should total war ever break out again—no matter how—our two countries would become the primary targets. It is an ironic but accurate fact that the two strongest powers are the two in the most danger of devastation. All we have built, all we have worked for, would be destroyed in the first 24 hours. And even in the cold war, which brings burdens and dangers to so many countries, including this Nation's closest allies—our two countries bear the heaviest burdens. For we are both devoting massive sums of money to weapons that could be better devoted to combating ignorance, poverty, and disease. We are both caught up in a vicious and dangerous cycle in which suspicion on one side breeds suspicion on the other, and new weapons beget counter-weapons.

In short, both the United States and its allies, and the Soviet Union and its allies, have a mutually deep interest in a just and genuine peace and in halting the arms race. Agreements to this end are in the interests of the Soviet Union as well as ours—and even the most hostile nations can be relied upon to accept and keep those treaty obligations, and only those treaty obligations, which are in their own interest.

So, let us not be blind to our differences—but let us also direct attention to our common interests and to the means by which those differences can be resolved. And if we cannot end now our differences, at least we can help make the world safe for diversity. For, in the final analysis, our most basic common link is that we all inhabit this small planet. We all breathe the same air. We all cherish our children's future. And we are all mortal.

Third: Let us reexamine our attitude toward the cold war, remembering that we are not engaged in a debate, seeking to pile up debating points. We are not here distributing blame or pointing the finger of judgment. We must deal with the world as it is, and not as it might have been had the history of the last 18 years been different.

We must, therefore, persevere in the search for peace in the hope that constructive changes within the Communist bloc might bring within reach solutions which now seem beyond us. We must conduct our affairs in such a way that it becomes in the Communists' interest to agree on a genuine peace. Above all, while defending our own vital interests, nuclear powers must avert those confrontations which bring an adversary to a choice of either a humiliating retreat or a nuclear war. To adopt that kind of course in the nuclear age would be evidence only of the bankruptcy of our policy—or of a collective death-wish for the world.

To secure these ends, America's weapons are nonprovocative, carefully controlled, designed to deter, and capable of selective use. Our military forces are committed to peace and disciplined in self-restraint. Our diplomats are instructed to avoid unnecessary irritants and purely rhetorical hostility.

For we can seek a relaxation of tensions without relaxing our guard. And, for our part, we do not need to use threats to prove that we are resolute. We do not need to jam foreign broadcasts out of fear our faith will be eroded. We are unwilling to impose our system on any unwilling people—but we are willing and able to engage in peaceful competition with any people on earth.

Meanwhile, we seek to strengthen the United Nations, to help solve its financial problems, to make it a more effective instrument for peace, to develop it into a genuine world security system—a system capable of resolving disputes on the basis of law, of insuring the security of the large and the small, and of creating conditions under which arms can finally be abolished.

At the same time we seek to keep peace inside the non-Communist world, where many nations, all of them our friends, are divided over issues which weaken Western unity, which invite Communist intervention or which threaten to erupt into war. Our efforts in West New Guinea, in the Congo, in the Middle East, and in the Indian subcontinent, have been persistent and patient despite criticism from both sides. We have also tried to set an example for others—by seeking to adjust small but significant differences with our own closest neighbors in Mexico and in Canada.

Speaking of other nations, I wish to make one point clear. We are bound to many nations by alliances. Those alliances exist because our concern and theirs substantially overlap. Our commitment to defend Western Europe and West Berlin, for example, stands undiminished because of the identity of our vital interests. The United States will make no deal with the Soviet Union at the expense of other nations and other peoples, not merely because they are our partners, but also because their interests and ours converge.

Our interests converge, however, not only in defending the frontiers of freedom, but in pursuing the paths of peace. It is our hope—and the purpose of allied policies—to convince the Soviet Union that she, too, should let each nation choose its own future, so long as that choice does not interfere with the choices of others. The Communist drive to impose their political and economic system on others is the primary cause of world tension today. For there can be no doubt that, if all nations could refrain from interfering in the self-determination of others, the peace would be much more assured.

This will require a new effort to achieve world law—a new context for world discussions. It will require increased understanding between the Soviets and ourselves. And increased understanding will require increased contact and communication. One step in this direction is the proposed arrangement for a direct line between Moscow and Washington, to avoid on each side the dangerous delays, misunderstandings, and misreadings of the other's actions which might occur at a time of crisis.

We have also been talking in Geneva about other first-step measures of arms control, designed to limit the intensity of the arms race and to reduce the risks of accidental war. Our primary long-range interest in Geneva, however, is general and complete disarmament—designed to take place by stages, permitting parallel political developments to build the new institutions of peace which would take the place of arms. The pursuit of disarmament has been an effort of this Government since the 1920's. It has been urgently sought by the past three ado ministrations. And however dim the prospects may be today, we intend to continue this effort—to continue it in order that all countries, including our own, can better grasp what the problems and possibilities of disarmament are.

The one major area of these negotiations where the end is in sight, yet where a fresh start is badly needed, is in a treaty to outlaw nuclear tests. The conclusion of such a treaty, so near and yet so far, would check the spiraling arms race in one of its most dangerous areas. It would place the nuclear powers in a position to deal more effectively with one of the greatest hazards which man faces in 1963, the further spread of nuclear arms. It would increase our security—it would decrease the prospects of war. Surely this goal is sufficiently important to require our steady pursuit, yielding neither to the temptation to give up the whole effort nor the temptation to give up our insistence on vital and responsible safeguards.

I am taking this opportunity, therefore, to announce two important decisions in this regard.

First: Chairman Khrushchev, Prime Minister Macmillan, and I have agreed that highlevel discussions will shortly begin in Moscow looking toward early agreement on a comprehensive test ban treaty. Our hopes must be tempered with the caution of history—but with our hopes go the hopes of all mankind.

Second: To make clear our good faith and solemn convictions on the matter, I now declare that the United States does not propose to conduct nuclear tests in the atmosphere so long as other states do not do so. We will not be the first to resume. Such a declaration is no substitute for a formal binding treaty, but I hope it will help us achieve one. Nor would such a treaty be a substitute for disarmament, but I hope it will help us achieve it.

Finally, my fellow Americans, let us examine our attitude toward peace and freedom here at home. The quality and spirit of our own society must justify and support our efforts abroad. We must show it in the dedication of our own lives—as many of you who are graduating today will have a unique opportunity to do, by serving without pay in the Peace Corps abroad or in the proposed National Service Corps here at home.

But wherever we are, we must all, in our daily lives, live up to the age-old faith that peace and freedom walk together. In too many of our cities today, the peace is not secure because freedom is incomplete.

It is the responsibility of the executive branch at all levels of government—local, State, and National—to provide and protect that freedom for all of our citizens by all means within their authority. It is the responsibility of the legislative branch at all levels, wherever that authority is not now adequate, to make it adequate. And it is the responsibility of all citizens in all sections of this country to respect the rights of all others and to respect the law of the land.

All this is not unrelated to world peace. "When a man's ways please the Lord," the Scriptures tell us, "he maketh even his enemies to be at peace with him." And is not peace, in the last analysis, basically a matter of human rights—the right to live out our lives without fear of devastation—the right to breathe air as nature provided it—the right of future generations to a healthy existence?

While we proceed to safeguard our national interests, let us also safeguard human interests. And the elimination of war and arms is clearly in the interest of both. No treaty, however much it may be to the advantage of all, however tightly it may be worded, can provide absolute security against the risks of deception and evasion. But it can—if it is sufficiently effective in its enforcement and if it is sufficiently in the interests of its signers—offer far more security and far fewer risks than an unabated, uncontrolled, unpredictable arms race.

The United States, as the world knows, will never start a war. We do not want a war. We do not now expect a war. This generation of Americans has already had enough—more than enough—of war and hate and oppression. We shall be prepared if others wish it. We shall be alert to try to stop it. But we shall also do our part to build a world of peace where the weak are safe and the strong are just. We are not helpless before that task or hopeless of its success. Confident and unafraid, we labor on—not toward a strategy of annihilation but toward a strategy of peace.

ADDRESS ON CIVIL RIGHTS

(JUNE 11, 1963)

Good evening, my fellow citizens:

This afternoon, following a series of threats and defiant statements, the presence of Alabama National Guardsmen was required on the University of Alabama to carry out the final and unequivocal order of the United States District Court of the Northern District of Alabama. That order called for the admission of two clearly qualified young Alabama residents who happened to have been born Negro.

That they were admitted peacefully on the campus is due in good measure to the conduct of the students of the University of Alabama, who met their responsibilities in a constructive way.

I hope that every American, regardless of where he lives, will stop and examine his conscience about this and other related incidents. This Nation was founded by men of many nations and backgrounds. It was founded on the principle that all men are created equal, and that the rights of every man are diminished when the rights of one man are threatened.

Today we are committed to a worldwide struggle to promote and protect the rights of all who wish to be free. And when Americans are sent to Viet-Nam or West Berlin, we do not ask for whites only. It ought to be possible, therefore, for American students of any color to attend any public institution they select without having to be backed up by troops.

It ought to be possible for American consumers of any color to receive equal service in places of public accommodation, such as hotels and restaurants and theaters and retail stores, without being forced to resort to demonstrations in the street, and it ought to be possible for American citizens of any color to register and to vote in a free election without interference or fear of reprisal.

It ought to be possible, in short, for every American to enjoy the privileges of being American without regard to his race or his color. In short, every American ought to have the right to be treated as he would wish to be treated, as one would wish his children to be treated. But this is not the case.

The Negro baby born in America today, regardless of the section of the Nation in which he is born, has about one-half as much chance of completing a high school as a white baby born in the same place on the same day, one-third as much chance of completing college, one-third as much chance of becoming a professional man, twice as much chance of becoming unemployed, about one-seventh as much chance of earning $10,000 a year, a life expectancy which is 7 years shorter, and the prospects of earning only half as much.

This is not a sectional issue. Difficulties over segregation and discrimination exist in every city, in every State of the Union, producing in many cities a rising tide of discontent that threatens the public safety. Nor is this a partisan issue. In a time of domestic crisis men of good will and generosity should be able to unite regardless of party or politics. This is not even a legal or legislative issue alone. It is better to settle these matters in the courts than on the streets, and new laws are needed at every level, but law alone cannot make men see right.

We are confronted primarily with a moral issue. It is as old as the scriptures and is as clear as the American Constitution.

The heart of the question is whether all Americans are to be afforded equal rights and equal opportunities, whether we are going to treat our fellow Americans as we want to be treated. If an American, because his skin is dark, cannot eat lunch in a restaurant open to the public, if he cannot send his children to the best public school available, if he cannot vote for the public officials who represent him, if, in short, he cannot enjoy the full and free life which all of us want, then who among us would be content to have the color of his skin changed and stand in his place? Who among us would then be content with the counsels of patience and delay?

One hundred years of delay have passed since President Lincoln freed the slaves, yet their heirs, their grandsons, are not fully free. They are not yet freed from the bonds of injustice. They are not yet freed from social and economic oppression. And this Nation, for all its hopes and all its boasts, will not be fully free until all its citizens are free.

We preach freedom around the world, and we mean it, and we cherish our freedom here at home, but are we to say to the world, and much more importantly, to each other that this is a land of the free except for the Negroes; that we have no second-class citizens except Negroes; that we have no class or cast system, no ghettoes, no master race except with respect to Negroes?

Now the time has come for this Nation to fulfill its promise. The events in Birmingham and elsewhere have so increased the cries for equality that no city or State or legislative body can prudently choose to ignore them.

The fires of frustration and discord are burning in every city, North and South, where legal remedies are not at hand. Redress is sought in the streets, in demonstrations, parades, and protests which create tensions and threaten violence and threaten lives.

We face, therefore, a moral crisis as a country and as a people. It cannot be met by repressive police action. It cannot be left to increased demonstrations in the streets. It cannot be quieted by token moves or talk. It is a time to act in the Congress, in your State and local legislative body and, above all, in all of our daily lives.

It is not enough to pin the blame on others, to say this is a problem of one section of the country or another, or deplore the fact that we face. A great change is at hand, and our task, our obligation, is to make that revolution, that change, peaceful and constructive for all.

Those who do nothing are inviting shame as well as violence. Those who act boldly are recognizing right as well as reality.

Next week I shall ask the Congress of the United States to act, to make a commitment it has not fully made in this century to the proposition that race has no place in American life or law. The Federal judiciary has upheld that proposition in a series of forthright cases. The executive branch has adopted that proposition in the conduct of its affairs, including the employment of Federal personnel, the use of Federal facilities, and the sale of federally financed housing.

But there are other necessary measures which only the Congress can provide, and they must be provided at this session. The old code of equity law under which we live commands for every wrong a remedy, but in too many communities, in too many parts of the country, wrongs are inflicted on Negro citizens and there are no remedies at law. Unless the Congress acts, their only remedy is in the street.

I am, therefore, asking the Congress to enact legislation giving all Americans the right to be served in facilities which are open to the public—hotels, restaurants, theaters, retail stores, and similar establishments.

This seems to me to be an elementary right. Its denial is an arbitrary indignity that no American in 1963 should have to endure, but many do.

I have recently met with scores of business leaders urging them to take voluntary action to end this discrimination and I have been encouraged by their response, and in the last 2 weeks over 75 cities have seen progress made in desegregating these kinds of facilities. But many are unwilling to act alone, and for this reason, nationwide legislation is needed if we are to move this problem from the streets to the courts.

I am also asking Congress to authorize the Federal Government to participate more fully in lawsuits designed to end segregation in public education. We have succeeded in persuading many districts to de-segregate voluntarily. Dozens have admitted Negroes without violence. Today a Negro is attending a State-supported institution in every one of our 50 States, but the pace is very slow.

Too many Negro children entering segregated grade schools at the time of the Supreme Court's decision 9 years ago will enter segregated high schools this fall, having suffered a loss which can never be restored. The lack of an adequate education denies the Negro a chance to get a decent job.

The orderly implementation of the Supreme Court decision, therefore, cannot be left solely to those who may not have the economic resources to carry the legal action or who may be subject to harassment.

Other features will be also requested, including greater protection for the right to vote. But legislation, I repeat, cannot solve this problem alone. It must be solved in the homes of every American in every community across our country.

In this respect, I want to pay tribute to those citizens North and South who have been working in their communities to make life better for all. They are acting not out of a sense of legal duty but out of a sense of human decency.

Like our soldiers and sailors in all parts of the world they are meeting freedom's challenge on the firing line, and I salute them for their honor and their courage.

My fellow Americans, this is a problem which faces us all—in every city of the North as well as the South. Today there are Negroes unemployed, two or three times as many compared to whites, inadequate in education, moving into the large cities, unable to find work, young people particularly out of work without hope, denied equal rights, denied the opportunity to eat at a restaurant or lunch counter or go to a movie theater, denied the right to a decent education, denied almost today the right to attend a State university even though qualified. It seems to me that these are matters which concern us all, not merely Presidents or Congressmen or Governors, but every citizen of the United States.

This is one country. It has become one country because all of us and all the people who came here had an equal chance to develop their talents.

We cannot say to 10 percent of the population that you can't have that right; that your children can't have the chance to develop whatever talents they have; that the only way that they are going to get their rights is to go into the streets and demonstrate. I think we owe them and we owe ourselves a better country than that.

Therefore, I am asking for your help in making it easier for us to move ahead and to provide the kind of equality of treatment which we would want ourselves; to give a chance for every child to be educated to the limit of his talents.

As I have said before, not every child has an equal talent or an equal ability or an equal motivation, but they should have the equal right to develop their talent and their ability and their motivation, to make something of themselves.

We have a right to expect that the Negro community will be responsible, will uphold the law, but they have a right to expect that the law will be fair, that the Constitution will be color blind, as Justice Harlan said at the turn of the century.

This is what we are talking about and this is a matter which concerns this country and what it stands for, and in meeting it I ask the support of all our citizens.

Thank you very much.

"ICH BIN EIN BERLINER"

(JUNE 26, 1963)

I am proud to come to this city as the guest of your distinguished Mayor, who has symbolized throughout the world the fighting spirit of West Berlin. And I am proud to visit the Federal Republic with your distinguished Chancellor who for so many years has committed Germany to democracy and freedom and progress, and to come here in the company of my fellow American, General Clay, who has been in this city during its great moments of crisis and will come again if ever needed.

Two thousand years ago the proudest boast was "civis Romanus sum." Today, in the world of freedom, the proudest boast is "Ich bin ein Berliner."

I appreciate my interpreter translating my German!

There are many people in the world who really don't understand, or say they don't, what is the great issue between the free world and the Communist world. Let them come to Berlin. There are some who say that communism is the wave of the future. Let them come to Berlin. And there are some who say in Europe and elsewhere we can work with the Communists. Let them come to Berlin. And there are even a few who say that it is true that communism is an evil system, but it permits us to make economic progress. Lass' sic nach Berlin kommen. Let them come to Berlin.

Freedom has many difficulties and democracy is not perfect, but we have never had to put a wall up to keep our people in, to prevent them from leaving us. I want to say, on behalf of my countrymen, who live many miles away on the other side of the Atlantic, who are far distant from you, that they take the greatest pride that they have been able to share with you, even from a distance, the story of the last 18 years. I know of no town, no city, that has been besieged for 18 years that still lives with the vitality and the force, and the hope and the determination of the city of West Berlin.

While the wall is the most obvious and vivid demonstration of the failures of. the Communist system, for all the world to see, we take no satisfaction in it, for it is, as your Mayor has said, an offense not only against history but an offense against humanity, separating families, dividing husbands and wives and brothers and sisters, and dividing a people who wish to be joined together.

What is true of this city is true of Germany—real, lasting peace in Europe can never be assured as long as one German out of four is denied the elementary right of free men, and that is to make a free choice. In 18 years of peace and good faith, this generation of Germans has earned the right to be free, including the right to unite their families and their nation in lasting peace, with good will to all people. You live in a defended island of freedom, but your life is part of the main. So let me ask you, as I close, to lift your eyes beyond the dangers of today, to the hopes of tomorrow, beyond the freedom merely of this city of Berlin, or your country of Germany, to the advance of freedom everywhere, beyond the wall to the day of peace with justice, beyond yourselves and ourselves to all mankind.

Freedom is indivisible, and when one man is enslaved, all are not free. When all are free, then we can look forward to that day when this city will be joined as one and this country and this great Continent of Europe in a peaceful and hopeful globe. When that day finally comes, as it will, the people of West Berlin can take sober satisfaction in the fact that they were in the front lines for almost two decades.

All free men, wherever they may live, are citizens of Berlin, and, therefore, as a free man, I take pride in the words "Ich bin ein Berliner!"

ADDRESS ON THE NUCLEAR TEST BAN TREATY

(JULY 26, 1963)

Good evening, my fellow citizens:

I speak to you tonight in a spirit of hope. Eighteen years ago the advent of nuclear weapons changed the course of the world as well as the war. Since that time, all mankind has been struggling to escape from the darkening prospect of mass destruction on earth. In an age when both sides have come to possess enough nuclear power to destroy the human race several times over, the world of communism and the world of free choice have been caught up in a vicious circle of conflicting ideology and interest. Each increase of tension has produced an increase of arms; each increase of arms has produced an increase of tension.

In these years, the United States and the Soviet Union have frequently communicated suspicion and warnings to each other, but very rarely hope. Our representatives have met at the summit and at the brink; they have met in Washington and in Moscow; in Geneva and at the United Nations. But too often these meetings have produced only darkness, discord, or disillusion.

Yesterday a shaft of light cut into the darkness. Negotiations were concluded in Moscow on a treaty to ban all nuclear tests in the atmosphere, in outer space, and under water. For the first time, an agreement has been reached on bringing the forces of nuclear destruction under international control—a goal first sought in 1946 when Bernard Baruch presented a comprehensive control plan to the United Nations.

That plan, and many subsequent disarmament plans, large and small, have all been blocked by those opposed to international inspection. A ban on nuclear tests, however, requires on-the-spot inspection only for underground tests. This Nation now possesses a variety of techniques to detect the nuclear tests of other nations which are conducted in the air or under water, for such tests produce unmistakable signs which our modern instruments can pick up.

The treaty initialed yesterday, therefore, is a limited treaty which permits continued underground testing and prohibits only those tests that we ourselves can police. It requires no control posts, no onsite inspection, no international body.

We should also understand that it has other limits as well. Any nation which signs the treaty will have an opportunity to withdraw if it finds that extraordinary events related to the subject matter of the treaty have jeopardized its supreme interests; and no nation's right of self-defense will in any way be impaired. Nor does this treaty mean an end to the threat of nuclear war. It will not reduce nuclear stockpiles; it will not halt the production of nuclear weapons; it will not restrict their use in time of war.

Nevertheless, this limited treaty will radically reduce the nuclear testing which would otherwise be conducted on both sides; it will prohibit the United States, the United Kingdom, the Soviet Union, and all others who sign it, from engaging in the atmospheric tests which have so alarmed mankind; and it offers to all the world a welcome sign of hope.

For this is not a unilateral moratorium, but a specific and solemn legal obligation. While it will not prevent this Nation from testing underground, or from being ready to conduct atmospheric tests if the acts of others so require, it gives us a concrete opportunity to extend its coverage to other nations and later to other forms of nuclear tests.

This treaty is in part the product of Western patience and vigilance. We have made clear—most recently in Berlin and Cuba—our deep resolve to protect our security and our freedom against any form of aggression. We have also made clear our steadfast determination to limit the arms race. In three administrations, our soldiers and diplomats have worked together to this end, always supported by Great Britain. Prime Minister Macmillan joined with President Eisenhower in proposing a limited test ban in 1959, and again with me in 1961 and 1962.

But the achievement of this goal is not a victory for one side—it is a victory for mankind. It reflects no concessions either to or by the Soviet Union. It reflects simply our common recognition of the dangers in further testing.

This treaty is not the millennium. It will not resolve all conflicts, or cause the Communists to forego their ambitions, or eliminate the dangers of war. It will not reduce our need for arms or allies or programs of assistance to others. But it is an important first step—a step towards peace—a step towards reason—a step away from war.

Here is what this step can mean to you and to your children and your neighbors:

First, this treaty can be a step towards reduced world tension and broader areas of agreement. The Moscow talks have reached no agreement on any other subject, nor is this treaty conditioned on any other matter. Under Secretary Harriman made it clear that any nonaggression arrangements across the division in Europe would require full consultation with our allies and full attention to their interests. He also made clear our strong preference for a more comprehensive treaty banning all tests everywhere, and our ultimate hope for general and complete disarmament. The Soviet Government, however, is still unwilling to accept the inspection such goals require.

No one can predict with certainty, therefore, what further agreements, if any, can be built on the foundations of this one. They could include controls on preparations for surprise attack, or on numbers and type of armaments. There could be further limitations on the spread of nuclear weapons. The important point is that efforts to seek new agreements will go forward.

But the difficulty of predicting the next step is no reason to be reluctant about this step. Nuclear test ban negotiations have long been a symbol of East-West disagreement. If this treaty can also be a symbol—if it can symbolize the end of one era and the beginning of another—if both sides can by this treaty gain confidence and experience in peaceful collaboration—then this short and simple treaty may well become an historic mark in man's age-old pursuit of peace.

Western policies have long been designed to persuade the Soviet Union to renounce aggression, direct or indirect, so that their people and all people may live and let live in peace. The unlimited testing of new weapons of war cannot lead towards that end—but this treaty, if it can be followed by further progress, can clearly move in that direction.

I do not say that a world without aggression or threats of war would be an easy world. It will bring new problems, new challenges from the Communists, new dangers of relaxing our vigilance or of mistaking their intent.

But those dangers pale in comparison to those of the spiraling arms race and a collision course towards war. Since the beginning of history, war has been mankind's constant companion. It has been the rule, not the exception. Even a nation as young and as peace-loving as our own has fought through eight wars. And three times in the last two years and a half I have been required to report to you as President that this Nation and the Soviet Union stood on the verge of direct military confrontation—in Laos, in Berlin, and in Cuba.

A war today or tomorrow, if it led to nuclear war, would not be like any war in history. A full-scale nuclear exchange, lasting less than 60 minutes, with the weapons now in existence, could wipe out more than 300 million Americans, Europeans, and Russians, as well as untold numbers elsewhere. And the survivors, as Chairman Khrushchev warned the Communist Chinese, "the survivors would envy the dead." For they would inherit a world so devastated by explosions and poison and fire that today we cannot even conceive of its horrors. So let us try to turn the world away from war. Let us make the most of this opportunity, and every opportunity, to reduce tension, to slow down the perilous nuclear arms race, and to check the world's slide toward final annihilation.

Second, this treaty can be a step towards freeing the world from the fears and dangers of radioactive fallout. Our own atmospheric tests last year were conducted under conditions which restricted such fallout to an absolute minimum. But over the years the number and the yield of weapons tested have rapidly increased and so have the radioactive hazards from such testing. Continued unrestricted testing by the nuclear powers, joined in time by other nations which may be less adept in limiting pollution, will increasingly contaminate the air that all of us must breathe.

Even then, the number of children and grandchildren with cancer in their bones, with leukemia in their blood, or with poison in their lungs might seem statistically small to some, in comparison with natural health hazards. But this is not a natural health hazard—and it is not a statistical issue. The loss of even one human life, or the malformation of even one baby—who may be born long after we are gone—should be of concern to us all. Our children and grandchildren are not merely statistics toward which we can be indifferent.

Nor does this affect the nuclear powers alone. These tests befoul the air of all men and all nations, the committed and the uncommitted alike, without their knowledge and without their consent. That is why the continuation of atmospheric testing causes so many countries to regard all nuclear powers as equally evil; and we can hope that its prevention will enable those countries to see the world more clearly, while enabling all the world to breathe more easily.

Third, this treaty can be a step toward preventing the spread of nuclear weapons to nations not now possessing them. During the next several years, in addition to the four current nuclear powers, a small but significant number of nations will have the intellectual, physical, and financial resources to produce both nuclear weapons and the means of delivering them. In time, it is estimated, many other nations will have either this capacity or other ways of obtaining nuclear warheads, even as missiles can be commercially purchased today.

I ask you to stop and think for a moment what it would mean to have nuclear weapons in so many hands, in the hands of countries large and small, stable and unstable, responsible and irresponsible, scattered throughout the world. There would be no rest for anyone then, no stability, no real security, and no chance of effective disarmament. There would only be the increased chance of accidental war, and an increased necessity for the great powers to involve themselves in what otherwise would be local conflicts.

If only one thermonuclear bomb were to be dropped on any American, Russian, or any other city, whether it was launched by accident or design, by a madman or by an enemy, by a large nation or by a small, from any corner of the world, that one bomb could release more destructive power on the inhabitants of that one helpless city than all the bombs dropped in the Second World War.

Neither the United States nor the Soviet Union nor the United Kingdom nor France can look forward to that day with equanimity. We have a great obligation, all four nuclear powers have a great obligation, to use whatever time remains to prevent the spread of nuclear weapons, to persuade other countries not to test, transfer, acquire, possess, or produce such weapons.

This treaty can be the opening wedge in that campaign. It provides that none of the parties will assist other nations to test in the forbidden environments. It opens the door for further agreements on the control of nuclear weapons, and it is open for all nations to sign, for it is in the interest of all nations, and already we have heard from a number of countries who wish to join with us promptly.

Fourth and finally, this treaty can limit the nuclear arms race in ways which, on balance, will strengthen our Nation's security far more than the continuation of unrestricted testing. For in today's world, a nation's security does not always increase as its arms increase, when its adversary is doing the same, and unlimited competition in the testing and development of new types of destructive nuclear weapons will not make the world safer for either side. Under this limited treaty, on the other hand, the testing of other nations could never be sufficient to offset the ability of our strategic forces to deter or survive a nuclear attack and to penetrate and destroy an aggressor's homeland.

We have, and under this treaty we will continue to have, the nuclear strength that we need. It is true that the Soviets have tested nuclear weapons of a yield higher than that which we thought to be necessary, but the hundred megaton bomb of which they spoke 2 years ago does not and will not change the balance of strategic power. The United States has chosen, deliberately, to concentrate on more mobile and more efficient weapons, with lower but entirely sufficient yield, and our security is, therefore, not impaired by the treaty I am discussing.

It is also true, as Mr. Khrushchev would agree, that nations cannot afford in these matters to rely simply on the good faith of their adversaries. We have not, therefore, overlooked the risk of secret violations. There is at present a possibility that deep in outer space, that hundreds and thousands and millions of miles away from the earth illegal tests might go undetected. But we already have the capability to construct a system of observation that would make such tests almost impossible to conceal, and we can decide at any time whether such a system is needed in the light of the limited risk to us and the limited reward to others of violations attempted at that range. For any tests which might be conducted so far out in space, which cannot be conducted more easily and efficiently and legally underground, would necessarily be of such a magnitude that they would be extremely difficult to conceal. We can also employ new devices to check on the testing of smaller weapons in the lower atmosphere. Any violations, moreover, involves, along with the risk of detection, the end of the treaty and the worldwide consequences for the violator.

Secret violations are possible and secret preparations for a sudden withdrawal are possible, and thus our own vigilance and strength must be maintained, as we remain ready to withdraw and to resume all forms of testing, if we must. But it would be a mistake to assume that this treaty will be quickly broken. The gains of illegal testing are obviously slight compared to their cost, and the hazard of discovery, and the nations which have initialed and will sign this treaty prefer it, in my judgment, to unrestricted testing as a matter of their own self-interests for these nations, too, and all nations, have a stake in limiting the arms race, in holding the spread of nuclear weapons, and in breathing air that is not radioactive. While it may be theoretically possible to demonstrate the risks inherent in any treaty, and such risks in this treaty are small, the far greater risks to our security are the risks of unrestricted testing, the risk of a nuclear arms race, the risk of new nuclear powers, nuclear pollution, and nuclear war.

This limited test ban, in our most careful judgment, is safer by far for the United States than an unlimited nuclear arms race. For all these reasons, I am hopeful that this Nation will promptly approve the limited test ban treaty. There will, of course, be debate in the country and in the Senate. The Constitution wisely requires the advice and consent of the Senate to all treaties, and that consultation has already begun. All this is as it should be. A document which may mark an historic and constructive opportunity for the world deserves an historic and constructive debate.

It is my hope that all of you will take part in that debate, for this treaty is for all of us. It is particularly for our children and our grandchildren, and they have no lobby here in Washington. This debate will involve military, scientific, and political experts, but it must be not left to them alone. The right and the responsibility are yours.

If we are to open new doorways to peace, if we are to seize this rare opportunity for progress, if we are to be as bold and farsighted in our control of weapons as we have been in their invention, then let us now show all the world on this side of the wall and the other that a strong America also stands for peace. There is no cause for complacency.

We have learned in times past that the spirit of one moment or place can be gone in the next. We have been disappointed more than once, and we have no illusions now that there are shortcuts on the road to peace. At many points around the globe the Communists are continuing their efforts to exploit weakness and poverty. Their concentration of nuclear and conventional arms must still be deterred.

The familiar contest between choice and coercion, the familiar places of danger and conflict, are all still there, in Cuba, in Southeast Asia, in Berlin, and all around the globe, still requiring all the strength and the vigilance that we can muster. Nothing could more greatly damage our cause than if we and our allies were to believe that peace has already been achieved, and that our strength and unity were no longer required.

But now, for the first time in many years, the path of peace may be open. No one can be certain what the future will bring. No one can say whether the time has come for an easing of the struggle. But history and our own conscience will judge us harsher if we do not now make every effort to test our hopes by action, and this is the place to begin. According to the ancient Chinese proverb, "A journey of a thousand miles must begin with a single step."

My fellow Americans, let us take that first step. Let us, if we can, step back from the shadows of war and seek out the way of peace. And if that journey is a thousand miles, or even more, let history record that we, in this land, at this time, took the first step.

Thank you and good night.

ADDRESS TO THE UN GENERAL ASSEMBLY

(SEPTEMBER 20, 1963)

Mr. President--as one who has taken some interest in the election of Presidents, I want to congratulate you on your election to this high office--Mr. Secretary General, delegates to the United Nations, ladies and gentlemen:

We meet again in the quest for peace.

Twenty-four months ago, when I last had the honor of addressing this body, the shadow of fear lay darkly across the world. The freedom of West Berlin was in immediate peril. Agreement on a neutral Laos seemed remote. The mandate of the United Nations in the Congo was under fire. The financial outlook for this organization was in doubt. Dag Hammarskjold was dead. The doctrine of troika was being pressed in his place, and atmospheric nuclear tests had been resumed by the Soviet Union.

Those were anxious days for mankind-and some men wondered aloud whether this organization could survive. But the 16th and 17th General Assemblies achieved not only survival but progress. Rising to its responsibility, the United Nations helped reduce the tensions and helped to hold back the darkness.

Today the clouds have lifted a little so that new rays of hope can break through. The pressures on West Berlin appear to be temporarily eased. Political unity in the Congo has been largely restored. A neutral coalition in Laos, while still in difficulty, is at least in being. The integrity of the United Nations Secretariat has been reaffirmed. A United Nations Decade of Development is under way. And, for the first time in 17 years of effort, a specific step has been taken to limit the nuclear arms race.

I refer, of course, to the treaty to ban nuclear tests in the atmosphere, outer space, and under water--concluded by the Soviet Union, the United Kingdom, and the United States--and already signed by nearly 100 countries. It has been hailed by people the world over who are thankful to be free from the fears of nuclear fallout, and I am confident that on next Tuesday at 10:30 o'clock in the morning it will receive the overwhelming endorsement of the Senate of the United States.

The world has not escaped from the darkness. The long shadows of conflict and crisis envelop us still. But we meet today in an atmosphere of rising hope, and at a moment of comparative calm. My presence here today is not a sign of crisis, but of confidence. I am not here to report on a new threat to the peace or new signs of war. I have come to salute the United Nations and to show the support of the American people for your daily deliberations.

For the value of this body's work is not dependent on the existence of emergencies-nor can the winning of peace consist only of dramatic victories. Peace is a daily, a weekly, a monthly process, gradually changing opinions, slowly eroding old barriers, quietly building new structures. And however undramatic the pursuit of peace, that pursuit must go on.

Today we may have reached a pause in the cold war--but that is not a lasting peace. A test ban treaty is a milestone--but it is not the millennium. We have not been released from our obligations--we have been given an opportunity. And if we fail to make the most of this moment and this momentum-if we convert our new-found hopes and understandings into new walls and weapons of hostility--if this .pause in the cold war merely leads to its renewal and not to its end--then the indictment of posterity will rightly point its finger at us all. But if we can stretch this pause into a period of cooperation--if both sides can now gain new confidence and experience in concrete collaborations for peace--if we can now be as bold and farsighted in the control of deadly weapons as we have been in their creation-then surely this first small step can be the start of a long and fruitful journey.

The task of building the peace lies with the leaders of every nation, large and small. For the great powers have no monopoly on conflict or ambition. The cold war is not the only expression of tension in this world-and the nuclear race is not the only arms race. Even little wars are dangerous in a nuclear world. The long labor of peace is an undertaking for every nation-- and in this effort none of us can remain unaligned. To this goal none can be uncommitted.

The reduction of global tension must not be an excuse for the narrow pursuit of self-interest. If the Soviet Union and the United States, with all of their global interests and clashing commitments of ideology, and with nuclear weapons still aimed at each other today, can find areas of common interest and agreement, then surely other nations can do the same--nations caught in regional conflicts, in racial issues, or in the death throes of old colonialism. Chronic disputes which divert precious resources from the needs of the people or drain the energies of both sides serve the interests of no one--and the badge of responsibility in the modern world is a willingness to seek peaceful solutions.

It is never too early to try; and it's never too late to talk; and it's high time that many disputes on the agenda of this Assembly were taken off the debating schedule and placed on the negotiating table.

The fact remains that the United States, as a major nuclear power, does have a special responsibility in the world. It is, in fact, a threefold responsibility--a responsibility to our own citizens; a responsibility to the people of the whole world who are affected by our decisions; and to the next generation of humanity. We believe the Soviet Union also has these special responsibilities--and that those responsibilities require our two nations to concentrate less on our differences and more on the means of resolving them peacefully. For too long both of us have increased our military budgets, our nuclear stockpiles, and our capacity to destroy all life on this hemisphere--human, animal, vegetable--without any corresponding increase in our security.

Our conflicts, to be sure, are real. Our concepts of the world are different. No service is performed by failing to make clear our disagreements. A central difference is the belief of the American people in self-determination for all people.

We believe that the people of Germany and Berlin must be free to reunite their capital and their country.

We believe that the people of Cuba must be free to secure the fruits of the revolution that have been betrayed from within and exploited from without.

In short, we believe that all the world--in Eastern Europe as well as Western, in Southern Africa as well as Northern, in old nations as well as new--that people must be free to choose their own future, without discrimination or dictation, without coercion or subversion.

These are the basic differences between the Soviet Union and the

United States, and they cannot be concealed. So long as they exist, they set limits to agreement, and they forbid the relaxation of our vigilance. Our defense around the world will be maintained for the protection of freedom--and our determination to safeguard that freedom will measure up to any threat or challenge.

But I would say to the leaders of the Soviet Union, and to their people, that if either of our countries is to be fully secure, we need a much better weapon than the H-bomb--a weapon better than ballistic missiles or nuclear submarines--and that better weapon is peaceful cooperation.

We have, in recent years, agreed on a limited test ban treaty, on an emergency communications link between our capitals, on a statement of principles for disarmament, on an increase in cultural exchange, on cooperation in outer space, on the peaceful exploration of the Antarctic, and on tempering last year's crisis over Cuba.

I believe, therefore, that the Soviet Union and the United States, together with their allies, can achieve further agreements-agreements which spring from our mutual interest in avoiding mutual destruction.

There can be no doubt about the agenda of further steps. We must continue to seek agreements on measures which prevent war by accident or miscalculation. We must continue to seek agreement on safeguards against surprise attack, including observation posts at key points. We must continue to seek agreement on further measures to curb the nuclear arms race, by controlling the transfer of nuclear weapons, converting fissionable materials to peaceful purposes, and banning underground testing, with adequate inspection and enforcement. We must continue to seek agreement on a freer flow of information and people from East to West and West to East.

We must continue to seek agreement, encouraged by yesterday's affirmative response to this proposal by the Soviet Foreign Minister, on an arrangement to keep weapons of mass destruction out of outer space. Let us get our negotiators back to the negotiating table to work out a practicable arrangement to this end.

In these and other ways, let us move up the steep and difficult path toward comprehensive disarmament, securing mutual confidence through mutual verification, and building the institutions of peace as we dismantle the engines of war. We must not let failure to agree on all points delay agreements where agreement is possible. And we must not put forward proposals for propaganda purposes.

Finally, in a field where the United States and the Soviet Union have a special capacity-in the field of space--there is room for new cooperation, for further joint efforts in the regulation and exploration of space. I include among these possibilities a joint expedition to the moon. Space offers no problems of sovereignty; by resolution of this Assembly, the members of the United Nations have foresworn any claim to territorial rights in outer space or on celestial bodies, and declared that international law and the United Nations Charter will apply. Why, therefore, should man's first flight to the moon be a matter of national competition? Why should the United States and the Soviet Union, in preparing for such expeditions, become involved in immense duplications of research, construction, and expenditure? Surely we should explore whether the scientists and astronauts of our two countries--indeed of all the world--cannot work together in the conquest of space, sending some day in this decade to the moon not the respresentatives of a single nation, but the representatives of all of our countries.

All these and other new steps toward peaceful cooperation may be possible. Most of them will require on our part full consultation with our allies--for their interests are as much involved as our own, and we will not make an agreement at their expense. Most of them will require long and careful negotiation. And most of them will require a new approach to the cold war--a desire not to "bury" one's adversary, but to compete in a host of peaceful arenas, in ideas, in production, and ultimately in service to all mankind.

The contest will continue--the contest between those who see a monolithic world and those who believe in diversity--but it should be a contest in leadership and responsibility instead of destruction, a contest in achievement instead of intimidation. Speaking for the United States of America, I welcome such a contest. For we believe that truth is stronger than error--and that freedom is more enduring than coercion. And in the contest for a better life, all the world can be a winner.

The effort to improve the conditions of man, however, is not a task for the few. It is the task of all nations--acting alone, acting in groups, acting in the United Nations, for plague and pestilence, and plunder and pollution, the hazards of nature, and the hunger of children are the foes of every nation. The earth, the sea, and the air are the concern of every nation. And science, technology, and education can be the ally of every nation.

Never before has man had such capacity to control his own

environment, to end thirst and hunger, to conquer poverty and disease, to banish illiteracy and massive human misery. We have the power to make this the best generation of mankind in the history of the world--or to make it the last.

The United States since the close of the war has sent over $100 billion worth of assistance to nations seeking economic viability. And 2 years ago this week we formed a Peace Corps to help interested nations meet the demand for trained manpower. Other industrialized nations whose economies were rebuilt not so long ago with some help from us are now in turn recognizing their responsibility to the less developed nations.

The provision of development assistance by individual nations must go on. But the United Nations also must play a larger role in helping bring to all men the fruits of modern science and industry. A United Nations conference on this subject he;d earlier this year at Geneva opened new vistas for the developing countries. Next year a United Nations Conference on Trade will consider the needs of these nations for new markets. And more than four-fifths of the entire United Nations system can be found today mobilizing the weapons of science and technology for the United Nations' Decade of Development.

But more can be done.

--A world center for health communications under the World Health Organization could warn of epidemics and the adverse effects of certain drugs as well as transmit the results of new experiments and new discoveries.

--Regional research centers could advance our common medical knowledge and train new scientists and doctors for new nations.

--A global system of satellites could provide communication and weather information for all corners of the earth.

--A worldwide program of conservation could protect the forest and wild game preserves now in danger of extinction for all time, improve the marine harvest of food from our oceans, and prevent the contamination of air and water by industrial as well as nuclear pollution.

--And, finally, a worldwide program of farm productivity and food distribution, similar to our country's "Food for Peace" program, could now give every child the food he needs.

But man does not live by bread alone-and the members of this organization are committed by the Charter to promote and respect human rights. Those rights are not respected when a Buddhist priest is driven from his pagoda, when a synagogue is shut down, when a Protestant church cannot open a mission, when a Cardinal is forced into hiding, or when a crowded church service is bombed. The United States of America is opposed to discrimination and persecution on grounds of race and religion anywhere in the world, including our own Nation. We are working to right the wrongs of our own country.

Through legislation and administrative action, through moral and legal commitment, this Government has launched a determined effort to rid our Nation of discrimination which has existed far too longin education, in housing, in transportation, in employment, in the civil service, in recreation, and in places of public accommodation. And therefore, in this or any other forum, we do not hesitate to condemn racial or religious injustice, whether committed or permitted by friend or foe.

I know that some of you have experienced discrimination in this country. But I ask you to believe me when I tell you that this is not the wish of most Americans--that we share your regret and resentment--and that we intend to end such practices for all time to come, not only for our visitors, but for our own citizens as well.

I hope that not only our Nation but all other multiracial societies will meet these standards of fairness and justice. We are opposed to apartheid and all forms of human oppression. We do not advocate the rights of black Africans in order to drive out white Africans. Our concern is the right of all men to equal protection under the law--and since human rights are indivisible, this body cannot stand aside when those rights are abused and neglected by any member state.

New efforts are needed if this Assembly's Declaration of Human Rights, now 15 years old, is to have full meaning. And new means should be found for promoting the free expression and trade of ideas--through travel and communication, and through increased exchanges of people, and books, and broadcasts. For as the world renounces the competition of weapons, competition in ideas must flourish--and that competition must be as full and as fair as possible.

The United States delegation will be prepared to suggest to the United Nations initiatives in the pursuit of all the goals. For this is an organization for peace--and peace cannot come without work and without progress.

The peacekeeping record of the United Nations has been a proud one, though its tasks are always formidable. We are fortunate to have the skills of our distinguished Secretary General and the brave efforts of those who have been serving the cause of peace in the Congo, in the Middle East, in Korea and Kashmir, in West New Guinea and Malaysia. But what the United Nations has done in the past is less important than the tasks for the future. We cannot take its peacekeeping machinery for granted. That machinery must be soundly financed-which it cannot be if some members are allowed to prevent it from meeting its obligations by failing to meet their own. The United Nations must be supported by all those who exercise their franchise here. And its operations must be backed to the end.

Too often a project is undertaken in the excitement of a crisis and then it begins to lose its appeal as the problems drag on and the bills pile up. But we must have the steadfastness to see every enterprise through.

It is, for example, most important not to jeopardize the extraordinary United Nations gains in the Congo. The nation which sought this organization's help only 3 years ago has now asked the United Nations' presence to remain a little longer. I believe this Assembly should do what is necessary to preserve the gains already made and to protect the new nation in its struggle for progress. Let us complete what we have started. For "No man who puts his hand to the plow and looks back," as the Scriptures tell us, "No man who puts his hand to the plow and looks back is fit for the Kingdom of God."

I also hope that the recent initiative of several members in preparing standby peace forces for United Nations call will encourage similar commitments by others. This Nation remains ready to provide logistic and other material support.

Policing, moreover, is not enough without provision for pacific settlement. We should increase the resort to special missions of factfinding and conciliation, make greater use of the International Court of Justice, and accelerate the work of the International Law Commission.

The United Nations cannot survive as a static organization. Its obligations are increasing as well as its size. Its Charter must be changed as well as its customs. The authors of that Charter did not intend that it be frozen in perpetuity. The science of weapons and war has made us all, far more than 18 years ago in San Francisco, one world and one human race, with one common destiny. In such a world, absolute -sovereignty no longer assures us of absolute security. The conventions of peace must pull abreast and then ahead of the inventions of war. The United Nations, building on its successes and learning from its failures, must be developed into a genuine world security system.

But peace does not rest in charters and covenants alone. It lies in the hearts and minds of all people. And if it is east out there, then no act, no pact, no treaty, no organization can hope to preserve it without the support and the wholehearted commitment of all people. So let us not rest all our hopes on parchment and on paper; let us strive to build peace, a desire for peace, a willingness to work for peace, in the hearts and minds of all of our people. I believe that we can. I believe the problems of human destiny are not beyond the reach of human beings.

Two years ago I told this body that the United States had proposed, and was willing to sign, a limited test ban treaty. Today that treaty has been signed. It will not put an end to war. It will not remove basic conflicts. It will not secure freedom for all. But it can be a lever, and Archimedes, in explaining the principles of the lever, was said to have declared to his friends: "Give me a place where I can stand--and I shall move the world."

My fellow inhabitants of this planet: Let us take our stand here in this Assembly of nations. And let us see if we, in our own time, can move the world to a just and lasting peace.

ADDRESS AT THE MORMON TABERNACLE

(SEPTEMBER 26, 1963)

Senator Moss, my old colleague in the United States Senate, your distinguished Senator Moss, President McKay, Mr. Brown, Secretary Udall, Governor, Mr. Rawlings, ladies and gentlemen:

I appreciate your welcome, and I am very proud to be back in this historic building and have an opportunity to say a few words on some matters which concern me as President, and I hope concern you as citizens. The fact is, I take strength and hope in seeing this monument, hearing its story retold by Ted Moss, and recalling how this State was built, and what it started with, and what it has now.

Of all the stories of American pioneers and settlers, none is more inspiring than the Mormon trail. The qualities of the founders of this community are the qualities that we seek in America, the qualities which we like to feel this country has, courage, patience, faith, self-reliance, perseverance, and, above all, an unflagging determination to see the right prevail.

I came on this trip to see the United States, and I can assure you that there is nothing more encouraging for any of us who work in Washington than to have a chance to fly across this United States, and drive through it, and see what a great country it is, and come to understand somewhat better how this country has been able for so many years to carry so many burdens in so many parts of the world.

The primary reason for my trip was conservation, and I include in conservation first our human resources and then our natural resources, and I think this State can take perhaps its greatest pride and its greatest satisfaction for what it has done, not in the field of the conservation and the development of natural resources, but what you have done to educate your children. This State has a higher percentage per capita of population of its boys and girls who finish high school and then go to college.

Of all the waste in the United States in the 1960's, none is worse than to have 8 or 9 million boys and girls who will drop out, statistics tell us, drop out of school before they have finished, come into the labor market unprepared at the very time when machines are taking the place of men and women—9 million of them. We have a large minority of our population who have not even finished the sixth grade, and here in this richest of all countries, the country which spreads the doctrine of freedom and hope around the globe, we permit our most valuable resource, our young people, their talents to be wasted by leaving their schools.

So I think we have to save them. I think we have to insist that our children be educated to the limit of their talents, not just in your State, or in Massachusetts, but all over the United States. Thomas Jefferson and John Adams, who developed the Northwest Ordinance, which put so much emphasis on education—Thomas Jefferson once said that any nation which expected to be ignorant and free, hopes for what never was and never will be. So I hope we can conserve this resource.

The other is the natural resource of our country, particularly the land west of the 100th parallel, where the rain comes 15 or 20 inches a year. This State knows that the control of water is the secret of the development of the West, and whether we use it for power, or for irrigation, or for whatever purpose, no drop of water west of the 100th parallel should flow to the ocean without being used. And to do that requires the dedicated commitment of the people of the States of the West, working with the people of all the United States who have such an important equity in the richness of this part of the country. So that we must do also.

As Theodore and Franklin Roosevelt and Gifford Pinchot did it in years past, we must do it in the 1960's and 1970's. We will triple the population of this country in the short space of 60 or 70 years, and we want those who come after us to have the same rich inheritance that we find now in the United States. This is the reason for the trip, but it is not what I wanted to speak about tonight.

I want to speak about the responsibility that I feel the United States has not in this country, but abroad, and I see the closest interrelationship between the strength of the United States here at home and the strength of the United States around the world. There is one great natural development here in the United States which has had in its own way a greater effect upon the position and influence and prestige of the United States, almost, than any other act we have done. Do you know what it is? It is the Tennessee Valley. Nearly every leader of every new emerging country that comes to the United States wants to go to New York, to Washington, and the Tennessee Valley, because they want to see what we were able to do with the most poverty-ridden section of the United States in the short space of 30 years, by the wise management of our resources.

What happens here in this country affects the security of the United States and the cause of freedom around the globe. If this is a strong, vital, and vigorous society, the cause of freedom will be strong and vital and vigorous.

I know that many of you in this State and other States sometimes wonder where we are going and why the United States should be so involved in so many affairs, in so many countries all around the globe. If our task on occasion seems hopeless, if we despair of ever working our will on the other 94 percent of the world population, then let us remember that the Mormons of a century ago were a persecuted and prosecuted minority, harried from place to place, the victims of violence and occasionally murder, while today, in the short space of 100 years, their faith and works are known and respected the world around, and their voices heard in the highest councils of this country.

As the Mormons succeeded, so America can succeed, if we will not give up or turn back. I realize that the burdens are heavy and I realize that there is a great temptation to urge that we relinquish them, that we have enough to do here in the United States, and we should not be so busy around the globe. The fact of the matter is that we, this generation of Americans, are the first generation of our country ever to be involved in affairs around the globe. From the ginning of this country, from the days of Washington, until the Second World War, this country lived an isolated existence. Through most of our history we were an unaligned country, an uncommitted nation, a neutralist nation. We were by statute as well as by desire. We had believed that we could live behind our two oceans in safety and prosperity in a comfortable distance from the rest of the world.

The end of isolation consequently meant a wrench with the very lifeblood, the very spine, of the Nation. Yet, as time passed, we came to see that the end of isolation was not such a terrible error or evil after all. We came to see that it was the inevitable result of growth, the economic growth, the military growth, and the cultural growth of the United States. No nation so powerful and so dynamic and as rich as our own could hope to live in isolation from other nations, especially at a time when science and technology was making the world so small.

It took Brigham Young and his followers 108 days to go from Winter Quarters, Nebraska, to the valley of the Great Salt Lake. It takes 30 minutes for a missile to go from one continent to another. We did not seek to become a world power. This position was thrust upon us by events. But we became one just the same, and I am proud that we did.

I can well understand the attraction of those earlier days. Each one of us has moments of longing for the past, but two world wars have clearly shown us, try as we may, that we cannot turn our back on the world outside. If we do, we jeopardize our economic well-being, we jeopardize our political stability, we jeopardize our physical safety.

To turn away now is to abandon the world to those whose ambition is to destroy a free society. To yield these burdens up after having carried them for more than 20 years is to surrender the freedom of our country inevitably, for without the United States, the chances of freedom surviving, let alone prevailing around the globe, are nonexistent.

Americans have come a long way in accepting in a short time the necessity of world involvement, but the strain of this involvement remains and we find it all over the country. I see it in the letters that come to my desk every day. We find ourselves entangled with apparently unanswerable problems in unpronounceable places. We discover that our enemy in one decade is our ally the next. We find ourselves committed to governments whose actions we cannot often approve, assisting societies with principles very different from our own.

The burdens of maintaining an immense military establishment with one million Americans serving outside our frontiers, of financing a far-flung program of development assistance, of conducting a complex and baffling diplomacy, all weigh heavily upon us and cause some to counsel retreat.

The world is full of contradiction and confusion, and our policy seems to have lost the black and white clarity of simpler times when we remembered the Maine and went to War.

It is little wonder, then, in this confusion, we look back to the old days with nostalgia. It is little wonder that there is a desire in the country to go back to the time when our Nation lived alone. It is little wonder that we increasingly want an end to entangling alliances, an end to all help to foreign countries, a cessation of diplomatic relations with countries or states whose principles we dislike, that we get the United Nations out of the United States, and the United States out of the United Nations, and that we retreat to our own hemisphere, or even within our own boundaries, to take refuge behind a wall of force.

This is an understandable effort to recover an old feeling of simplicity, yet in world affairs, as in all other aspects of our lives, the days of the quiet past are gone forever. Science and technology are irreversible. We cannot return to the day of the sailing schooner or the covered wagon, even if we wished. And if this Nation is to survive and succeed in the real world of today, we must acknowledge the realities of the world; and it is those realities that I mention now.

We must first of all recognize that we cannot remake the world simply by our own command. When we cannot even bring all of our own people into full citizenship without acts of violence, we can understand how much harder it is to control events beyond our borders.

Every nation has its own traditions, its own values, its own aspirations. Our assistance from time to time can help other nations preserve their independence and advance their growth, but we cannot remake them in our own image. We cannot enact their laws, nor can we operate their governments or dictate our policies.

Second, we must recognize that every tion determines its policies in terms of its own interests. "No nation," George Washington wrote, "is to be trusted farther than it is bound by its interest; and no prudent statesman or politician will depart from it." National interest is more powerful than ideology, and the recent developments within the Communist empire show this very clearly. Friendship, as Palmerston said, may rise or wane, but interests endure.

The United States has rightly determined, in the years since 1945 under three different administrations, that our interest, our national security, the interest of the United States of America, is best served by preserving and protecting a world of diversity in which no one power or no one combination of powers can threaten the security of the United States. The reason that we moved so far into the world was our fear that at the end of the war, and particularly when China became Communist, that Japan and Germany would collapse, and these two countries which had so long served as a barrier to the Soviet advance, and the Russian advance before that, would open up a wave of conquest of all of Europe and all of Asia, and then the balance of power turning against us we would finally be isolated and ultimately destroyed. That is what we have been engaged in for 18 years, to prevent that happening, to prevent any one monolithic power having sufficient force to destroy the United States.

For that reason we support the alliances in Latin America; for that reason we support NATO to protect the security of Western Europe; for that reason we joined SEATO to protect the security of Asia—so that neither Russia nor China could control Europe and Asia, and if they could not control Europe and Asia, then our security was assured. This is what we have been involved in doing. And however dangerous and hazardous it may be, and however close it may take us to the brink on occasion, which it has, and however tired we may get of our involvements with these governments so far away, we have one simple central theme of American foreign policy which all of us must recognize, because it is a policy which we must continue to follow, and that is to support the independence of nations so that one bloc cannot gain sufficient power to finally overcome us. There is no mistaking the vital interest of the United States in what goes on around the world. Therefore, accepting what George Washington said here, I realize that what George Washington said about no intangling alliances has been ended by science and technology and danger.

And third, we must recognize that foreign policy in the modern world does not lend itself to easy, simple black and white solution. If we were to have diplomatic relations only with those countries whose principles we approved of, we would have relations with very few countries in a very short time. If we were to withdraw our assistance from all governments who are run differently from our own, we would relinquish half the world immediately to our adversaries. If we were to treat foreign policy as merely a medium for delivering self-righteous sermons to supposedly inferior people, we would give up all thought of world influence or world leadership.

For the purpose of foreign policy is not to provide an outlet for our own sentiments of hope or indignation; it is to shape real events in a real world. We cannot adopt a policy which says that if something does not happen, or others do not do exactly what we wish, we will return to "Fortress America." That is the policy in this changing world of retreat, not of strength.

More important, to adopt a black or white, all or nothing policy subordinates our interest to our irritations. Its actual consequences would be fatal to our security. If we were to resign from the United Nations, break off with all countries of whom we disapprove, end foreign aid and assistance to those countries in an attempt to keep them free, call for the resumption of atmospheric nuclear testing, and turn our back on the rest of mankind, we would not only be abandoning America's influence in the world, we would be inviting a Communist expansion which every Communist power would so greatly welcome. And all of the effort of so many Americans for 18 years would be gone with the wind. Our policy under those conditions, in this dangerous world, would not have much deterrent effect in a world where nations determined to be free could no longer count on the United States.

Such a policy of retreat would be folly if we had our backs to the wall. It is surely even greater folly at a time when more realistic, more responsible, more affirmative policies have wrought such spectacular results. For the most striking thing about our world in 1963 is the extent to which the tide of history has begun to flow in the direction of freedom. To renounce the world of freedom now, to abandon those who share our commitment, and retire into lonely and not so splendid isolation, would be to give communism the one hope which, in this twilight of disappointment for them, might repair their divisions and rekindle their hope.

For after some gains in the fifties the Communist offensive, which claimed to be riding the tide of historic inevitability, has been thwarted and turned back in recent months. Indeed, the whole theory of historical inevitability, the belief that all roads must lead to communism, sooner or later, has been shattered by the determination of those who believe that men and nations will pursue a variety of roads, that each nation will evolve according to its own traditions and its own aspirations, and that the world of the future will have room for a diversity of economic systems, political creeds, religious faiths, united by the respect for others, and loyalty to a world order.

Those forces of diversity which served Mr. Washington's national interest—those forces of diversity are in the ascendancy today, even within the Communist empire itself. And our policy at this point should be to give the forces of diversity, as opposed to the forces of uniformity, which our adversaries espouse, every chance, every possible support. That is why our assistance program, so much maligned, of assisting countries to maintain their freedom, I believe, is important.

This country has seen all of the hardship and the grief that has come to us by the loss of one country in this hemisphere, Cuba. How many other countries must be lost if the United States decides to end the programs that are helping these people, who are getting poorer every year, who have none of the resources of this great country, who look to us for help, but on the other hand in cases look to the Communists for example?

That is why I think this program is important. It is a means of assisting those who want to be free, and in the final analysis it serves the United States in a very real sense. That is why the United Nations is important, not because it can solve all these problems in this imperfect world, but it does give us a means, in those great moments of crisis, and in the last 21/2 years we have had at least three, when the Soviet Union and the United States were almost face to face on a collision course—it does give us a means of providing, as it has in the Congo, as it now is on the border of the Yemen, as it most recently was in a report of the United Nations at Malaysia—it does give a means to mobilize the opinion of the world to prevent an atomic disaster which would destroy us all wherever we might live.

That is why the test ban treaty is important as a first step, perhaps to be disappointed, perhaps to find ourselves ultimately set back, but at least in 1963 the United States committed itself, and the Senate of the United States, by an overwhelming vote, to one chance to end the radiation and the possibilities of burning.

It may be, as I said, that we may fail, but anyone who bothers to look at the true destructive power of the atom today and what we and the Soviet Union could do to each other and the world in an hour and in a day, and to Western Europe—I passed over yesterday the Little Big Horn where General Custer was slain, a massacre which has lived in history, 400 or 500 men. We are talking about 300 million men and women m 24 hours.

I think it is wise to take a first step to lessen the possibility of that happening. And that is why our diplomacy is important. For the forces making for diversity are to be found everywhere where people are, even within the Communist empire, and it is our obligation to encourage those forces wherever they may be found. Hard and discouraging questions remain in Viet-Nam, in Cuba, in Laos, the Congo, all around the globe. The ordeal of the emerging nations has just begun. The control of nuclear weapons is still incomplete. The areas of potential friction, the chances of collision, still exist.

But in every one of these areas the position of the United States, I believe, is happier and safer when history is going for us rather than when it is going against us. And we have history going for us today, but history is what men make it. The future is what men make it.

We cannot fulfill our vision and our commitment and our interest in a free and diverse future without unceasing vigilance, devotion, and, most of all, perseverance, a willingness to stay with it, a willingness to do with fatigue, a willingness not to accept easy answers, but instead, to maintain the burden, as the people of this State have done for 100 years, and as the United States must do the rest of this century until finally we live in a peaceful world.

Therefore, I think this country will continue its commitments to support the world of freedom, for as we discharge that commitment we are heeding the command which Brigham Young heard from the Lord more than a century ago, the command he conveyed to his followers, "Go as pioneers . . . to a land of peace."

Thank you.

President John F. Kennedy

REMARKS AT AMHERST COLLEGE

(OCTOBER 26, 1963)

Mr. McCloy, President Plimpton, Mr. MacLeish, distinguished guests, ladies and gentlemen:

I am very honored to be here with you on this occasion which means so much to this college and also means so much to art and the progress of the United States. This college is part of the United States. It belongs to it. So did Mr. Frost, in a large sense. And, therefore, I was privileged to accept the invitation somewhat rendered to me in the same way that Franklin Roosevelt rendered his invitation to Mr. MacLeish, the invitation which I received from Mr. McCloy. The powers of the Presidency are often described. Its limitations should occasionally be remembered. And therefore when the Chairman of our Disarmament Advisory Committee, who has labored so long and hard, Governor Stevenson's assistant during the very difficult days at the United Nations during the Cuban crisis, a public servant of so many years, asks or invites the President of the United States, there is only one response. So I am glad to be here.

Amherst has had many soldiers of the king since its first one, and some of them are here today: Mr. McCloy, who has long been a public servant; Jim Reed, who is the Assistant Secretary of the Treasury; President Cole, who is now our Ambassador to Chile; Mr. Ramey, who is a Commissioner of the Atomic Energy Commission; Dick Reuter, who is head of the Food for Peace. These and scores of others down through the years have recognized the obligations of the advantages which the graduation from a college such as this places upon them to serve not only their private interest but the public interest as well.

Many years ago, Woodrow Wilson said, what good is a political party unless it is serving a great national purpose? And what good is a private college or university unless it is serving a great national purpose? The library being constructed today, this college, itself—all of this, of course, was not done merely to give this school's graduates an advantage, an economic

President John F. Kennedy

advantage, in the life struggle. It does do that. But in return for that, in return for the great opportunity which society gives the graduates of this and related schools, it seems to me incumbent upon this and other schools' graduates to recognize their responsibility to the public interest.

Privilege is here, and with privilege goes responsibility. And I think, as your president said, that it must be a source of satisfaction to you that this school's graduates have recognized it. I hope that the students who are here now will also recognize it in the future. Although Amherst has been in the forefront of extending aid to needy and talented students, private colleges, taken as a whole, draw 50 percent of their students from the wealthiest 10 percent of our Nation. And even State universities and other public institutions derive 25 percent of their students from this group. In March 1962, persons of 18 years or older who had not completed high school made up 46 percent of the total labor force, and such persons comprised 64 percent of those who were unemployed. And in 1958, the lowest fifth of the families in the United States had 41/2 percent of the total personal income, the highest fifth, 44 1/2 percent. There is inherited wealth in this country and also inherited poverty. And unless the graduates of this college and other colleges like it who are given a running start in life—unless they are willing to put back into our society those talents, the broad sympathy, the understanding, the compassion—unless they are willing to put those qualities back into the service of the Great Republic, then obviously the presuppositions upon which our democracy are based are bound to be fallible.

The problems which this country now faces are staggering, both at home and abroad. We need the service, in the great sense, of every educated man or woman to find 10 million jobs in the next 21/2 years, to govern our relations—a country which lived in isolation for 150 years, and is now suddenly the leader of the free world—to govern our relations with over 100 countries, to govern those relations with success so that the balance of power remains strong on the side of freedom, to make it possible for Americans of all different races and creeds to live together in harmony, to make it possible for a world to exist in diversity and freedom. All this requires the best of all of us.

Therefore, I am proud to come to this college whose graduates have recognized this obligation and to say to those who are now here that the need is endless, and I am confident that you will respond.

Robert Frost said:

Two roads diverged in a wood, and I—

I took the one less traveled by,

And that has made all the difference.

I hope that road will not be the less traveled by, and I hope your commitment to the Great Republic's interest in the years to come will be worthy of your long inheritance since your beginning.

This day devoted to the memory of Robert Frost offers an opportunity for reflection which is prized by politicians as well as by others, and even by poets, for Robert Frost was one of the granite figures of our time in America. He was supremely two things: an artist and an American. A nation reveals itself not only by the men it produces but also by the men it honors, the men it remembers.

In America, our heroes have customarily run to men of large accomplishments. But today this college and country honors a man whose contribution was not to our size but to our spirit, not to our political beliefs but to our insight, not to our self-esteem, but to our self-comprehension. In honoring Robert Frost, we therefore can pay honor to the deepest sources of our national strength. That strength takes many forms, and the most obvious forms are not always the most significant. The men who create power make an indispensable contribution to the Nation's greatness, but the men who question power make a contribution just as dispensable, especially when that questioning is disinterested, for they determine whether we use power or power uses us.

Our national strength matters, but the spirit which informs and controls our strength matters just as much. This was the special significance of Robert Frost. He brought an unsparing instinct for reality to bear on the platitudes and pieties of society. His sense of the human tragedy fortified him against self-deception and easy consolation. "I have been," he wrote, "one acquainted with the night." And because he knew the midnight as well as the high noon, because he understood the ordeal as well as the triumph of the human spirit, he gave his age strength with which to overcome despair. At bottom, he held a deep faith in the spirit of man, and it is hardly an accident that Robert Frost coupled poetry and power, for he saw poetry as the means of saving power from itself. When power leads man towards arrogance, poetry reminds him of his limitations. When power narrows the areas of man's concern, poetry reminds him of the richness and diversity of his existence. When power corrupts, poetry cleanses. For art establishes the basic human truth which must serve as the touchstone of our judgment.

The artist, however faithful to his personal vision of reality, becomes the last champion of the individual mind and sensibility against an intrusive society and an officious state. The great artist is thus a solitary figure. He has, as Frost said, a lover's quarrel with the world. In pursuing his perceptions of reality, he must often sail against the currents of his time. This is not a popular role. If Robert Frost was much honored during his lifetime, it was because a good many preferred to ignore his darker truths. Yet in retrospect, we see how the artist's fidelity has strengthened the fibre of our national life.

If sometimes our great artists have been the most critical of our society, it is because their sensitivity and their concern for justice, which must motivate any true artist, makes him aware that our Nation falls short of its highest potential. I see little of more importance to the future of our country and our civilization than full recognition of the place of the artist.

If art is to nourish the roots of our culture, society must set the artist free to follow his vision wherever it takes him. We must never forget that art is not a form of propaganda; it is a form of truth. And as Mr. MacLeish once remarked of poets, there is nothing worse for our trade than to be in style. In free society art is not a weapon and it does not belong to the sphere of polemics and ideology. Artists are not engineers of the soul. It may be different elsewhere. But democratic society—in it, the highest duty of the writer, the composer, the artist is to remain true to himself and to let the chips fall where they may. In serving his vision of the truth, the artist best serves his nation. And the nation which disdains the mission of art invites the fate of Robert Frost's hired man, the fate of having "nothing to look backward to with pride, and nothing to look forward to with hope."

I look forward to a great future for America, a future in which our country will match its military strength with our moral restraint, its wealth with our wisdom, its power with our purpose. I look forward to an America which will not be afraid of grace and beauty, which will protect the beauty of our natural environment, which will preserve the great old American houses and squares and parks of our national past, and which will build handsome and balanced cities for our future.

I look forward to an America which will reward achievement in the arts as we reward achievement in business or statecraft. I look forward to an America which will steadily raise the standards of artistic accomplishment and which will steadily enlarge cultural opportunities for all of our citizens.

And I look forward to an America which commands respect throughout the world not only for its strength but for its civilization as well. And I look forward to a world which will be safe not only for democracy and diversity but also for personal distinction.

Robert Frost was often skeptical about projects for human improvement, yet I do not think he would disdain this hope. As he wrote during the uncertain days of the Second War:

Take human nature altogether since time began... And it must be a little more in favor of man, Say a fraction of one percent at the very least... Our hold on the planet wouldn't have so increased.

Because of Mr. Frost's life and work, because of the life and work of this college, our hold on this planet has increased

Made in the USA
Coppell, TX
17 December 2023

26347884R00177